ON YOUR OWN

Discovering Your New Life and Career Beyond the Corporation

PERIODICAL → WORKPLACE TRENDS

ON YOUR OWN

Discovering Your New Life and Career Beyond the Corporation

C. D. Peterson

John Wiley & Sons, Inc.

New York • Chichester • Weinheim • Brisbane
Singapore • Toronto

This text is printed on acid-free paper.

Copyright © 1997 Carl D. Peterson
Published by John Wiley & Sons, Inc.

All rights reserved. Published simultaneously in Canada.

This publication is designed to provide accurate and authoritative
information in regard to the subject matter covered. It is sold with
the understanding that the publisher is not engaged in rendering legal,
accounting, or other professional services. If legal advice or other expert
assistance is required, the services of a competent professional person
should be sought.

Library of Congress Cataloging-in-Publication Data

Peterson, C. D. (Carl D.)
    On your own: discovering your new life and career beyond the
corporation / by C. D. Peterson.
        p.   cm.
    Includes bibliographical references.
    ISBN 0-471-14845-8 (paper: alk. paper)
    1. New business enterprises—Management.   2. Small business—
Management.   3. Self-employed.   I. Title.
HD62.5.P465   1997
658'.041–DC20   96-35572
                                                                 CIP

Printed in the United States of America

10 9 8 7 6 5 4 3 2 1

To Odessa, Wendy, Stephanie, and Chris

Contents

PART III
Four Routes to Ownership: Buying a Business, Owning a Franchise, Starting a Business, Becoming a Consultant
83

Preface

"I wasn't let go in the latest cutbacks. I should be very thankful—jobs are hard to get. It's just that I ended up with all the work from the people who left my department. Now I'm worried that if I can't keep up, they'll fire me. Regardless of what they say, I think more cutbacks are coming. I really need this job."

That paragraph opens this book. It captures some of the anxieties people are feeling in a workplace where *reengineering* discredits experience, where *Continuous Quality Improvement* negates predictability, and where *constant change* creates constant threat to those enduring the changes.

People who have long been retired might wonder what the fuss is about. "When was it written that work should be fun?" they might ask. "Work is work." Of course they are right, but they worked under an old rule that was often unspoken but seldom broken. It was a rule that valued experience, provided predictability, and blunted the force of change. The rule simply stated:

Do a good job and you'll keep a good job.

It didn't always work, but even when textile jobs moved south, people could follow. When small farming ceased to be viable, manufacturing jobs were being added at a prodigious rate. Jobs changed gradually; they did not just vanish overnight, as have thousands of jobs in banking.

Today's anxieties spring from the historical reality that many people started working under that old rule. Many of us still retain some of the deep-rooted belief in mutual loyalty. This book tries to recognize that fact and offers several specific paths to a life and career beyond the corporation—a life of self-reliance.

One path leads back to your present job and company, exploring what you might change in your present situation to create viability. Another leads to examining other jobs and other companies. We will also explore some seemingly off-beat options such as bartering and seminar leadership.

Another path, however, constitutes the bulk of this book. This path leads to the four routes to business ownership: buying a business, buying a franchise, starting a business, and forming a consulting practice.

Whether you choose employment or ownership, you must find your way to becoming your own "economic enterprise." As your own economic enterprise you will invest in yourself through training and education, and you will need to promote yourself so that people will know who you are, where you are, and how good you are.

For at least ten years, with increasing shrillness, writers and commentators have been chronicling the millions of layoffs and the personal and social upheaval that result. They offer a menu of causes—foreign competition, corporate greed, intellectual sloth—and several political, social, and economic theories about what can be done. *On Your Own* offers a basic, practical, and personal approach. The strategy is to create options; the goal is self-reliance.

C. D. Peterson

Acknowledgments

A writer may believe passionately in an idea for a book, but publishers decide what books are published and how they are marketed. My idea was simple: to write a book that would really help people who find themselves—by choice or fate—on their own. I intended no fanciful tales about corporate dreamers who drop out and whittle artworks in Vermont, and no adoring anecdotes about some billionaire's "secrets"—told to anyone who will listen—of entrepreneurship. The book was to be a well-structured, straightforward work, full of tested advice and practical ideas, accompanied by useful worksheets and references. It was to be a book for people dealing seriously with the reality of being on their own.

The publisher that gave me the opportunity to do the book my way, without the pandering promise of simplicity and a wagonload of vacuous anecdotes that can seduce buyers, was John Wiley & Sons, Inc. The editor who secured that opportunity is Michael Hamilton, who edited an earlier book for me, *An Introduction to Business Brokerage*. Mike believed that a professionally oriented book, based on real experiences with business buyers, sellers, and those in transition, would appeal to readers. Let's hope Mike is right!

I received help from Attorney Fred Baker of Baker, Moots, and Pelligrini, who practices in Danbury, Connecticut. He provided up-to-date advice on legal topics.

Mr. John Durkin, of Financial Underwriters in Danbury, gave me a lot of help with the personal finance material.

Given my full-time job, this book was written in the very late hours of the evening and on those weekends when I was not working. My wife, Odessa, provided ungrudging tolerance and absolute support, and she kept the task of writing fun for me.

C. D. Peterson

PART I

Reality Check

"I wasn't let go in the latest cutbacks. I should be very thankful—jobs are hard to get. It's just that I ended up with all the work from the people who left my department. Now I'm worried that if I can't keep up, they'll fire me. Regardless of what they say, I think more cutbacks are coming. I really need this job."

Talk to enough working people today and you will certainly hear similar words. These are good people, the survivors. They were judged valuable in courts of harsh economic necessity. Unfortunately, much like the firms they work for, the accumulated equity of a person's past performance—in some cases a life's work—has been seriously devalued. Consider how companies' activities today affect those who work for them.

Reengineering erases former understandings of the rules of work and, with them, people's personal reputations for performance.

What management says: "Reengineering means we have to forget about the way things used to be done. The old ways are out. We need new ways to do the work."

What people hear: "All my years of hard work don't mean a thing. It's 'what have you done for me lately' from now on."

Continuous Quality Improvement, by definition, promises only that change is constant and that the prospect of meeting the basic human need for predictability is gone.

(*Continued*)

(Continued)

What management says: "We can't rest on our successes. Improving quality must go on indefinitely, continuously. Quality is a pursuit that will never end."

What people hear: "We'll never have time to savor our accomplishments, no time to practice what we've learned or to feel comfortable with our skills. The pressure we're feeling now will never go away."

Change is necessary, but the view of change differs between those who initiate change and those who are affected by it.

What management says: "Like it or not, we have to face reality. This is business today."

What people hear: "Like it or not, we have to face reality. Life stinks."

CHAPTER 1

The New Realities of Corporate Employment

At midcareer, a self-reliant person can always find bright spots. Nonetheless, reality can sometimes paint a dark picture. People today cannot entrust their lives and futures to the institutions and practices that have existed since the end of the Depression. These served well in the past, but a new century will require new perspectives. The final decade of this century will be a forge in which individual self-determination will be tested.

1990 began the decade of self-reliance. Corporations abandoned paternalism and cast off any traces of obligatory loyalty. Government help at all levels is shrinking. International competition respects only economic strength and vigor.* As in America's early days, each of us needs to kindle a pioneering spirit of rugged individualism. Tough as it may seem after giving and receiving corporate loyalty, it is going to be up to you to take care of yourself and your family—to be self-reliant beyond the corporation.

Organizations will continue to be the major source of employment and, after waves of downsizing, will slowly stabilize as the baby boomers begin to retire at the end of this decade and a labor shortage sets in. Only a few years ago large corporations such as IBM, GM, and Sears were being called "dinosaurs." Today they are stable, and IBM reports that it is hiring 10,000 people a year in its services division. Being self-reliant and working as

---

*Consider that a company can pay one year's wages to a software engineer in Bangalore for what it would cost to buy just one month of the same skills in Seattle.

a team member within an organization are not in conflict. A good team player is not only reliant, but reliable.

What Happened to Loyalty and Job Security?

Before we discuss what it will take to be self-reliant in the second half of the 1990s, we need to have a common understanding of the forces that have shaped the dilemma we now face and a common awareness of the problem to be solved.

For most people reading this book, what follows will be old and sad news, but they can take heart that their plight is recognized and seize the means for self-reliance that this book provides. Others may find all this to be startling news, but that, too, is good because such people need strong motivation to do the work to become self-reliant.

Looking back, we can see that loyalty grew from the years when professional managers wrested power away from the founding owner-barons and created the orderly pyramid organization, the organization that is now being flattened and stripped of its tidy structure.

Background

When World War II ended, the United States was the world's sole economic power with undamaged, newly built industrial plants and unchallenged, freshly developed technology. The G.I. Bill sent millions of the middle class to college, while government policies and loan programs fueled a housing (and baby) boom from Levittown, New York, to Long Beach, California.

The Eisenhower years brought billions of dollars into highways and bridges, providing jobs and a new infrastructure. The United States at mid-century was strong and secure.

From Strength to Weakness

Strength, however, led directly to a new phenomenon. The strong U.S. dollar was being spent overseas, where new competitors, fresh from rebuilding their war-ravaged businesses, were aggressively challenging us in our own markets. In the 1960s the balance of payments shifted and the United States became a net importer.

In 1971 the exchange rates were allowed to float and the dollar fell. Although this made U.S. goods easier to sell, it also made the now very large flow of imported goods more expensive to buy, so that prices crept upward. The oil crises arrived, and by the mid-1970s inflation was at a full gallop. At first corporate profits benefited from inflation. Companies granted expensive and self-perpetuating cost-of-living formulas for wage increases. Because these and other cost increases could easily be passed on by raising prices, investments in capital and technology to improve efficiency and productivity were neglected.

The 1980s brought little but financial market legerdemain, creating only temporary service jobs, debt, and a few millionaires.   ⤷ DEF?

From Security to Jeopardy

Near the end of the 1980s *Business Week* (Oct. 5, 1987) observed:

> Companies became trapped in the worst of all possible worlds. By the late 1970s even though profits still seemed strong, productivity growth was slowing to a crawl. The competitiveness of American manufacturers, as measured by their share of world markets was sagging. The Federal Reserve Board pushed up interest rates to fight inflation, and the dollar soared. American companies had to cope with higher credit costs while being priced out of markets overseas and surrendering big chunks of their domestic markets to cheaper and better imports.
>
> [In the late 1980s the] adjustment has been painful. Plant closings, layoffs, ⟶ DEF? restructuring, mergers, and acquisitions have provided the "leitmotiv" of the corporate drama for at least five years. Some industries have undergone wholesale elimination of excess capacity in a process of consolidation designed to carve up a shrinking pie among fewer companies.

In the years since this article appeared, things have worsened. Layers of managers, thousands of workers, and much of the cadre of financial services hires have been laid off as companies face the ferocity of international competition against world standards of quality, price, and value.

The Picture Today

Now, unless you take action, it will be you, the individual, who will be faced with threats to your paycheck from many sides. The very things that ✳ companies do to improve their own security imperils the security of their workforce. Your company's programs to improve productivity and lower costs cause layoffs in the short term. The president and CEO of Data General announced on a national news show that his company's improvements in manufacturing processes would allow the firm to shrink from 5 million square feet of space to 2 million square feet and still produce the same number of products. He foresaw more and more layoffs not only for his firm, but for others in his industry, as productivity improvement becomes an ongoing process during good times, not an occasional event when things are bad.

These so-called structural layoffs usually result in a migration of people to new jobs in new industries or new locations. This time, however, international competition is eliminating jobs everywhere, often permanently. Even the U.S. Army is reducing its workforce, using civilian techniques of offering retirement packages and seeking volunteers, but also resorting to coercive tactics by withholding reenlistment contracts.

New Factors

This is not a blip caused by a recession. This is an historic restructuring of the U.S. work force that's taking place over many years.
                              Dan Lacey, Editor of *Workplace Trends*

Americans have weathered employment contractions before. In the past, business cycles seldom hit all businesses at once, and ways were found to prime the economic pump. Today the economy labors under huge governmental debt, which limits its ability to intervene. Political sentiment to reduce debt further restricts intervention.

Federal government debt and, in some cases, policy have sucked up funds that previously flowed into state treasuries and the programs they supported. The layoff of state workers such as state police and state university employees—unheard of in times past—has become commonplace. State programs aimed at social, welfare, medical, and other such services are under severe pressure.

As might be expected, the financial pressure at the state level has been leveraged down to the local level. Local budget meetings have become contentious and often divisive affairs pitting young parents against the elderly, environmentalists against business people, and eventually neighbor against neighbor. In my own county, local budgets in several towns are rejected three and four times, until cuts are made in such previously sacred accounts as teachers' salaries and school programs. These rejections occur at now-packed town meetings that traditionally had been attended by few residents.

Between the Cracks—More Cracks

Although some resources have been directed to improving our factories, our productive methods, and our infrastructure, new problems demand attention.

Insolvencies among companies and their insurers have put pension funds at risk. You may know some retirees who never imagined they would face the prospect of poverty as they are trapped between reduced or dried-up pensions and rising medical costs. Rising health-care costs are forcing firms, unable to offset or pass on the increases, to shift the added cost to employees. These co-payments and higher deductibles can strip hundreds of dollars a month from a paycheck. State governments furlough massive segments of their operations, cutting services to their economies and wages to their employees.

Perhaps even more ominous are the tears showing up in the social fabric. Topics such as immigration, protectionism, welfare reform, and job quotas are back in the limelight. These issues focus on income redistribution—on recutting the economic pie to favor one group over another to achieve some degree of desired equity. These issues arise when that pie stagnates or shrinks. They also divide the people and add no value to the country's wealth.

Commentators blame the national debt and job shrinkage for such diverse problems as the emergence of extremist politicians, the extraordinary level of child poverty, and the upsurge in street gangs.

Finally, it has not escaped notice that the income of Americans is being redistributed. The rich are getting richer, and the income gap is widening. The richest 5 percent of the population has seen its after-tax, after-inflation income grow by 60 percent over the last 15 years, while the bottom two thirds of the population watched its real income *decline* by more than 10 percent.

Changing Perspectives and New Expectations

We have reached a watershed in American life as the prospect of ever-rising prosperity has come to an end. No longer can each generation automatically look forward to better jobs, bigger homes, more leisure, and greater security. In fact, only one generation in our country's history, the generation that matured in the 1940s, enjoyed the explosive growth in opportunities that has recently ended. To the dismay of today's young and the sadness of their parents, younger generations will be lucky to live nearly as well as their forebears.

Periodicals have chronicled stories of middle-class people facing daily economic peril. The business section of the *New York Times* (Nov. 17, 1991) detailed the agony of families "trapped in the impoverished middle class," where even a modest life is slipping away. *Business Week* (Oct. 21, 1991) told of people who "don't have enough money to walk through the mall," and then devoted a cover story (Mar. 9, 1992) to "downward mobility." More recently the *New York Times* (Jan. 1, 1996) marked the baby boomers' hitting 50 years old with a featured article lead-in that stated "longer lives, yes, but less time to pay for it all."

As early as mid-1991, the *Wall Street Journal* reported that U.S. living standards were slipping and had begun the slide even before the recession. An autumn of political denial failed to overcome popular intuition and daily experience, eventually putting this momentous condition at the center of American focus, and costing an incumbent president his expected reelection.

One Person's Reality

One poignant story is of Susan Balee, a well-educated woman who, as she put it, "commited the crime of poverty." With her last $170, Ms. Balee went to court to pay a ticket for driving with an expired registration. After observing a procession of defendants receive various metes of justice, she learned from the cashier that her expected fine of $167.50 had been increased to $203. Flirting with the top limit of her credit card, she managed to draw the needed cash and pay the fine. She described her feelings in *Northeast*, the magazine of the *Hartford Courant* (Oct. 6, 1991):

> I went to court feeling self-righteous, but I left feeling humble. It used to be that there was a wide margin between me and the majority of the people who were called to that courtroom. But suddenly it seemed that there was very little difference between us at all. I had an education, but I couldn't get a decent job with it. I was married, but my husband was forced to live in another state for his job, and I was forced to raise my daughter without his help. I could still say "Have credit card, will travel," but how long would it be before I would have to abandon even that motto? How long before I couldn't afford to make the minimum payments? I was a member of the well-educated middle class, but I felt the cracks beginning to open beneath my moccasins. It wouldn't be that hard to slide into the underclass—a few bad months and we could fall through the cracks.

Most individuals have bet on the system. A good education brought to bear with solid work habits is supposed to guarantee the good (and most likely better) life. For over 10 years, however, the system that said "Do a good job and you'll keep a good job" has been changing to one that says "I can pay you if you can solve my problems, lower my costs, or increase my income—if I have room for you."

Managements have applied this philosophy openly—some would say ruthlessly—even to their top-level executives: When executives at Westinghouse, Goodyear, IBM, Apple, and the White House were terminated, management made no bones about the fact that the executives had not been performing.

Downward Mobility

In the early 1980s many of us heard stories about shocked senior and middle-level executives who experienced unexpected joblessness. Television and print media did in-depth pieces on some of these new unemployed and introduced their audiences to "downsizing" strategies, "outplacement" companies, and "networking" techniques. Now, in the late

1990s, there are stories about the enormous stress gripping some of these same people as they face joblessness a *second time*, further in debt, older, and with much diminished confidence.

The American Management Association reported that the 12-month period ending June 30, 1991, was the worst period for job cutting in history. Though individual cuts were smaller, more companies pursued downsizing. For the first seven months of 1992, staff cuts ran 2.3 percent ahead of 1991.

White-collar workers are receiving most of the publicity in this period because it is the first time they have been on the unemployment lines and in line for food stamps, but blue-collar workers are not exempt. General Motors alone used a variety of incentives to encourage 12,000 workers to leave and is still pushing for more, possibly as many as 74,000. General Electric and others are using similar programs.

Data from the U.S. Bureau of Labor Statistics show that many of the jobless do not recover. Even in the good times of the 1980s, as many as 14 percent never found work. Those who did were reemployed at an overall *decrease* in wages of 11.8 percent. In addition, 25 percent of those reemployed took cuts of 20 percent or more, and 25 percent lost health insurance. Not counted as unemployed are another 11 percent who were full-time workers but who are now part-time, self-employed, or unsalaried in a family enterprise.

The Plight of the Employed

Those who are employed also face problems. Tough times have created a whole new cadre of business celebrities: tough-minded managers. Gone are the charismatic CEOs who inspired us, and the fast-food franchise kings who showed us how simple success could be. The covers of magazines today feature the grim faces of managers who "cut fat to the bone" and who are "fighting a struggle for survival" as they consolidate, merge, scuttle sick operations, and shed workers. As these leaders install this new culture into their businesses and as other firms copy their model, the American worker who *is* employed is paying a price in higher stress and lower job satisfaction.

Reduced Job Satisfaction

The abrupt stop of the growth elevator of the 1980s caused many people to bang into the ceiling. For some the economic brake had the added drag of discrimination. For many, the vision of the firm providing them with increasing responsibilities, more varied and interesting assignments, and ample opportunity to grow and to experience personal fulfillment became dim. Lowered positive expectations coupled with negative concerns about basic job security have led to widespread dissatisfaction.

The *Harvard Business School Bulletin* of April 1991 contains a lengthy article about graduates of the school who are dissatisfied with their careers and the substantial consulting activities now devoted to helping such people seek fulfillment through various career transition techniques. Growing unhappiness has contributed to a continuing wave of entrepreneurship and to books with titles like *Is Coffee Break the Best Part of Your Day?* * and *Staying Up When Your Job Pulls You Down.* †

Stress

Confronting dissatisfaction, a basic thrust of this book, connotes some power of action. Enduring stress, however, connotes a wearing away of health and well-being, a sapping of the power necessary to effect change.

The most obvious source of stress on working people is the fear of losing their jobs. This chapter has so far painted a grim picture of employment prospects, one being reinforced at this writing by several merging insurance companies' announcements of more planned layoffs.

No longer protected by past service, loyalty, or recognized accomplishments, employees experience frustration and fear of economic impotence, the feeling of helplessness. Economic impotence undermines feelings of personal financial security. A crushing load of personal debt commonly adds to the stress. Credit-card borrowing and extended car loans have stretched many borrowers to their limit, only a few paychecks from insolvency.

From Asset to Liability

In a particularly harsh turn of events, the single most important asset of most Americans has, for some, become a nightmarish liability. Spurred by the seemingly endless prosperity of the 1980s and attendant soaring house values, owners borrowed heavily against the bloated equity in their homes, taking on heavy second mortgage payments. Now, as they see or hear of others losing their homes to foreclosure, and with job loss a real possibility, these borrowers know it can happen to them.

Yet another kind of stress is also gripping working people: the more familiar but now more pervasive stress of time pressure. Cutbacks by and large have focused on people and not the work they do, so the employees who remain after a cutback often carry a heavier workload.

Fax machines, voice mail, pagers, and the like have wiped out the luxury of "turnaround time" and "out-of-pocket time." Because these devices

---

*Dick Leatherman, Human Resource Development Press, Amherst, MA, 1990.
†Joanne Bodner and Venda Raye-Johnson, Perigee Books, New York, 1991.

have been installed in hotels and resorts, vacations no longer let you "get away from it all." It all follows you.

International business, with its time differences, means doing business at all hours, and frequent international travel has long been known to be a source of stress.

One specific manifestation of increased stress is the increase in sleeping disorders.* When people start losing their jobs or fearing they might lose their jobs, they start losing sleep. The loss of sleep often leads to depression, which hurts job performance, which puts the individual in greater jeopardy of being terminated.

And Now for the Good News . . .

As a way to make a point, this chapter has intentionally painted a bleak picture of the economy, corporate America, political futility, and the specter of this country's first generational maelstrom of downward mobility. But good news can still be found. Consolidations and mergers may make U.S. entities better able to compete with our larger international rivals.

The Internal Revenue Service has approved rules that allow employers to make pension contributions weighted toward older workers, helping companies to retain and attract these experienced people.

One powerful piece of good news can remove worries about an employment "doomsday" scenario. The work population in the United States is declining, and that means a labor shortage looms in the future. Even with weak employment, the underlying labor force is growing at only one third the rate it did after previous downturns began.

The record-breaking cutbacks have barely nudged up the number of unemployed who are actively seeking work. You may be puzzled by the fact that with weak employment and well-publicized massive layoffs, the unemployment rate has remained fairly constant at around 6 percent. Job seekers who just drop out account for some of the relief on the rate, but perhaps a more important factor is the passing of the surge in baby boomers and women who entered the workforce for the first time in the 1970s and 1980s.

Many of today's job seekers with in-demand skills are able to *and do* turn down less-than-great jobs. Others are able to bargain with employers and trade money for more free time, a growing desire among dual-wage-earning families. As an example of what in-demand skills can mean, recent

*Dr. Arthur Kotch, Medical Director of Danbury (CT) Hospital's Sleep Disorders Center, estimates that insomnia, sleep apnea, and narcolepsy cost the economy more than $15 billion a year.

graduates of several schools who took masters' degrees focused on the latest manufacturing engineering techniques, were swamped with offers, and were able to command salaries as high as $90,000. For skilled minorities and females, it is actually a sellers' market. Entrepreneurs with marketable ideas, sharp skills, and solid determination are still starting businesses and profiting from their efforts and risk taking. Trucking deregulation has spawned nearly 30,000 new companies since 1980.

The good news in this chapter shows that highly skilled people are always in demand. People, especially those at midcareer, who can develop and match their accumulated knowledge and extensive experience to the changing needs of the marketplace will have skills with earning power and can afford to be choosy about how to make a living even beyond the corporation. In fact, more experienced business executives often have an advantage when pursuing owership as an alternative to employment. Their experience translates into more confidence, better judgment, and more realistic objectivity. If you are at midcareer, your status brings with it your established reputation and, most likely, considerable resiliency and resourcefulness. More experienced people may have fewer financial commitments and more useful business contacts.

Other good news points to the fact that if you can afford to wait, there will be jobs aplenty as demand curves up over supply. However, if you cannot afford to wait until the next century, if you want more control over your life, if you want more satisfaction from earning income and building wealth, then read on and discover how you can build a new life and career beyond the corporation *now*.

PART II

Look Before You Leap

Discovering your new life and career beyond the corporation may well lead you to a business or professional practice of your own, but before you take that leap, consider some basic steps to self-reliance that will apply no matter what route you decide to follow.

People must now see themselves as *personal enterprises,* almost as if they were human factories or businesses whose task it is to generate income and create personal wealth and security for themselves. Just like corporate businesses, these human versions need investment (training) and marketing (promotion) to keep producing income over a lifetime.

The goal is self-reliance. Start by reinventing yourself as your own personal economic enterprise.

CHAPTER 2

Reinvent Yourself as Your Own Personal Enterprise

Self-reliance depends first on your ability *to produce value competitively*. Whether you plan to work for a company or own your own business, your efforts must provide something the market wants and that delivers higher value than the market could buy somewhere else.

Rule No. 1 for the 1990s

You must be able to describe clearly and quickly how *you* do one of two things: *add to revenue* or *lower costs*. Whether you are an employee or an owner, learn this Rule No. 1 for the 1990s.

Any plan for self-reliance will have to deal with the major complication of choice. There are many ways to produce value competitively; how do you choose which way to develop and what to build on? You can follow a conventional approach and adjust your skills and knowledge to changes in the environment as they occur. Although this is better than not adjusting, it does put your personal enterprise at risk while you catch up to changes. Alternatively, as the economy reinvents itself, you can follow a different approach and choose to reinvent yourself. By consciously examining your own marketability, you can develop a plan aimed at doing what you want to do and being what you want to be. *Employability*, not employment, should be your goal. The process has three parts: (1) *learn what the market demands;* (2) *assess your personal resources;* and (3) *integrate your life values.* View this process as research and development for your personal enterprise.

The Dynamics of Demand

Whether you used your MBA on Wall Street or mastered robots on an auto assembly line in Detroit, you know something about demand: It can change. If you chose to undertake the training to become a physical therapist, you know another thing about demand: It can exist even in the worst of times. If you have been a middle-level manager, "coordinating" or "administrating," you know something else about demand: It can vanish completely and permanently.

Learn How Employment Value Is Determined by Employers

Because self-reliance depends partly on the market's demands, you need ways to analyze where demand exists and, more important, where it will exist in the future. You can assess demand by industry type, by individual company, by occupation, and by type of knowledge and skill.

> The greatest blacksmith of his time couldn't fix the engine in a Model T Ford.

Demand by Industry Type

One way to assess employment demand is by industry type. It is obvious that growth industries will add jobs, but so will static industries, and even declining industries will need new people from time to time. Growth or decline in an industry may be cyclical or structural.

Cyclical Industries. The paper industry is a positive example of a cyclical industry. International supply and demand do grow over time, but they do so in waves of increases and declines. The U.S. paper industry is competitive on the world scene and continues to invest for the future. Within the paper industry, some segments will grow (paper for copy and fax machines) and others will decline (paper for the old tabulating cards), but for the foreseeable future, with or without recycling, paper is a solid cyclical industry. In the short run the paper industry sees cutbacks and additions, and it does engage in productivity improvements that cost specific occupations. Yet a person with skills in high demand by the paper industry has a good foundation on which to build self-reliance.

Less positive examples of cyclical industries are the automobile and tire businesses. While supply and demand may grow over the long term, these U.S. industries, with many old, high-cost plants, are now in a poor position. Foreign manufacturers have made big share gains. Productivity improvements and major cutbacks may continue for some time, making these industries less desirable places to be unless your skills are those that help make the improvements.

Noncyclical Industries. The structure of demand for some industries does not follow a repetitive cycle but rather a life cycle that the industry goes through only once. The nature of the business requires that it constantly develops new products and services as older ones complete their cycles. At the beginning of the cycle the industry is a growth industry, such as cable television is right now. At the end of the cycle, without new products or services, the industry declines, much as the hatting industry has.

Other Industry Factors

Cyclicality, or the lack of it, is only one factor in assessing industry demand. Here are two more.

Supply and Demand. Some industries, such as nonacute health care and personal computers, are facing a demand that seems to have no end. Others, such as aerospace and defense, looked solid just a few years ago, but now appear to be entering a long period of decline.

Employment Intensity. Farming produces a growing output with fewer workers, while retail stores hire thousands of people when sales are static. Health care is employee intensive, whereas cable television is not. It's not enough to pick a growth industry; you need to recognize how that growth translates into jobs.

A plan for self reliance cannot ignore these important factors, as they can render the value of your skills useless and are mostly beyond your control. You can learn about industries at any good library. *Business Week* and other magazines publish annual industry round-up editions. Directories such as Dun's and others provide facts and rankings. Stock brokers can analyze and compare industries in many ways.

Demand by Company

Growth industries include losing companies, and there are winners in declining industries. Your chances of attaining self-reliance depend on your choice about which company you work for. While the chances of an entire industry going from good to bad is rare, it is not rare for individual companies to change from stars to dogs and back again.

During your career you may decide that the company you are with has become a risk to your self-reliance. The implication of such a decision may appear to be self-centered, but consider it no different from the decision a company makes when it fires a worker who is not helping its survival. A caring company may try to correct a slumping worker and you might try to help your slumping company, but self-interest should eventually dominate. At some point you may face the need to choose your own economic well-being over your loyalty to your firm. The choice is yours, but make it consciously. Don't wait around while Rome burns. Better yet, sniff for smoke regularly. If you get caught by surprise, you may end up buried in a crowd of job seekers unleashed on the market at the same time.

You can evaluate prospective companies by talking with employees, suppliers, competitors, and others. If the company is a public one, you can read its annual report and talk with stock brokers. Business libraries maintain files and directories of articles on thousands of companies.

Most job creation comes from new and smaller companies, and from those exploiting new technology. You can check the study of the 500 fastest-growing small companies published annually by *Inc.* magazine, and the growth study of larger companies published each year by *Forbes* magazine.

Demand by Occupation

Several studies have been done on future demand by occupation. The most well known is the Workforce 2000 study of the U.S. Department of Labor. Figure 2–1 shows the 20 occupations that are growing fastest in terms of percent growth. Figure 2–2 shows the 20 occupations that will add the greatest *number* of jobs—perhaps 40 percent of the total—between now and the year 2000.

Some jobs appear on both lists, which means that they are adding lots of jobs very quickly. Those jobs include computer systems analysts, computer programmers, and allied health-care professionals.

Demand by Specific Type of Knowledge and Skill

In any occupation, the specific skills and knowledge needed to succeed change with the advent of new methods, new needs, and new technologies.

Paralegals	Travel agents
Medical assistants	Computer systems analysts
Home health aides	Physical and corrective therapy
Radiologic technicians	assistants
Data processing equipment	Social welfare service aides
repairers	Occupational therapists
Medical record technicians	Computer programmers
Medical secretaries	Human services workers
Physical therapists	Respiratory therapists
Surgical technologists	Corrections officers and
Operations research analysts	jailers
Securities and financial	
services sales reps	

Figure 2-1. The 20 fastest-growing occupations (percent growth). (*Source: Workforce 2000*, Federal Publication.)

Learn How Demand Changes

Figure 2–3 lists the 10 slowest-growing or declining occupations today. Like the lists of hot jobs, this list also changes with time.

To find out what specific skills and knowledge are in demand today, read the help wanted classified and display ads in the newspapers. The *National Business Employment Weekly* is one good source of large display ads, which tend to spell out job requirements clearly. Employment agencies and executive recruiters are other sources of data about today's in-demand skills.

Nursing—A Study in Demand

Hospital beds are half empty in much of the country, as managed care and other forces restrict admissions and limit the length of admissions that do occur. The need for nurses might be expected to fall, but nursing is one of the country's fastest-growing occupations. Why? One dynamic involves the nature of the profession, with its shift hours and turnover. A more important set of reasons, however, stems from the obvious fact that while people may not be treated in hospitals, they are being treated somewhere. That somewhere may be a subacute facility, a nursing home, at home, or in such new settings as assisted-living apartments.

The challenge for nurses is to reinvent themselves to take advantage of the new demands.

Salespersons, retail	Cashiers
Registered nurses	Guards
Janitors and cleaners	Computer programmers
Waiters and waitresses	Food counter, fountain, and
General managers and	related workers
executives	Food preparation workers
General office clerks	Licensed practical nurses
Secretaries, except legal and	Teachers, secondary schools
medical	Computer systems analysts
Nursing aides and orderlies	Accountants and auditors
Truck drivers	Teachers, kindergarten and
Receptionists and information	elementary school
clerks	

Figure 2-2. The 20 fastest-growing occupations (number of jobs). (*Source: Workforce 2000*, Federal Publication.)

An important source is your own company. Your company's human resources department or others in management should be able to give you ideas about which skills are in demand. Also, sharpen and use your own powers of observation.

Tomorrow's Knowledge and Skills

Having today's skills and knowledge is fine, but that won't ensure career self-reliance. The biggest problem many people face is the possible obsolescence of their value. Perhaps they don't know enough or can't do as much as the next person to help their company lower costs or increase revenue.

Developing your skills and knowledge is an ongoing process. A critical part of your decision making about your development is *future* requirements. Your judgment of what kinds of skills and knowledge *will be* needed will determine in great measure how successful you are at achieving self-reliance. You can get help deciding on tomorrow's skills.

Tool operator	Musician
Inspector, grader, tester	College/university professor
Welder	Judge
Vending machine service/repair	Petroleum engineer
Broadcasting technician	Government official

Figure 2-3. The 10 slowest-growing jobs. (*Source: Workforce 2000*, Federal Publication.)

In a poignant "My Turn" column in *Newsweek* magazine, a man in his fifties described his recent firing and the personal trauma surrounding the event and its effect on him. At one point he told readers how he tried to read the help wanted ads *but couldn't even understand the language of the requirements.* He was bitter about his company but did not acknowledge his own responsibility to keep his skills and knowledge current.

Leaders in your field are one source of information about future needs. Leaders are typically the people who recognize and implement new ideas. They are likely to have a vision of the problems and opportunities ahead.

Academics most often do the research and experimentation that shape the future. Knowing what these people are doing and thinking about can give you a special insight into tomorrow's skills and knowledge.

Analysts may not actually describe the skills and knowledge needed, but they do describe the problems and opportunities—that's what you need to know. If you can see the problems and opportunities, you can see ahead to what it will take to meet them. Financial analysts, industry analysts, and technical, political, and economic analysts may all have keys to the future.

If your company employs strategic planning analysts, they should be able to give you a good picture of the problems and opportunities your firm will face in the future. A discussion might reveal a new thrust or emphasis requiring new skills and knowledge. (Don't forget to sniff for smoke about what might be headed for obsolescence.)

Trade and technical associations are good sources of trends and issues. Spot a trend early enough and you may be able to see the problems and opportunities that will develop. These will illuminate what knowledge and skills will be needed.

Personal Assessment

Once you understand what the market wants today and will want in the future, you will be ready for the next step in reinventing yourself: conducting a personal assessment.

Find and overcome your weaknesses; find and exploit your strengths. Personal assessments are more typically called *assessments.* Assessment techniques have been around for decades. They evolved mainly from the fields of industrial psychology and human resources. Assessments use interviews, tests, and other exercises to explore *interests, personality traits, skills*, and *knowledge.*

Assessors use a body of test data accumulated over the years and professional skill to draw some correlations between a person's analyzed results in these four areas and the requirements of various occupations. From the test results and interviews, they can suggest the kinds of work environment and content most likely to be suited to you. Assessors integrate analyses of a person's aptitudes and preferences to produce their reports.

If you have not done such an assessment recently, you may find it useful to do so. Among the dozens of books that deal with personal assessment are Bolles' *What Color Is Your Parachute?*, his *The Three Boxes of Life . . .* , and Krannich's *Careering and Re-careering for the 1990's.** *What Color Is Your Parachute?* includes a section on locating career counselors.

Elements of a Personal Assessment

Appraising your personal enterprise involves taking an inventory of your assets and liabilities. Personal assessment uses certain terms—skills, knowledge, traits, and interests—to take inventory, and you should understand them.

Skills are things you can *do.* They are behaviors you acquire by practice and that you can demonstrate by actions. Figure 2–4 lists examples of skills.

Knowledge is what you *know.* When reason acts on knowledge, there is understanding. You acquire knowledge by observation in its broadest sense, and you can demonstrate it by answering questions. Figure 2–5 gives some examples of knowledge.

The difference between skills and knowledge is important. You can probably acquire the knowledge you need to achieve self-reliance, but the same may not be true for skills. Skills are behaviors you gain through practice, not study.

Juggling will serve as an example. You can learn all the knowledge about juggling that exists—how it works, the laws of physics involved, the history of juggling, and the names and motions of every trick. However, despite all the practice you might devote to juggling, it is possible that you may never acquire the skills to do it properly.

As another example, *medical equipment sales* would rank high on the occupational growth charts in Figures 2–1 and 2–2. Health care is a growth

*Richard N. Bolles, *What Color Is Your Parachute?*, Ten Speed Press; Berkeley, CA, 1996. Richard N. Bolles, *The Three Boxes of Life and How to Get out of Them,* Ten Speed Press; Berkeley, CA, 1992. Ronald K. Krannich, *Careering and Re-careering for the 1990's,* Impact Publications; Woodbridge, VA, 1991.

Acting	Leading
Adapting	Lifting
Administering	Listening
Calculating	Lying
Charming	Managing
Coaching	Negotiating
Conceptualizing	Organizing
Convincing	Perceiving
Creating	Planning
Cutting	Playing
Dancing	Promoting
Designing	Reading
Driving	Running
Estimating	Selling
Fishing	Speaking
Flying	Supervising
Growing	Team building
Influencing	Threatening
Innovating	Translating
Interpreting	Welding
Judging	Writing
Juggling	

Figure 2-4. Typical skills.

field and will need added sales coverage. It is likely that you could learn about the equipment, its features and benefits, the market, the territory, the customers, and the competition. You would have little trouble learning how to manage your time and sales call pattern. But whether you could master the skills of selling—the probe, the presentation, overcoming objections, the tentative close, and all the other techniques of the face-to-face sales situation—is an unknown.

Traits are things you are, characteristics or attributes that are hard to change in adulthood. Figure 2-6 lists just a few traits. Behavioral traits

Architecture	Markets
Company	Mathematics
Competition	People
Computer	Places
Customs	Processes
Facts	Products
Geography	Technology
History	Things
Language	Transportation

Figure 2-5. Examples of kinds of knowledge.

Articulate	Leader
Assertive	Manipulative
Beautiful	Naive
Charismatic	Old
Confident	Patient
Coordinated	Persistent
Creative	Risk taking
Decisive	Short
Disciplined	Shy
Excitable	Sickly
Fast	Strong
Glib	Tall
Honest	Ugly
Imaginative	Withdrawn
Inquisitive	

Figure 2–6. Traits—characteristics and attributes.

such as being "creative" or "mature" are hard enough to examine in ourselves, and nearly impossible for others to help us assess because traits are not seen. We can't see "self-motivated"; we can see only behavior that *we interpret* as reflecting self-motivation.

One widely used test to analyze personality traits is the Myers-Briggs Type Indicator. The test sets up four dimensions of personality and, by combination, reports results as one of 16 "types." Figure 2–7 lists the four dimensions. Using the underlined initials, the results would be reported as, for example, ENFP—someone who is Extroverted, Intuitive, Feeling, and Perceiving.

Interests or preferences can be analyzed using such tests as the Jackson Vocational Interest Survey or the Strong Interest Inventory. Figure 2–8 presents the Strong Interest Inventory classifications.

Interests are often examined as *occupational* (enterprising, artistic, helping, etc.), *basic* (teaching, sales, advising, law, business, etc.), and through *comparisons*, which compare your interests to those of people in specific jobs such as librarian, bank manager, language teacher, and so on.

Extroversion versus Introversion
Sensing versus Intuition
Thinking versus Feeling
Judging versus Perceiving

Figure 2–7. Myers-Briggs types.

Realistic
Conventional
Enterprising
Investigative
Artistic
Social

Figure 2-8. Strong Interest Inventory classifications.

Limitations of Personal Assessment

Although personal assessment is widely used, it has limitations in relevance and scope.

Relevance. Any assessment represents only a snapshot in time. It does not consider your potential to add skills and knowledge or to develop different interests. It does not recognize that you can initiate changes in yourself. An assessment may have limited relevance to your situation and is not a final judgment. It is a tool to guide your initiatives for your future development.

Scope. Unless your assessment involves in-depth personal interviews, it will miss critical factors that affect your career development choices. Your capacity for change has already been mentioned. Other factors not considered within the scope of typical assessments relate to *financial resources, social connections, talent,* and *personal matters.*

Financial resources, or the lack of them, can have a big influence on your plan for career self-reliance. Buying a ski resort may satisfy all the assessment criteria you established, but without the money to buy it, you will need another career alternative—say, becoming the manager.

If you face the prospect of putting three children through college at one time or have other large financial obligations, your career plan has to consider ways to meet those responsibilities. This is not to say that you cannot reject those obligations. People with a passion for their goal have left spouses, walked away from debt, told their children to put themselves through college, and so on. At the other end of the spectrum are people near retirement who have prepared well financially and as a result have few financial constraints when developing a plan for career self-reliance.

Social connections and status can open many career doors. You can build a career plan around your ability to reach board chairmen, for example. The children of actors have a much easier time starting a career in the entertainment business. High visibility in your community may help you to enter politics, real estate, banking, or personal services.

Typical assessments miss the fact that your particular social values may play a big part in your career planning. Your commitment to an issue such as ecology or child abuse may be so strong that it will drive your career plan and development choices.

Talent—natural mental, creative, or artistic ability—can be overlooked in ordinary assessments because it is not part of standardized testing, yet talent can easily be the most important component of your personal enterprise.

Personal matters outside the scope of many assessment exercises include the impact of childhood events, unresolved conflicts, and similar psychological issues. Other personal considerations may involve your inability or unwillingness to relocate, a medical condition, your desire for leisure, your religious beliefs, or even your commitment to health and fitness.

Personal Assessment: Imperfect but Necessary

Appraising your personal enterprise, no matter how deeply you go, is admittedly an imperfect exercise. Your interests, traits, knowledge, and skills are complex and changing. Nonetheless, your personal enterprise, like any business enterprise, needs to be appraised as a way of determining its present capabilities and its investment needs.

Find Your Life Values: Do What You Love

Contemplate lifestyle issues. Unlike other business enterprises, your personal enterprise is based on you, a living human being, composed of more than just an inventory of assets and liabilities. You posses an intellect that acts on both logic and emotion. Examine the power of strong emotion—passion—as you think about reinventing yourself. Many of us who work with people in transition and with those seeking more self-reliance have come to recognize the implications of pursuing a passion.

It takes energy, effort, and sacrifice to go to night school, do book research, take a second job, learn a skill, save a nest egg, or do without some of life's pleasures, but that's just what it takes to learn and develop. You can find agreement on that point in self-help books and other motivational programs, which all stand on the premise that strong desire and a clear goal are prerequisites to achieving human potential.

When people marshall traits, knowledge, skills, and vocational preferences behind a true passion, they can reshape their personal resources, overcome deficiencies, and even reorient their values. Sacrifices become investments as work becomes pleasure.

Zero in on your passion. Finding your passion may take some work. Look for it in those things you do that make you feel good. Think back on jobs or projects that gave you satisfaction. Do you recall ever having been "in a groove" or "high on life?" (Why was that?) Where does your mind take you when it wanders? (Don't you want to spend real time there?)

Career counselors ask their clients to write an autobiography, including the obituary they want for themselves. They ask clients to confess their "wannabe" fantasies. When people first try these exercises and begin their search, they commonly construct barriers to finding their passion. They load their examination with "oughts" and "shoulds," adopting roles and living by standards they allow others to set for them.

Work toward simplifying your life and toward stripping away those burdens and any others—unhealthy relationships, meaningless time wasters, and bad habits. Make room for your passion.

Make your passion part of your career plan. Integrating your passion into a career plan for self-reliance takes creativity. "I love to fish, but I can't make a living at it" would seem to dismiss the whole idea until we think about the Orvis Company and all the other firms that make and market fishing equipment and services. A love of cooking may not translate directly to a career as a chef. It may, however, lead you to full- or part-time involvement in one of the careers listed in Figure 2–9. You can use your functional business skills—marketing, finance, and human resources—as

Butcher	Kitchen installation
Cafeteria manager	Kitchen utensils manufacturing
Catering	Nutritional consulting
Farming	Owning a bakery
Food critic	Owning a luncheon truck
Food products manufacturing	Owning a restaurant
Food service contracting or	Owning a specialty food store
subcontracting	Publishing a newsletter
Food, supply, or equipment	Raising organic vegetables
wholesaling	Selling appliances
Home economist	Selling specialty foods
Inspecting food or restaurants	Teaching cooking
Joining a cooking club	Writing cookbooks
Kitchen design	

Figure 2–9. Cooking-related careers.

an employee if not as an owner of a food, restaurant, or cooking-related business.

One more example may help make the point. Even if you love the outdoors and fresh air, you may not see yourself as a farmer; but how about the possibilities shown in Figure 2–10?

Conform your passion and practicality. You will need to subject any company or job opportunity to the same practical tests you will use when considering a business of your own later in this book:

- How much money you need to earn
- How much money you want to earn
- Location
- Risk
- Growth potential
- Competition
- Physical working conditions
- Status and image
- People intensity

Passion can overcome barriers, but some of these important criteria are, for the most part, beyond your control.

Get help pursuing your passion. There are some excellent books to help you examine and pursue your passion. Two of them deserve mention.

Building supply yard owner	Lumber worker
Civil engineer	Mail carrier
Construction company owner	Marina manager
Country club manager	Milkman
Fisherman	Pool maintenance
Forest ranger	Resort owner
Garden center owner	Road builder
Gardener	Road crew boss
Golfer, tennis player, baseball player, etc.	Ski instructor
	Surveyor
Grounds keeper	Utility lineman
Landscape architect	Yard maintenance company
Law enforcement officer	owner
Lifeguard	

Figure 2–10. Careers for people who love the outdoors.

One is *Do What You Love, the Money Will Follow*, by Marsha Sinetar.*
In her book, Dr. Sinetar provides a series of inspirational pushes to her
reader to "discover your right livelihood." Another excellent source is
Work with Passion, by Nancy Anderson.† Ms. Anderson provides a series
of specific exercises to help you find and plan how to do what you love
for a living.

Setting a Goal

Your route to self reliance depends on your destination, your goal. This
book presents four options, business ownership, employment choices in
and outside your company, "hot" jobs, and some possibly off-beat alternatives. The chapter has also suggested ways to assess your skills, knowledge, and interests so you can conduct an appraisal of the present state of
your personal enterprise.

Building a Career/Life Plan
to Establish Your Earning Power

Don't choose your goal based solely on your *present* state. Decide first
what you want to do and what you want to become. Find your passion.
Next, using your appraisal, determine how your skills and knowledge measure up to the career you have chosen.

Your challenge is to fill any gap in qualifications with a plan of personal
development. This represents the "investment" in your personal enterprise
that will be developed in the next chapter. Only if the qualification gap is
vast and full of requirements beyond your known limits should you adjust
the goal. Even then, if in doubt, go for it. Albert Einstein was a poor stu-
dent, Leon Uris failed English, James Earl Jones once stuttered, Woody
Allen flunked a film class, and Abe Lincoln lost a dozen elections on his
way to the White House.

Why not try your first choice and adjust later if necessary? The joy of
pursuing a paramount goal will lend resolve to your efforts and strengthen
your self-reliance.

*Dell Publishing; NY, 1987.
†Carroll & Graf Publishers; NY, 1990.

CHAPTER 3

Self-Invest to Build Personal Value

Secretaries once honed their dictation and typing skills, then they mastered word processing. Now, to be in demand, office support staff need the skills to do graphics for presentations, manage complex communications systems, and more. Soon they will be learning the skills to exploit the new CD interactive technology. If you haven't mastered CD interactive technology, consider your personal enterprise at a competitive risk.

Draftsmen once mastered tedious drawing skills. Then they used templates, followed years later by the early XY plotters. They learned the first crude computer-aided design (CAD) techniques only a few years ago, and now they create movable, three-dimensional, video-imaged models from databases of design elements. Tomorrow, instead of designing parts and then assemblies, these technicians will create, view from different perspectives, and even operate complete machines that don't yet exist. This is called simulation/animation. If you haven't already thought about how to use a video camera to feed images into your computer, you may learn it from your competition.

Building Personal Value

Commit yourself to never-ending education and training. Your new life and career will require investment. It is not enough to *be* in demand; you must anticipate and prepare for changes in order to *stay* in demand, even in your chosen field. Some professions require continuing education as a matter of course—aviation, real estate, medicine, and accounting, to name a few. To stay in demand, you must treat your personal enterprise as though it, too, requires never-ending education and training.

Decide what you are now and what you want your value to be. You face more of a task than simply keeping your present technical skills up to date, especially if your new life calls for you to change what you do or where you do it. Education alone does not mean self-reliance, as many well-educated (and unemployed) managers, airline pilots, and others will tell you. You have choices of *what* investments to make in yourself, *how* to make them, and what investment *strategy* to follow.

Devise a self-investment strategy that balances expertise with flexibility. Whether you plan to make your investments in yourself by gradually adding to your present skills or by pursuing a full-time program to gain new ones, you need a defined strategy. The two extremes of self-investment strategy are either to become an expert in one field or a generalist in several. A balance between the two will give your personal enterprise its best security.

Become an expert, totally focused. One investment strategy is to become a world-class expert in some specialty. You will then be in demand by those who need what you do. Your personal enterprise will have a competitive advantage, and you should command a premium price. Your expert status might spawn other opportunities, such as writing and speaking, and will help you in your efforts at self-promotion (see Chapter 4).

However, relying solely on expertise as a strategy presents risks to your personal enterprise. The specialty you have chosen may be subject to the pressures of a small market or to obsolescence. In a small market, buyers can exert pressure on your value because you have limited opportunities or alternatives to sell. Obsolescence can overtake even "modern" specialties, such as those connected narrowly with the defense industry.

Change is a constant, and overreliance on this strategy exposes you to the vagaries and whims that can accompany change.

Become a generalist, staying flexible. You can adopt a strategy at the other extreme, and add as many skills as possible to your personal enterprise. If the skills you choose are in demand, you will be in demand. You will be well positioned to react to changes in your environment. Because you understand several functions, you will work better in teams.

Your flexibility will enable you to recognize and adapt to new demands and opportunities.

But accumulating a large number of new skills takes time, energy, and other resources. Taken to extreme, it is likely that you will not be able to gain proficiency in any of them. While none of your competitors may have as many skills, it's a good bet that several of them have better skills, and that will relegate you to picked-over and less desirable assignments.

Achieve balance between flexibility and expertise. You can reach a balance by using an "inchworm" strategy. Stretch yourself to acquire a new skill, but then gather yourself up and take the time to become competent at it. Another method is to acquire a group of similar skills—say, computer fundamentals and basic software literacy—at one time, so the learning is mutually reinforcing.

Base your mix of expertise and flexibility on the overall development goal you set at the end of Chapter 2. You will always be recycling your skills, adapting them into newly marketable forms. A career was once like a chess game, with known moves and rules, but today it is more like a quick-reflex video game, with unexpected, often random, twists and turns. A mistake can mean the game—your career—is over.

Develop yourself as an economic resource; choose a mix of hard and soft skills. *Hard skills* include swapping interest rates, operating a backhoe, constructing benefits plans, selling financial products, and doing desk-top publishing. *Soft skills* encompass such things as working in teams, making timely decisions, and adapting to changes.

Your investment in becoming proficient in hard skills will make you better qualified to increase revenue or reduce costs, which make up the marketable value of your personal enterprise. Gaining soft skills will make you able to apply your hard skills and realize that value. Developing these skills together will make you a more functional and complete economic resource.

Hard Skills

Certain hard skills and basic knowledge are nearly mandatory for your personal enterprise to be competitive.

Language Skills

Language skills are the foundation of all the skills in your personal enterprise. If you have strong language skills, you have a true competitive advantage. The generally poor level of these skills draws fire from education, government, and business leaders. Many Americans cannot read well enough to follow written instructions, or write well enough to compose a simple paragraph.

You can enhance your personal enterprise by sharpening your English-language skills, and you can do even more for yourself by mastering other languages. The formation of a European Economic Community, the reemergence of Eastern Europe, the potential for capitalism in the former Soviet Union, and the surging power of the Pacific Rim economies all present opportunities for those with in-demand skills, but those skills are worth little if they can't be employed because of a language barrier.

Consider for a moment how much larger the market for your services would be if you spoke just one other language. As might be expected, English-language training is a billion-dollar business in Japan.

Mathematics and Science Skills

Mathematics and science, the foundations of technology, are also in bad shape in our general population. Critics say that the monetary reward of financial and business careers has been siphoning the best and the brightest of us away from the sciences. Although scientific breakthroughs still happen in Silicon Valley, Cambridge, and elsewhere, we can look with some embarrassment at the fact that nearly all recent innovations in manufacturing and quality improvement have come from Japan.

The ability to apply quantitative techniques to solve problems is a hard skill in short supply. If you can add skills such as the capability to do statistical analysis or to construct mathematical models to the other skills in your personal enterprise, you will be more in demand. In Chapter 1 we saw the specific example of manufacturing graduates who also had engineering (mathematical) training being able to command up to $90,000 starting salaries.

Investment in your science skills and their application will give you an ability to innovate, to make improvements, and to create. As a result, the investment will add to your value and make you more self-reliant.

Computer Skills

Computer competency means more than simply being literate. Every part of every modern enterprise uses computers. This chapter began with examples of how secretarial work and drafting have embraced these skills and have been changed by them. These changes are occurring in all disciplines. Manufacturing schedules push the limits of resource utilization and require on-line systems to function. Cash management has become a minute-by-minute activity requiring computerized networks. Handheld electronic counters take shelf inventories in stores, while consumer purchasing activity is instantly recorded by bar code scanners for analysis of every sale. And you and your family are almost certainly in several computer databases; just check your mail box to see the evidence.

Here are six computer fundamentals and their primary functions.

1. *Hardware and operating systems* are the "black box" parts of the computer world. Most people need only a general understanding of how computers actually do what they do. You usually can acquire this knowledge with experience.
2. *Word processing* is the electronic version of typing, editing, composing, and revising text. Many brands of software programs offer spell checking, a thesaurus, graphic composition capabilities, and more.
3. *Spreadsheets* are the basis for most financial and mathematics work. Spreadsheets create electronic boxes by using one set of labels across the top and another set of labels down the side. For example, you might put the 12 months across the top and the elements of a budget down the side, creating boxes of budget elements for each month. You can then perform any mathematical function you wish on the data in these boxes. Spreadsheets also handle text to support the presentation of the information.
4. *Databases* are essentially files. These might be customer files, parts lists, or anything similar. Database software programs allow you to manage those files. One common use is with mailing lists. Today's software is very powerful, containing integrated elements of word processing and computation.
5. *Desktop publishing* software allows you to generate wide ranges of type styles and sizes and permits the use of graphics from simple icons to elaborate scanned-in pictures, depending on the software program.
6. *Planning and scheduling* programs focus on time management and are variations of spreadsheets.

You can buy software that combines several functions, typically word processing, database management, and a spreadsheet component.

Selling Skills

Selling is a hard skill that can give you both singular and added value. The singular value of being able to sell comes from the ability to increase revenue. If you are skilled at convincing customers to pay money for a product or service, you have an in-demand skill no matter how bad the state of the economy is. Coupling selling skills with your primary hard skills can only add value to your personal enterprise.

People tend to think of selling as a discrete function performed by full-time salespeople, but many employees in a company have the opportunity to sell if they have the skills. The credit manager with sales skills knows how to satisfy customers even when saying "no." The engineer who can sell adds valuable credibility in contacts with technical buyers. Few sales calls are more effective than those made by a team from sales, service, and manufacturing.

Selling *skill* is often transferable from one product or service to another, as long as you can acquire the needed *knowledge*.

These skills—language, science and mathematics, computer skills, and sales skills—are just four broad examples of easily demonstrated hard skills.

Soft Skills

Unfortunately, the woods are full of people with hard skills who can't function in organizations. Some possess no interpersonal skills, others trip over politics, and still others cannot adjust to change. Soft skills, though less easy to define and prescribe, can be every bit as important to your personal enterprise.

Interpersonal Skills

Interpersonal skills include everything from your ability to communicate to your competence as a supervisor. Negotiating, building relationships, resolving conflict, and establishing a positive work climate are all examples of skills involving interactions with other people.

Leadership is the most powerful and most written about interpersonal skill. Many feel that leadership, like creativity, is in part a trait—"leaders are born, not made." This implies that some of the behaviors can be learned, but effectiveness isn't assured.

Don't spend too much time on this debate. Rather, invest in gaining interpersonal skills because your plan for self-reliance will depend in great measure on your skills in dealing with others. Being self-reliant does not mean being a loner. Strategic alliances, support groups, partnerships, and even employment relationships may all be part of your strategy of self-reliance beyond the corporation.

Team Skills

Team skills, whether as a team member or leader, have increasing value as more and more companies adopt this form of organization. Understanding group behavior, exerting influence in a group, and being able to adapt your goals to those of the group represent typical team skills.

Because teams can be "self-managing," many of the self-reliance skills you develop as an individual will be needed by the team as a unit.

Profit-Making Skills

A focus on revenues and costs is not new, but we now recognize and identify it as a separate and important one. Broadly defined, it means:

- Having the skills to make your actions, no matter in what capacity, increases revenue or lowers costs and thereby contributes to profits
- Seeing the business from the viewpoint of the customer and applying creativity to satisfying customer needs and creating opportunities to generate revenue
- Getting the most out of the resources you manage so that you improve efficiency and lower costs

To increase revenue and lower costs, you need to understand how your business, client, or employer makes money. You need to know their objectives and strategies. To be most effective, your skills in this area should include a good understanding of what others do and how to work with them to achieve this focus.

Decision-Making Skills

Timely decision skills are essential to turn your revenue/cost focus into action. You need the skills to make correct decisions, normally a combination of gathering knowledge and applying analysis, and you need the skills to make decisions quickly. Organizational speed now connotes a strategic strength. Competitive battles are being won or lost on how quickly a product or service can be brought to market. Huge cost savings can come from shortening development time or reducing the time that money is owed. If you can contribute to that strength, you have additional in-demand skills.

Information-Gathering Skills

Information gathering is absolutely essential to decision making. Although it is a soft skill, finding, retaining, and interpreting information takes hard work and a kind of resourcefulness that typifies the idea of self-reliance. Two variables—what and where—are at work.

What information to gather depends on how you ask the question. If you ask what information is needed, most people either won't know or will ask for far more information than they need. Tons of green-and-white-striped computer printouts languish in offices as proof. Instead of asking what information is needed, ask what decisions are to be made. Once you know the decisions to be made, you can figure out what information you require to make them.

Where to get information depends on what it is and how important it is. Commissioning a major consulting study, visiting a competitor, doing a library literature search, or making a phone call to someone who has an answer to a question could all be appropriate at one time or another. The second trick to gathering information, then, requires you to cultivate as deep a file of resources as you can. If you have done a good job of identifying what information you need, building a resource file about where to find it will be easier.

Political Skills

Political skills have always been valuable, but with the advent of flatter, less formal hierarchies of decision making and power, your personal enterprise must be politically skilled. Political skills relate to your ability to understand and function in the culture and informal power structure of an organization. Political skill means knowing what behavior is and is not valued, what the standards are for appearance and work habits, how information actually flows, and who influences that flow. The ultimate results of political activity produce and implement decisions. Observe and analyze decisions and how they are made. When a decision seems to be illogical, you may be missing the politics of it. Seek to understand who had what influence on the outcome and why.

Advice on this soft but often brutal skill has been written about in everything from Nicolo Machiavelli's *The Prince* to Susan Haden Elgin's *The Gentle Art of Verbal Self Defense* (Dorset Press, 1980).

Other Soft Skills

Versatility is a skill that requires two components, broad competence and adaptability. If you make the investments to add a good mix of hard and soft skills, and to balance expertise with flexibility, you will add this valuable skill to your personal enterprise.

Other soft skills you might want to gain are those concerned with *quality* and those related to *international business*. The focus on these two areas indicates they are trends, not fads.

Acquiring Knowledge and Skills

Develop a plan to acquire the knowledge and skills you want. Once you have chosen a strategy for investing in yourself and have decided what investments to make, decide how you will make those investments. You have a rich array of resources available to you. Some, such as universities, are costly; others, such as libraries, are virtually free.

Pursue skills acquisition through institutions. A variety of institutions can help you acquire the skills you want.

High schools, colleges, and universities offer full- and part-time programs, day and evening courses, credit and noncredit courses, and often special programs to meet specific needs of their market. Some institutions may specialize in your field.

A few institutions advertise, and all have some form of catalog. Increasingly, these institutions use direct mail to solicit enrollments, and you should get on the mailing lists of institutions that offer programs in your desired skills.

Private institutions such as computer centers or real estate schools offer specialized training, whereas some, such as The Learning Annex or The California Institute of Integral Studies, offer courses in everything from film making to flirting, all at very reasonable prices.

Look for private institutions in the Yellow Pages and get on their mailing lists.

The *armed services* have always offered training and a way to afford it. The period of service required of you need not be full time or active duty. The armed services now offer programs that will build a fund for tuition once you complete your service. The services do, of course, employ an openly discriminatory, though completely understandable, hiring policy regarding age and physical fitness.

Government training programs are offered by cities, states, and the federal government. The *U.S. Government Manual* is a guide to federal programs. Federal training programs are the responsibility of the Department of Labor. Here are some specific programs and phone numbers to find more information about them:

- Office of Trade Adjustment Assistance. This office oversees programs that provide reemployment services such as training, job search and relocation allowances, and weekly cash payments to people who have lost their jobs because of foreign imports. (202) 523-0555.
- Bureau of Apprenticeship and Training. This office oversees and promotes apprenticeship programs. (202) 535-0540.
- Office of Job Training Programs. This office is responsible for administering the Job Training Partnership Act of 1982. The goal of the act is to train or retrain and place eligible individuals in permanent, unsubsidized employment, preferably in the private sector. (202) 535-0236.
- Veterans' Employment and Training Service. This service directs programs through a nationwide network of field offices and in cooperation with the states. (202) 532-9116.

State and local programs can be found by contacting the appropriate employment office or an office of human resources development.

Take advantage of work-related training. In addition to institutions, a rich source of training is your place of work, even if your company does not offer formal training programs. Don't wait for someone to offer training to you, take the initiative and find out what is available. If your company does not offer some form of training that you think it should, take the added initiative to propose a program.

Formal training is offered by many companies. Now that you know what knowledge and experience you want, you can take the initiative and seek out the programs that fit your plan. Don't overlook conferences and other similar events that you might be able to attend.

On-the-job training is a valuable and often overlooked way to get the experience you are after. You can ask to have responsibilities added to your job. Volunteer for special assignments, project teams, and task forces. One good way to do this is to identify a problem or opportunity that needs multiple skills to solve, and at the same time identify the people (including yourself) who will be needed to do the job.

Create a rationale for cross-training with other people. Companies are or should be looking for ways to increase flexibility and keep head counts low. Having people cross-trained in many skills and tasks is a good way to do it.

Seek out people in your company who might help you learn. Show your appreciation with lunch or a small gift. Spend your own unpaid time, if you must, to observe, ask questions, and learn. These are investments in your personal enterprise and will add to your self-reliance.

Apprenticeships offered by companies and unions are tried-and-true ways to invest in yourself. If you have made the investments in basic skills such as language and math, you should be able to compete well for entry into these programs.

Apprentice yourself to an expert, formally or informally. Finding mentors, people willing to invest time and effort in your development, requires that you find people whose own objectives complement yours. Finding people who will spend the time simply because they are altruistic will be serendipitous. More likely, you will find people who like you and who see in your potential the means to achieve their own or the company's goals.

The real challenge is not so much for you to find a mentor, but for a mentor to find you. Some techniques to help make that happen are covered in Chapter 4, but the single best thing you can do is superlative work.

Gain knowledge and skills on your own. If you haven't spent much time learning on your own, you are in for a surprise. The marketplace for training, development, and self-improvement is huge. Seminars, tapes, books, products, courses, counseling, workshops, and retreats ranging from mountain climbing (to build your confidence) to isolation (to find your "center") are offered by companies and individuals.

You can find information about these offerings in advertisements in magazines and newspapers, and some will arrive via direct-mail campaigns. You can also contact The American Society for Training and Development (1630 Duke Street, Alexandria, VA 22313) or the Human Resources Information Network (9585 Valpariso Court, Indianapolis, IN 46268), which provide substantial databases of available programs.

Richard Bolles has assembled an extensive list of counseling resources at the back of his *What Color Is Your Parachute?.**

Regulation in this marketplace, particularly in the self-help arena, is spotty, so shop very carefully. Some promoters aim their material at peoples' deepest needs for security and self-actualization and make wonderfully appealing claims for success. As usual, if something sounds too good to be true, it probably is.

Libraries deserve special mention. They, and to a lesser extent bookstores, represent gold mines for people with the initiative to explore and exploit them. At little or no cost, you can have access to many of the same ideas, products, and services offered for sale in the market. More important, libraries organize information for you in exactly the way you are looking for it, by subject.

Libraries also deserve special mention because of the developments in library technology in just the last few years. Most public and university libraries are now part of computer systems that give them—and you—access to materials in dozens of other libraries. Libraries are increasingly becoming subscribers to computerized on-line and CD-ROM databases and the Internet. This means that you have access to millions of up-to-date facts on your subjects of interest.

Also, libraries are becoming increasingly active in career issues by taking initiatives to assemble resource lists, offering special speakers' programs, and becoming network centers.

Other learning on your own can include a reading program. To stay alert to your world you need to read the right newspapers, books, and magazines. Taking an active part in your trade or professional association can help. By following the steps we have outlined in developing your program for self-reliance, you can have a clear set of investment objectives, and this will help you focus your efforts.

Getting Help with Your Development Plan

Expect to be pleasantly surprised when you seek help in preparing your development plan. Your boss and your company's human resources department are easy places to start. Even if you seek a future outside the corpo-

*Ten Speed Press; Berkeley, CA, 1996.

ration, your present company will be willing to help so as to achieve its own goals. High schools and colleges offer counseling help. Librarians can help. You can hire professionals from the list of resources mentioned elsewhere in this chapter. You might simply team up with others in your situation and be resources for each other as you prepare your personal development plans.

The American characteristic of helping and even cheering those who are working to get ahead is still alive and well, as you will discover.

It's All Up to You

All the help and resources in the world by themselves can't make you more knowledgeable or more skilled or put you more in demand. To be sure, serendipity and luck will play a part in your development, but luck only benefits the well prepared. Luck occurs where preparation meets opportunity.

No one can build knowledge and skill using excuses. If you can find the time to watch TV, you can find the time to take a course. If you don't have a lot of money, use the library and on-the-job training.

You may find these investments hard to make. They may call for sacrifices in time, money, and effort. But you will be investing in your own personal enterprise, investing in your skills and knowledge, providing yourself with something no person and no corporation can take away from you—your self-reliance.

CHAPTER 4

Now That You're Sharp, Get Recognized . . . and Make Opportunities Come to You

From the first page of this book you have been told that in-demand skills are necessary for a midcareer personal enterprise to succeed. You already know that good work habits and job performance are necessary elements for success. The right skills, good work habits, and great performance are *necessary*, but they are not *sufficient* to guarantee self-reliance. Remember:

> The best economic insurance you can obtain is having skills that are in demand and having lots of employers, headhunters, and other influential people who know who you are, where you are, and how good you are.

What you *don't* want is to be out of a job, running in the pack with others as they mass-mail resumes, chase want ads, and network frantically. You need to insure against that risk by actively generating a steady flow of interest in your personal enterprise.

Before we discuss the many ways you can generate a flow of interest in your personal enterprise, you need to understand the conventional ways to find a job. Though this is not a book on job searching, we will cover the basic techniques.

Basic Techniques of Job Searching

For years people in recruiting and outplacement have advocated four well-established methods of job searching:

1. Responding to advertisements
2. Contacting executive recruiters
3. Contacting companies directly
4. Networking

Today we still use all of our methods, but with different emphasis and some new variations. Recent economic conditions have reduced the normal formation and flow of job opportunities into the employment market. Responding to ads is therefore less productive because there are fewer ads—and more applicants. Recruiters are a less fertile source for the same reason: Their inventory of jobs is low. A less obvious factor affecting these two traditional methods is cost. Newspaper ads and recruiters are expensive, and many companies have a databank of people on file and don't need help finding candidates. Similarly, *contacting companies* produces fewer results because of the oversupply of applicants and the scarcity of openings. Networking, offered by some experts as the preferred technique, now suffers from overuse and clutter.

Your first step in the job search process should be to decide on an appropriate career direction. Earlier chapters discussed what you need to set your direction. Once you have a career direction, you can establish transition objectives: the industries, positions, geographic areas, companies, and people you want to contact. Your job campaign strategy will flow from these objectives.

The next step is to select a campaign method. Experts strongly advocate a balanced approach using all four campaign methods.

Responding to Advertisements

When responding to ads, competition makes it tough to get attention, much less get a job. To get attention you must be different. The best way to be different is to be interesting, and that means focusing on issues of interest to the company or recruiting firm that placed the ad. You should tailor all your ad responses to the specific ad. This means that you should customize both your cover letter *and* your resume to match each ad.

Convert your actions to accomplishments and your experiences to results. If the ad talks about "being a team player," you should find a way to talk not only about your experience as a team player but also about the results. The same is true for catch phrases such as "cost conscious," and the ubiquitous "results oriented." Describe your actions, but highlight your accomplishments. If specific experience, skills, or education are mentioned in the ad, try to address them directly and positively. Your midcareer status represents a plus, because it gives you the ability to match experience to need. Customizing may require some homework. The more you know about the company and what it needs, the stronger your ad response can be.

To increase exposure, scan as many newspapers as possible, including several weeks of back issues, to find appropriate ads.

Contacting Executive Recruiters

At this stage of your career you may know several recruiters, but if you are like most people, you haven't really built a relationship with them. Today you must be able to cultivate a personal relationship with recruiters, and that requires a focused program, not mass broadcast mailings. First focus on recruiters who specialize in your industry or functional area. Plan on periodic phone contact. Send clippings of your accomplishments, publications, and so on. Find ways you can be helpful to the recruiter, such as helping him or her get a search assignment.

Recruiters *do* need attractive candidates, but as a candidate you must create the opportunity to meet with them. The competition to be on a recruiter's list is stiff. Your friends may be able to help you make contact.

Contacting Companies Directly

You can bypass the crush of ad responders and recruiters by contacting companies directly. This once involved the drudgery of digging through directories by hand, copying names and addresses, and typing individual letters. Now you can use computerized databases of companies, available at most libraries, or through their internets, to locate appropriate companies. Here's what to do:

1. Target firms that match your career options. Today's databases can sort companies by type, location, size, and performance.
2. Learn all you can about the firms you target. Get annual reports for public companies. Read articles in newspapers and magazines to learn about issues. Search out financial results and the names of key people. Your research may require the use of public or college libraries and may involve requesting information by phone.
3. Write to specific people and, where possible, key in on real company issues and your successful experience dealing with them as a way to stand out in today's crowded and competitive market.

Networking

Networking, the personal direct marketing technique, is accepted as the most effective of the four job search methods. Today, though, even this channel is crowded with job seekers. Experts advocate targeting the best probable sources of job leads and no longer recommend the cold-call "information" contact to strangers unless you have a special story to tell the person. People in hiring roles complain today about the number of phone calls they get from people who "just want to learn about your company."

Many people learned the old rules of networking.

Old Rules for Networking

1. Always view everybody as a potential network member.
2. Always be ready to network.
3. Keep records of everyone you meet.
4. Put ticklers in your records and stay in touch with everyone.

Today people recognize that the old rules lead to shallow and overloaded networks that do little to help you stay in demand. Most networks end up as little more than piles of business cards with notes scribbled on the back. Networks now need to be managed by new rules.

New Rules for Networking

1. View your network as a long-term commitment.
2. Pick network members who can help you and whom you can help.
3. Build quality relationships, not quantity contacts.
4. Produce results for your network members and let them know how to produce results for you.

Start your network through friends, family, and others who know you and who will actively help. The farther along you are in your career, the longer and more productive that list can be.

Your first objective is to use your network to learn about job opportunities. The second objective is to ask members of your network for help in getting to the contacts you want to reach. By bridging from someone known to the desired contact, you avoid the cold call.

Searching the Internet

Yes, now you can search for jobs on the Internet. Try an index such as Yahoo (www.yahoo.com) or a site such as www.careermosaic.com.

The Targeted Resume or Job Proposal

A powerful new strategy is based on the *job proposal*. With this strategy you develop a *business proposal* aimed at convincing a hiring manager in a specific company to create a position for you. The proposal requires research and creativity to know what problems and opportunities your target company most likely faces. A literature search and talking with people who know the company or the industry are two ways to learn. In your proposal, spell out the kind of job you envision and what your duties would be. Focus on how you can solve specific problems and thus *increase revenue* or *reduce costs*. Keep a sharp focus on those two outcomes and present yourself as an *investment* rather than an *expense*. If possible, use your network to arrange a personal introduction or at least a sponsored delivery of your job proposal.

This innovative approach distinguishes you from the crowded field of job seekers and makes you a potential problem solver. If the job proposal doesn't yield a permanent job, it may at least lead to project or consulting assignments which may be attractive.

Searching for a job requires extensive work to plan, implement, and control an effective campaign. You can find job search help at libraries and bookstores and from outplacement firms.

Don't Stop When You Find a Job

Sad as it may seem, your new job may end up just like your old one—you might be cut back, outsourced, or downsized. Keep your contacts alive. Update your resume at once. By all means, treat your new job as though you will be there forever, but treat yourself as though it could be gone tomorrow.

The Job Proposal: An Example

Dave Jarred lost his job as manager of discount chain store sales for Rilco, a large hardware manufacturing company. Dave was well known and respected by discount chain purchasing agents around the country.

Another firm, Down East Hardware, was a regional manufacturer of specialty hardware items sold only through hardware stores. Dave had seen and liked their products. He wondered why Down East had never tried to sell to discount chains. After reading Down East's product literature and annual report, and after doing a search for articles about them at the library, Dave did some personal research through his industry contacts. His work turned up that Down East made good products, manufactured efficiently, and maintained very slow though solid financial growth. Sales activity focused on hardware stores exclusively.

Dave took some samples of Down East's products, showed them to his buyer friends at the discount chains, and asked if the products were of interest. He learned what these buyers liked and didn't like about the products, terms, prices, and packaging.

Dave then wrote a job proposal.

Promoting Your Personal Enterprise

If you are choosing the option of business ownership, much of what follows will also be of use to you, especially if your business is a consulting practice.

In this book, *Promotion* embraces three components: *what* you are promoting, *to whom* you are promoting, and *how* you promote.

What You Are Promoting

What you are promoting is simply you: your personal enterprise, its accomplishments, its features, and its other interesting and unique facets. Most of all you are promoting the ways your personal enterprise can be of benefit to others. As we have emphasized, the market value of your enterprise rests principally on your ability to increase revenue or reduce costs, but Figure 4–1 is a more expansive list of the benefits others might seek

Mr. Stan Block
President
Down East Hardware
Old Route 1
Augusta, ME 00000

Dear Mr. Block:

I believe Down East's products, with some adaptation, could
sell very well in the discount store market. My background is
in sales management to the discounters. I took the initiative
of showing your products to some of the key buyers in this
segment and what I learned convinced me that your company
has an opportunity to enter this large and growing market.

The buyers I spoke with universally liked the products. They
shared with me their requirements for packaging, pricing,
and terms, none of which seem outside your capability. These
buyers estimated that discounters do about the same amount
of volume in your type of products as do the hardware
stores, which means you are only reaching half the market
now.

I would like to respectfully propose that we meet to discuss
how I might develop and execute a business and marketing
plan for Down East to enter the discount market.

Sincerely,

David Jarred

To increase sales	To avoid criticism
To save money	To avoid trouble
To save time	To profit from opportunities
To save effort	To gain control over their lives
To feel good	To solve a problem
To be popular	To be safe and secure
To win praise	To please someone important to
To gain recognition	them
To conserve possessions	To end confrontation or sales
To increase their well being	pressure
To be in style	To be different
To copy others	To obey the law
To protect their reputation	

Figure 4–1. What others may need from you.

from you. The list is stated in terms of *needs*. *What* you are promoting are your abilities to satisfy those needs.

To Whom You Are Promoting

Under some extraordinary conditions, everybody could be the target of your promotion, but that's unlikely. Some will be too indirectly connected to your objective, and others may simply not be relevant. The mistake most people make, however, is to consider *too few* people as promotional targets.

Understanding the Size of Your Audience

Read this list and think for a moment about how each of these people might help you stay in demand.

- *Your boss* influences your job, your performance appraisal, your pay, your promotions, and your image. He or she will probably be a reference that others, both inside and outside your company, will want.
- *Other bosses* may control the job you want. They may also have credibility as boosters or detractors of your image.
- *Co-workers (past and present)*, by virtue of their numbers, represent a large network of people in positions every day to see job openings, opportunities, and threats to your personal enterprise.
- *Recruiters* are obvious targets for your promotional efforts. Most recruiters keep files on people they consider would make top candidates for assignments. Recruiters often specialize and take pride in knowing who are the top people in their field of specialization.
- *Employers in your industry* may be the most important targets for you, because your skills and knowledge should be worth more to them. However, they can't know who you are, where you are, and how good you are if someone doesn't tell them. Don't risk your personal enterprise on a hope that these important people will know about you.
- *Faculty members* come into contact with lots of people and are credible references.
- *Employers in your area* are vital to your personal enterprise if you need or want to stay in your area. The more limited the employer base is, the more important is your need to be known to them.
- *Public accountants and auditors* deal with companies every day. They know which firms have problems and which have opportunities. Their recommendations often carry a lot of weight with their clients.
- *Consultants* are in much the same situation as public accountants;

they spend their time with company managers who have confidence in them.

- *Bankers* see many businesses and, like public accountants, know of opportunities and problems. Bankers, on occasion, know more and know sooner about *planned* activities, both good and bad. A banker's recommendation is a strong asset for your personal enterprise.
- *People in your industry* who may not be actual employers, such as analysts, commentators, and regulators, may still have valuable knowledge and powerful influence.
- *Professional associates* know better than almost anyone else what you can do and what an appropriate opportunity would look like. These people do have to know what you want from them.
- *Civic club members* are usually community activists who have diverse affiliations and broad spheres of influence. These are the people who could remark about you, "Oh, yes. I know that person from Rotary," or whatever the club.
- *Charitable organizations* give you an opportunity to "do well by doing good." Your involvement will most certainly be welcome, and your leadership and contribution will almost always give you positive visibility. Charity work attracts influential people.
- *Alumni*, whether known to you or not, may have loyalty to your school. That can be an opportunity for you if their loyalty is coupled with needs which match your career objectives.
- *Friends* are an often-overlooked resource. You may assume that your friends know exactly what your career plan is and that they will always be alert for opportunities on your behalf. Don't risk that assumption. People sometimes don't want to burden friends. That's another assumption you should test.
- *Neighbors*, like friends, are often overlooked because people fail to see them in any other context.
- *Classmates* arc recognized as a resource, but all too often the only time classmates hear from one of their own is when the person is out of work and wants help. If you practice the art of self-promotion well, your classmates will see any call for help on your part as justified. If your self-promotion is successful, they will already be helping you.
- *Media people* can be the hardest to reach but the easiest to leverage. One mention in *Business Week*, the *Wall Street Journal*, or even your local paper can mean instant visibility, and possibly celebrity.
- *Customers* can tell you what's going on in the marketplace. With little effort they can make you known to others in your trade. Customers are your link to other parts of your industry.
- *Suppliers* are another link to other parts of your industry and another resource who can easily refer you to key people.

- *Dentists and doctors* should be seen as the helping professionals they are. They are almost always well disposed to help you in other parts of your life.
- *Clergy* have a broader role as helping professionals and have emerged as leaders in helping people with career support. In some parts of the country the clergy actively manage career networks and transition centers.
- *Fellow commuters* are natural targets for your self-promotion. Common experience along with diversified contacts can mean strong mutual benefits.
- *Competitors* should see the most value in who you are, but sometimes they and you are prohibited ethically or legally from being in contact.
- *People who promote to you* are in the same marketplace in at least one way. They can be good network contacts.

Make up a list of your own, adding others and giving at least some general priority to them.

Promoting Yourself

If you have worked in or observed public relations and advertising, you may recognize some of the techniques of promotion. Even to experienced businesspeople, though, the parallels to personal promotion are not always apparent, because public relations and advertising typically promote a product or a service, not a person. Major political elections can give you some insight into a narrow, media-focused type of publicity being used as part of a full personal promotional campaign.

You have many ways to promote your personal enterprise. Your challenge is to construct your program of self-promotion so that it does what you want it to do. That means setting some objectives.

Objectives for Self-Promotion

Objectives for self-promotion could include any of the following:

- Getting in print
- Getting considered for future jobs
- Creating favorable awareness
- Overcoming a bad image or event
- Doing a favor/creating an obligation or appreciation
- Getting an introduction to someone
- Getting recommended
- Establishing yourself as an expert

- Showing appreciation
- Getting money
- Gaining professional status
- Getting a promotion or raise
- Creating a "fan club"
- Gaining visibility
- Attracting a mentor
- Getting elected or chosen

Be very specific—and honest—about what you want to accomplish.

With your targets in sight and your objectives set, you are ready to build your plan for self-promotion using the techniques best suited to your needs.

Techniques for Self-Promotion

Following is a "menu" of 27 techniques that successful self-promoters recommend to help you stay in demand.* You may not be able (or willing) to use all of them, but don't make the mistake of doing no self-promotion of your personal enterprise. Imagine what that would do to a conventional business. Imagine, too, what advantages your competitors have if they *do* self-promote.

1. Prepare. You will need to prepare for your promotional activities. If you don't have business cards or if you want cards that don't present your employer's name, get your own. They can be very plain, with just your name, address, and phone number, but buy high-quality cards. Apply the same standards to your personal stationery.

Determine how you will handle secretarial functions. If you can't handle them on your own, you can hire secretarial services, or perhaps pay a friend. If the load is going to be heavy or of critical importance to your personal enterprise, you may want to invest in acquiring your own capabilities. You will almost certainly need an answering machine and a fax.

2. Initiate your own performance review. Waiting for an annual review of your performance or some random feedback on what the boss thinks of you is a passive and risky use of your career time. One or a series of "self-initiated performance reviews" can help you stay in control of this critical relationship.

As the name implies, in these sessions you will propose, ask, or confirm what is expected from you and then seek your boss' agreement. The

*For more on self-promotion, see Jeffrey Lant, *The Unabashed Self-Promoter's Guide*, Jeffrey Lant Associates; Cambridge, MA, 1992.

first step toward a self-initiated performance review is to gain the boss' agreement to the idea. It is hard to imagine a boss who would not respond positively to your suggestion of something that will help your performance.

There are two objectives to a self-initiated performance review: receiving information and gaining positive visibility. Your declared intent for the meeting is to review your job performance. If you have an agreed-upon set of objectives with your boss, present your progress toward them. If you don't have stated mutual objectives, offer up the objectives you have set for yourself and present your progress toward them. Try to quantify your results in terms of higher revenue or lower cost. "Conducted XYZ survey" may be what you did, but "Conducted XYZ survey which led to a four-day reduction in accounts receivable" is what you want to convey to show the value of your personal enterprise.

3. Understand what others want and expect. Use the review to learn what your company and your boss feel is important to them. Understand their objectives, problems, and opportunities. Ask about specific ways they are trying to increase revenue or reduce costs and listen for opportunities for your personal enterprise to take on those tasks. Then ask (and suggest) how you can best contribute to those tasks. Put your formal job description aside. Ask to take on the task that will contribute most to your boss' and the company's objectives. These are your personal enterprise's most important clients.

This is also the time to ask for assignments which will broaden your experience and contribute to your professional development.

4. Milk meetings for all they are worth. For some nose-to-the-grindstone people, attending meetings, conventions, and shows is a distracting waste of time. For people promoting their personal enterprise, these activities can be goldmines of opportunity to learn, grow, and meet people.

The actual content of these events may or may not be of particular value to your personal enterprise, but events around them are often useful. Social activities and seminar sessions will bring you in contact with people in your field, people who should know who you are, where you are, and how good you are. Even the attendance list can contain a wealth of contact names for you.

No judgment is made here on the subject of mutual loyalty between companies and employees. Let duty, ethics, and just plain fairness keep you from taking advantage of your employer.

5. Make organizational membership a platform for getting known. The two considerations for effective organization membership are to choose organizations that can truly benefit you and to work hard for the organizations you join. Choose organizations that have objectives aligned with your own, that have members you want to be with, and that can provide you with opportunities for visibility.

Contribute to your organization. Hard work and worthwhile results are the underpinnings of effective promotion just as they are of any undertaking.

6. Assume leadership in organizations. For real visibility, don't just join organizations, lead them. Find the jobs that will get you seen. One high-visibility job in organizations, committees, and task forces is to be the secretary. The secretary can influence the agenda, has access to membership rolls, and gains notice as the signatory to meeting notices and minutes. In his or her role as the group's communicator, the secretary is often afforded direct contact with all the members and with outside groups.

7. Work at everyday communications and social activity. It may seem calculating to keep and refer to lists of people's birthdays or their children's names. You may find it hard to put people on a "contact schedule" to ensure that they remember you. And using social activity to further your personal enterprise may make you feel like a user. As long as you have no intention of taking advantage of people and are perfectly willing to reciprocate, you might view these actions at better, more purposeful communications as simply another skill you need to develop and use.

Insincere, programmed, and inappropriate communications will be recognized by people for the pro-forma activities they are. Your good judgment will tell you when your self-promotion activities need to be overt or subtle and when they need to be put aside altogether.

8. Cultivate a genuine interest in others. Your communications, networking, and other self-promotion activities will make you feel less selfish if you can cultivate real interest in others. No one can make you feel interest, but you can develop the skills to learn about people, to understand them, to appreciate their differences, to find out about their goals, fears, problems, opportunities, and even their dreams. People are interesting. If you open yourself up to this kind of exploration and make the learning investment, you stand a good chance of developing interest in others.

9. Get involved in political activity. Holding office or serving on boards and commissions will bring you a very high level of recognition, but there are other kinds of political involvement. You can be active in party activities such as fund raising, hosting events, or serving on committees.

A bonus of your involvement in political activity is that politics is a popular subject for press coverage and a natural arena for networking.

10. Take part in charity and other volunteer work. Choose volunteer organizations you want to work with on the basis of mutual benefit. You must be willing to contribute the time, effort, and other resources the organization needs if you expect to receive the benefits you want. This method of gaining recognition has one big advantage in that these organizations will gladly accept your active involvement. If your involvement brings visibility for you, it brings visibility to the organization, too.

You will gain the most visibility if you serve in a leadership role. For example, being responsible for the group's publicity will put you in contact with members of the media.

11. Get quoted. If you have ever wondered why some people constantly seem to get calls from publications and end up being quoted, wonder no more. They don't get calls out of the blue: They work purposefully to make those calls happen.

No matter what your field, there are journals, magazines, house organs, or newsletters that act as forums for ideas and commentary. If your field is broad, national publications such as *Business Week* and the *Wall Street Journal* might be relevant. Getting quoted requires three things:

1. Having something worth quoting
2. Finding out who might quote you
3. Making sure those who might quote you know about you

12. Have something worth quoting. You have a big advantage if you are at midcareer, because you have almost certainly developed some special expertise. You have built an inventory of facts, experiences, opinions, and ideas in your "expert domain." Here's a golden chance to use them to gain recognition and credibility.

Start by analyzing what topics in your field are hot topics of discussion. Maybe there is a new technological breakthrough, a piece of pending legislation, a need to reduce costs, a new competitive pressure, or even some issue of style, trend, or taste. Pore over your relevant publications and, if appropriate, the radio and television shows that cover your field, and find some thing in your expert domain that is getting heavy coverage.

Now you know what people want to read about. The next step is to develop something quotable. For a quote to be interesting it should not only add to the body of knowledge, it should offer something fresh and have an unusual insight or slant. It might point out something that was missed in previous coverage of the subject.

If you feel you have a problem writing or expressing your quotable thoughts clearly, get some help. Read a book. Take a course. If all else fails, hire a writer.

13. Find out who might quote you. Finding out who might quote you is really straightforward detective work. Start by reading articles in your field that carry a writer's byline and put the writer's name in your database. If there is no byline, call or write the publication and find out who wrote the piece. In the case of trade publications where the whole magazine or newsletter is on your topic, get the names of the editorial staff, starting with the editor, right from the masthead printed somewhere in the first few pages of the magazine. For radio and television programs you will need the name of the show's producer.

You may have opportunities to be quoted in your local press, which would have an interest in you as a local expert on almost any subject. Find out who on the local paper covers your subject or your area.

You can get ideas and help locating publications and editors from *Writer's Market*, which contains over 4,000 listings of book, magazine, periodical, and trade journal editors, and from *Editor & Publisher Year Book*, which lists editors and publishers of nearly every newspaper in the world.*

14. Make sure those who might quote you know about you. Nearly all working writers and editors keep a file of experts on whom they call to verify facts, get ideas, and generally deepen their understanding of a subject. You have to get into that file and stay in that file. This means that you have to let the person know who you are and what your expert domain is. Use the telephone or a letter or some combination to make the first contact and offer a quotable observation on your subject. Describe your qualifications as an expert and your continuing pursuit of the subject. Offer to be of help any time the writer or editor is covering the subject.

Follow up this initial contact with a purposeful program of ongoing communications. Give the writer or editor feedback. They, like all of us, enjoy receiving compliments on their work. Drop notes and comments to the writer or editor about trends you see, experiences and events, and other observations you think would be of interest.

Repeat this process with others—other writers, others who speak on your topic, association executives, academics, researchers, and anyone else who might just pick up the phone and ask you for your (quotable) thoughts.

If this seems like a lot of effort, remember this: Once you have been quoted it is more likely that you will be quoted again. When you have been quoted several times, you become an expert. Your name, when quoted as an expert, is what others clip and file and use as a source when they want

---

*Glenda Neff (ed.), *Writer's Market*, Writer's Digest Books; Cincinnati, OH (annual); *Editor & Publisher Yearbook*, Editor & Publisher Co.; NY (annual).

an expert. In a relatively short time this one self-promotion technique can catapult you into stardom and really put you in demand.

15. Write articles (or even letters) that get noticed. As an expert you can do more than get quoted; you can get published. Select your target publications and your topic using the same techniques mentioned above.

Do some research on the publications you have targeted. Learn their style and format. Uncover the names of the editors and their area of responsibility. *Writer's Market* and *Editor & Publisher* can be very helpful. Above all, get to understand their readers and what their readers want. Editors view everything that comes across their desks with an eye to their readers' interests. If you appear not to understand the readers, your submission will be rejected.

The accepted procedure for getting published in a periodical starts with a "query letter" sent to the editor responsible for your subject area. In the query letter you should outline your idea for a proposed article and state your qualifications to write it. Explain briefly how you will approach your subject and, most important, why it should appeal to the readers. Double space any sample material you submit. If you have been published previously, say so. *Writer's Market* and back issues of *Writer's Digest* magazine provide sample query letters.

Some busy editors receive an avalanche of mail, so make things easy for them by enclosing a self-addressed stamped envelope.

If you receive an assignment, get clear guidance on the length desired and the due date. Have the editor describe what he or she wants the article to do, or what special focus is wanted. If you have concerns about your writing style, ask about ways the editor might help you.

If the publication pays for submissions like yours, consider it a bonus.

16. Consider providing high-visibility "pro bono" consulting. This is another way to do well by doing good. Churches, schools, hospitals, and other community service organizations need advice and help to solve problems and operate more effectively. As an experienced person, your personal enterprise has skills and knowledge that can be useful to them.

Apply the criteria of mutual benefit mentioned above to choosing the institutions. Research them to uncover the kinds of opportunities and problems they face, and then determine how your expertise can be applied to them. Use the best combination of direct contact and networking to approach them and offer a proposal of help. Don't be overly specific; you need to hear from people in the organization about what they see as their key needs.

Your work will provide benefit to the organizations, so don't be ashamed to gain the visibility you want.

17. Become a lecturer. Public speaking isn't for everybody, but with some training most people can learn to address an audience. Many of the institutions mentioned in Chapter 3 offer public speaking courses. Don't limit the potential to gain recognition for your personal enterprise to just your business or professional expertise. Your travels, hobbies, collections, and personal experiences may be of real interest to many groups.

Once again, you must do research and planning to secure lecture assignments. Decide what types of groups you want to reach. Find out if they do or would use guest lecturers and develop a list of lecture topics you could deliver to them. Lecturing to a group that can't help you is a waste of your time, and lecturing on a topic of no interest to a group is a waste of its time.

Use direct contact and networking to reach the groups you have targeted. If the group has other chapters or units, it may be an easy matter to arrange for more than one lecture engagement.

A Tip from Professionals

Professional lecturers advise an excellent way to gain more assignments. They urge you to conclude each talk with a statement to the audience that you are excited about your topic and that you would be pleased to present it to other interested groups.

You may want to consider giving public lectures if your subject has broad enough interest and your skills are well enough refined. You can use the techniques mentioned above to gain media publicity, but you may need to advertise or use direct marketing to get attendees.

18. Create or participate in seminars. Developing your expertise continues to be a cornerstone in your plan for self-reliance and to stay in demand. Once developed, your expertise can qualify you to be a panelist in seminars. Because you may be one of several participants, this is an easy way to get your feet wet and to learn how to be in front of an audience.

Your industry, professional, or trade associations are good places to look for existing seminar opportunities. Start a file on all the seminars in your field, and make note of the names of the organizers. Contact them and offer to be a panelist.

Of course, you can develop seminars to offer through your associations or to offer on your own. Developing and delivering seminars has become such a popular avenue for midcareer people that a whole seminar support industry has sprung up. Available "how to" books and tapes cover all phases of seminar development, from deciding on a topic to packaging a seminar to very detailed tips on marketing and promoting.

Much of the pioneer work in seminar development was led by the late Howard Shenson, whose book, *How to Develop and Promote Successful Seminars and Workshops* (John Wiley, New York, 1990), is still a valuable resource.

19. Develop and teach courses on your specialty. Many of the institutions mentioned in Chapter 3, as well as your own company, may have a desire to offer courses in your area of expertise. Your programs can be as short as one day or as long as a full semester. You may be able to gain some accreditation for your program, adding to its value. Take the same initiatives described earlier to approach key decision makers with a proposal. The midcareer person possesses the advantage of experience, always a plus in teaching.

Teaching lends credibility to your personal enterprise and affords added ways to gain visibility, often supported by the institution offering your program.

20. Create, conduct, and publicize surveys. Surveys are often *marketing* programs, not educational exercises. A customer satisfaction survey may show brand A to be most preferred. An industry survey of problems may show a high incidence of a problem that product X solves. It is likely that brand A and product X sponsored or conducted those surveys as another way to promote them.

Your surveys can be more subtle. Your objective is self-promotion, not the sale of a product, and recognition can be achieved by simply providing useful information to people. Begin by deciding what information your promotional targets want or need. If you don't know, ask. Give your targets a list of topics in your area of expertise that you think might be of interest to them. Tell them that you plan a series of informational communications and want to know their interests. Ask them to rank the topics "much interest," "some interest," or "no interest." This will help you set priorities.

Next, structure questions to develop the data to answer these questions. You can conduct your survey by researching literature or by interrogating people by mail, by phone, or in person. You can survey individuals or groups. Your survey can be highly focused, somewhat structured, or totally open ended, depending on the data you need. Finally, write up the results of your survey in a way that your targets will find useful and will enjoy.

If you have done the work suggested above to know editors and publishers, you may be able to get your survey published. Your credibility will be enhanced by authoring a survey, further increased by having it published, and bolstered over and over by the use of reprints.

Becoming Famous by Creating a Survey: A Case Study

Ken Williams learned that his job as director of public relations for St. James Hospital was being combined into the marketing department, and that he was to be let go. Married and with a young family, Ken had little time to waste in replacing his income. He decided to set himself apart from others by creating and promoting his own survey, "The Williams Survey of Key Health Care Issues." He followed a simple and fast seven-step process:

1. He made a list of six health care topics which he knew to be hot:

   What new ways are being found to limit inappropriate use of the Emergency Room?
   How is your hospital preparing for Managed Care?
   How are you handling the 24-hour rule imposed by some insurers on new mothers?
   What are you doing about electronic/universal medical records versus patient confidentiality?
   How will the cuts in Washington affect hospitals in our area?
   What new ways do you use to measure patient satisfaction?

2. He faxed and mailed the questionnaire to a dozen hospital colleagues he knew around the state, asking for their (quick) response.
3. In a few days he had back their responses and compiled them into a report.
4. He released the survey report to his local newspapers and to several hospital trade journals.
5. He included the survey report in his prospecting letters to potential employers.
6. He included it along with his resume in responding to known opportunities.
7. As newspapers and magazines began to print his survey, he included those clippings in his mailings.

Ken generated four interviews, three follow-up media inquiries, and established himself—and his survey—as an expert source of health-care information—all in less than a month.

21. Give gifts, mementos, books, and so on. Buying recognition through the giving of gifts can be risky and costly, but it is something you can carefully control. With good manners and common sense it can be very effective.

The keys to successful giving are appropriateness and timeliness. Appropriateness means that your gift is in good taste, is something the other person will appreciate, and is relevant to your relationship. Good manners dictate that your gifts be neither so meager that they embarrass nor so lavish that they obligate.

Timeliness is important because it can influence the perception of your motivation for gift giving. Don't try to deceive people about your motivation. Most people will know that you are trying to build goodwill, but don't make your motivation appear like bribery due to poor timing. Giving a gift just before an event where the recipient can do something to benefit you is shallow and ill advised. Giving a gift after you have received help can be viewed simply as proper appreciation.

22. Clip and send articles of interest. Clipping and sending articles from newspapers and periodicals is an easy and inexpensive way to gain and maintain visibility with others. It involves—and shows—personal effort on your part. To enhance the personal touch, hand write a note to send along with the clipping.

Common sense is again your guide. Sending articles that your recipient has likely already seen should only be done if you are offering some comment or analysis along with it. Sending too many clippings makes your purpose look superficial. Sending clippings that will be useful and interesting. However, don't be overly shy in sending clippings about yourself. Reasonable pride in an accomplishment is acceptable to most people.

23. Publicize! Promote your family, pets, home, food, hobbies, clothes, travels, and more. Dr. Jeffrey Lant, author of *The Unabashed Self-Promoter's Guide,* offers detailed advice for avid self-promoters to turn nearly every aspect of their lives into media events. In one example he mentions how you could author an article about your spouse's fabulous chocolate cookies and get it published in the food section of your newspaper. That effort might yield promotion of the cookies, increased standing for your spouse, and a nice plug for you and your company, product, or service.

Lant's suggestions for using other family members and lifestyle habits follow similar guidelines. The promotion of your personal enterprise is essential to achieve self-reliance. Lant believes that you should leave no stone unturned. As outrageous as this idea might seem, the nub is sound: Opportunities for publicity are everywhere. Lant refers to himself and others who follow his ideas as "shameless" self-promoters, but a greater shame might lie in failing to promote your personal enterprise.

24. Use targeted audience networking. You may feel that networking—expanding your circle of personal contacts by purposefully asking for introductions and leads—has been overdone. Strangers calling strangers and asking for favors and advice *has* been overdone, and the abuses have generated resentment toward the whole idea of networking. In many cases the whole exercise is wasted because the object of the contact is not really able to be of any help anyway.

Networking done properly is still the most powerful technique for gaining recognition. Networking can get you the contacts you need for other kinds of self-promotion in the media, the business community, and elsewhere.

Good networking takes good manners. More than mere politeness, good manners means that you show consideration for the people you are dealing with. Contact them at sensible times, always ask for their permission to continue the contact, have the courtesy to know something about them, make only appropriate inquiries, and, most of all, have some idea of how to reciprocate the help you are seeking. Reciprocation can range from helping your contacts get introductions they want to giving them business. I've heard of one appreciative networker who made a contribution to his contact's favorite charity.

Kate Wendleton, founder of the New York-based Five O'Clock Club, a job search network, strongly advises networkers to avoid most of the kind of wholesale, shotgun networking aimed at one-time benefits. She recommends building *and then maintaining* genuine, longer-lasting networks based on mutual benefits.

It may seem to you that these approaches take too much time, but you can squander far more time flitting around dozens and dozens of hard-to-maintain, marginally helpful, possibly resentful contacts.

Some groups exist for the sole purpose of networking. These are not civic or professional groups, which are discussed later, but rather groups whose primary goal is the promotion of members' wants and needs for contacts.

Transition support groups, many promoted by churches, exist to help people make job contacts. Long-term relationships among the group members are neither sought nor expected.

"Tips" groups or "leads" groups are relatively new kinds of long-term networks designed to generate business leads for their members. Typically, 25 or so *noncompetitors* meet weekly to exchange very specific information about business activities and opportunities for the group's members. One member might ask another for an introduction to a desired potential customer. Members ask for help finding suppliers and employees. Continued membership in the group often requires a certain level of activity and contribution.

Setting Up a "Tips" Group

Follow these simple steps and you can have your own "tips" group

1. List three or four people (not your competitors) who call on the same customers you do.
2. Invite them to have coffee or lunch to exchange information about your mutual or potentially mutual customers.
3. At your first meeting, determine how you can help each other and if anyone else should be added to your group.
4. Set a schedule for meeting.

---

25. Master memorable introductions—the "Two-Minute Drill." Skilled group networkers know they don't have much time to make a clear, memorable, and *useful* impression on people. They have devised the "two-minute drill," which is a well-thought-out minipresentation of who they are, what they do, the kinds of help they are seeking, and the kinds of help they can provide. The drill may not always be two minutes. The presentation is tailored to each situation and person, but the networkers have the ideas and words well defined in their heads at all times.

One standard closing to these encounters has you exchanging business cards. Experienced networkers immediately—and in plain view—write on the back of the card to capture reminders of the conversation, the person, and any planned follow-up. Another standard closing is "do you know anyone who . . . ," which is how networkers make new connections.

Whether you are networking formally or just meeting people, your skill at the two-minute drill can be a useful technique to promote your personal enterprise.

26. Create your own self-promotion network. You can start your own self-promotion network group using the same steps shown above to start a "tips" group. The goal for this network is somewhat different and more specific: You will be associating for the purpose of personally supporting and helping each other get recognized.

Help in the beginning might include giving each other ideas and developing self-promotion programs. More specific cooperation could take the form of help with introductions, support for club membership or public office, and direct assistance such as calling you to the attention of the public or some specific audience.

Using Your Own Self-Promotion Network

Throwing a party in your own honor is easier if someone else makes all the arrangements.

Laura Ames was seeking work as a commercial artist and designer. The people who could give her assignments were the art directors of local ad agencies and publications. Laura assembled a showing of her portfolio of work and turned for help to her self-promotion network, three people committed to helping each other get attention. Together they organized a showing of Laura's work, hosted and promoted by her network partners, who extended the invitations. The showing, held after working hours at a popular spot, included wine and cheese and the expectation that those attending would have the opportunity to mingle with their peers. The event attracted the right people, and Laura established her base of business contacts.

An added value of a personal self-promotion network is that individual members can better avoid the risk of appearing too pushy, crass, or ill mannered by openly promoting themselves. As each others' "press agents," network members can make far more direct and favorable comments about each other than they could make about themselves. Your self-promotion network can become the equivalent of a trade association for your personal enterprise.

27. Integrate your self-promotional activities. Your objectives, targets, and techniques for self-promotion will overlap. Minimize duplication, avoid omissions, and make your efforts most efficient by developing an integrated plan. One useful device for integrating multipart plans is the matrix. Construct a "self-promotion matrix" by listing your targets down the left side and your techniques across the top. If you list your most important targets and objectives first, the upper part of your matrix will give you a good focus on your priorities. In the boxes formed by the matrix, put the specific action you plan to take.

Remember to include your place of employment as a target. Try to ensure that the recognition you earn outside earns recognition for you inside your firm as well.

The matrix will reveal gaps, duplication, and excesses in your efforts. You should be able to see how one technique might be broadened to meet several objectives or to reach more than one target. Evaluate the costs and benefits of your activities and the matrix will show you whether you have placed your efforts on your priorities.

The matrix elements can be transferred into a calendarized plan to give you an event/work schedule. Finally, the matrix will show you the effort or lack of it you are giving to promoting your personal enterprise and building your self-reliance.

You can get help with your self promotion from Ilise Benum, publisher of a newsletter called *The Art of Self Promotion.**

Summary

If you are at midcareer, it is likely that you may view this whole idea of self-promotion as improper. "Blowing your own horn" registers as a negative with those raised on an ethic of modesty. Just remember that you stand as your own personal enterprise, and today, with the passing of employment loyalties, you carry the responsibility to ensure security for your enterprise.

While you might think of yourself as a "shameless" self-promoter, a greater shame might lie in failing to promote your personal enterprise.

*Ilise Benum, Box 23, Hoboken, NJ 07030; (201) 653-0783.

CHAPTER 5

Consider Your Conventional Employment Options

The greatest number of options for most people are still in the world of conventional employment—working full time for monetary compensation. If you have the time to look before you leap, explore options within your present company and in other firms.

Examine "Inplacement"—Reemployment within Your Present Company

If you are employed, you have a number of conventional employment options within your own company.

Stay Where You Are

Perhaps because it is so obvious, people often overlook the option of staying where they are. However, the decision to hold your ground and concentrate on creating a more satisfying situation, or removing the barriers to your happiness and career growth, is perfectly legitimate. We saw in Chapter 4 that staying where you are does not mean you can tune out, sit back, and relax, even at midcareer. This option need not mean boredom, stress, or unhappiness either. It does mean that you may have an option to remain in your present job and yet find and build a higher degree of satisfaction. Four factors affect job satisfaction, and you can address each of them in your efforts to improve your situation.

1. *Job content.* If your job is too dull or too varied, too demanding or too simple, or if it is unsatisfactory in any aspect of its content, you can feel stressed and pressured. A rational employer will make an effort to construct the content of your job to suit you better because it is in both your interests to do so. Initiative on your part to make well-defined suggestions will make it easier for you to get the changes considered. Consider submitting a revised (or new) job description to your boss.

   Reengineering the workplace occupies prime space in the business literature and on the seminar circuit. Learn the concepts and reengineer your own job.

2. *Working conditions.* Unsatisfactory working conditions may mean excessive hours or travel, uncomfortable surroundings, insufficient resources to do your job, or any number of things ranging from hazardous materials to unsafe practices. Decide what specific unsatisfactory working conditions can reasonably be modified, and then make the effort with your employer to change them. If safety, health, or other agencies should play a role, involve them. The more constructive your proposals are, the more likely they will be adopted. Try to offer alternatives, and always recognize the cost implications of your suggestions.

3. *Behavioral problems.* Behavioral or interpersonal issues are common and can exist with co-workers, customers, suppliers, subordinates, the general public, your employer, and, yes, yourself. Behavioral problems are pervasive in all of life, and you must deal with them as a part of living. If you haven't acquired the skills to build working relationships, confront problems constructively, and resolve conflicts, get them now. Your company may offer courses in these skills. If not, visit a library, find some seminars, or, if you think your problem is serious, seek professional help.

4. *Compensation.* Pay, benefits, and other elements of compensation are notorious job dissatisfiers. If your employer has any experience, he or she is prepared to deal with your concerns about salary and compensation issues. Get data from your human resources department, other companies, or from outside agencies so that you can be factual and creative in your approach. Here's a tip: Tie your arguments as closely as you can to your good performance and comparable pay in your industry. Try to demonstrate how you helped to either add to revenue or lower costs.

The key to improving your satisfaction in your present job is to confront any of these factors that are causing your discontent. Few people attack these problems head-on, possibly because of some old assumptions about how people have to adapt to work rather than the other way around. More likely today is a fear that complaining malcontents will be high on the list when layoffs are planned or can easily be replaced by a host of eager job seekers. *Whatever your problem, solving it can be your simplest and most profitable option.*

Consider Promotion, Demotion, and Side Stepping

The traditional notions of in-company mobility involve the more or less formal matching of your business skills, knowledge, and performance with your employer's needs, typically as part of your employer's development program and at your employer's initiative. If they even exist, many such company programs atrophy after a little use, and some are failures from the beginning. Here is another area where you can exercise initiative. By knowing your company thoroughly, you will know where it is growing or contracting. You will know or can find out where it needs new, better, or added skills.

Base your initiative on more than a conventional look at your job experience and the jobs that experience might suggest. Examine all parts of your education and any specialized training you have had. Even your hobbies may give you some special qualifications. Your strong desire and a good work history might convince a hiring manager to give you an opportunity in a different field.

As an example, many companies today have recognized that the weakness of the dollar makes U.S. goods a bargain for foreign buyers. As these companies prepare to enter the export market, they will need people with international skills—languages, cultural and political savvy, in-country experience, and similar skills. An employee who has or can obtain these needed skills can use them as the basis for a career initiative.

Your most powerful initiative is to recognize what skills will be in demand, to develop your skills and knowledge on your own, and to manage your own in-company mobility to ensure that you stay in demand.

Restructure Your Job or Create a New One

Every company has its special problems and opportunities, which can go unnoticed and unaddressed for years. Among the most in-demand skills are those that can save your company money or increase its revenue. These are ripe areas for exploration. The first step is to conduct a systematic search for such problems or opportunities. When you have identified a few, decide which ones (be realistic) would be most interesting and rewarding to work on, and which would have the biggest payoff for your company. The next step is to train yourself or get the training needed to be a "subject matter expert" in those areas.

This tactic is growing in popularity as people become more self-reliant. Once you have the in demand skills you want (see Chapters 2, 3, and 4) and have analyzed the problems and opportunities in your company, you will be in a position to propose a job that matches up the two. Be crystal clear when you describe how you can solve problems (lower costs) or take advantage of opportunities (increase revenue).

A Nurse Goes Where the Action Is

Anne L. had worked at Downtown Hospital for almost ten years. In the last two years she had seen the hospital's patient census drop from over 400 to barely 300. Managed care was putting pressure on doctors, hospitals, and patients to reduce admissions to the hospital and to shorten the stays of those who were admitted. Fewer patients in the hospital meant that fewer nurses and staff were needed.

Anne recognized that to reduce costs, managed care required detailed attention to each patient's case. Anne not only recognized the need, she reasoned that the need would grow and that as a nurse she was well positioned for the task. The hospital had just formed a "case management" department, and Anne went to learn what skills and knowledge were required. She found out that her nursing background was essential but that she would have to learn about the many intricacies surrounding benefits plans and about the applicable rules and regulations associated with case management.

She found help from co-workers in the hospital's administration, from reading benefit plans, and from attending conferences at the state hospital association. Anne is now a case manager, and the hospital, after a major downsizing, has a patient census hovering around 250.

Become Familiar with the World of "Outplacement"— Employment Options Outside Your Present Company

This is not a job search book. Books on all aspects of finding a job can be found at bookstores everywhere. Job search fundamentals were covered in Chapter 4, but in this chapter we want to develop and explore employment options that may not have been obvious to you.

Do the Same Job You Are Doing Now, but in a Different Setting

You can do the same thing you are doing now in a variety of different settings:

- Another company in your industry, where your industry knowledge will enhance the value of your job skills
- A larger company, where you can grow more professionally in your present skills
- A smaller company or division, where you can broaden and add to your skills
- A different geographic location, where your skills and knowledge might be in higher demand

Take on a Different Job

As we have seen, you can use past experiences, formal training, hobbies, or just plain desire to get a job in a whole new field inside your company. Of course, you can do the same thing outside your company as well.

- You can use the strategies to *create a job* in another company, as suggested in Chapter 4.
- Some jobs, such as real estate sales, require little previous special background, as the essential skills and knowledge are usually provided in some way by the hiring firm.
- Police, fire, and craft apprenticeship programs in some fields allow for untrained new entrants, though educational and physical qualifications do exist.
- Other jobs require few skills at all. Entry-level and unskilled positions exist almost everywhere, though in some places the competition is keen among the unskilled unemployed.
- Sometimes brass nerve and a silver tongue can get a person a job for which he or she is not qualified. If that person is a quick study, success is not impossible.
- "Celebrity" can bring job offers to the unqualified. Professional athletes are sometimes given a chance at jobs because the people hiring them believe the athletes can become qualified and that their marketing or other value to the firm is worth the risk and expense of the learning curve. If your career has brought you any celebrity status at all, you can leverage it to advantage.
- New industries create new jobs and new career opportunities. By definition, the people who first fill these jobs will be unskilled at them.

A New Industry Made into Law

In the winter of 1996, President Clinton signed a law revolutionizing the communications industry. Barriers to competition between and among phone, cable, and other communications companies are now all but gone. Fold into this new structural free-for-all the myriad opportunities yet to be even conceived in applications of the Internet/World Wide Web.

At midcareer you could put your experience to use uncovering applications in this new industry.

Labor shortages are uncommon now but forecasters predict a big shortage in the future, and those shortages may bring a desperation to hiring firms that will force them to hire the unqualified.

The point of this short chapter is to demonstrate that being at midcareer creates no insurmountable barrier to reshaping and reinvigorating your working life.

CHAPTER 6

Consider Some (Slightly Off-Beat) Alternative Opportunities

Maybe a full-time, full-pay company job is not for you. Maybe corporate demand for your knowledge and skills has evaporated, and you don't want to retool for another go. You have alternatives. Part of staying in demand is knowing how to locate special—some might say off-beat—opportunities.

These alternatives might serve as interim or temporary arrangements. They can become long-term arrangements for those who form new expectations. They can keep skills and contacts alive and can add to the demand for your personal enterprise.

These opportunities are not fantasy trips; they are very real alternatives. Some are new; some are just overlooked. You may not qualify for some and you may not want others, but you should know about all of them. Here, in alphabetical order, are 20.

Remember the Armed Services

No longer do the armed services accept just anyone. The armed services are cutting back and downsizing just like civilian institutions, and they are carefully controlling their human resources. They are still seeking new enlistees, although perhaps now they are looking for only a "fewer good men," and perhaps even fewer of those at midcareer.

Understand Bartering

Singing for your supper may not be an alternative for you, but trading labor or skills for housing, services, or goods is a real possibility. In this country's early days, when self-reliance was imperative, barter was the principal form of exchange.

Barter Need Not Be Direct

Think about three-way barter. For example, your landlord does not need your advertising skills, but the landscaper does. So you develop an advertising campaign for the landscaper and agree that it has a value of $1,000. The landscaper in turn takes care of the property for the landlord to that amount, and the landlord gives you $1,000 credit on your rent.

Consider Care Giving

The elderly, the sick, and the children of working parents need care, and the skills involved in giving care are not all professional skills.

The opportunities are not exclusively in the voluntary sector. Many are paying jobs available to independent contractors, while others are available through organizations.

You should know that home health-care givers and other so-called extenders for health professionals represent a very fast-growing segment of our economy as more and more people want more and more health-care services at lower cost.

Help the "Sandwiched Generation"

Many working people, especially women, face the pressure of caring for both their children and their aging parents. In some cases the care extends to grandchildren also. These people are sometimes called the "sandwiched generation." The workload can lead to fatigue, guilt, and even depression. As one who has experienced life, you can help. Perhaps you can find several people who need this help, and that might lead to a new career for you.

Be a Courier or Chauffeur

Delivering documents to secret agents abroad isn't much called for now, but some people still want their cars driven from Miami to New York. And many people want to leave the driving to someone else on occasion. Because demand for drivers is so uneven, livery companies welcome people who can fill in when needed.

Downscale

Scaling back your material goals and your career ambitions can open up many new options for you. Casting off a high-pressure success image can mean less stress and more satisfaction than a fast track that has no checkered flag. Amy Saltzman, in her book *Downshifting* (Harper Collins, New York, 1991) calls the process "reinventing success on a slower track." This reinvention can include accepting life on the vocational plateau, seeking less demanding (and presumably more available) jobs, or maybe just finding some different company or rural geography where life is richer in ways other than upscale achievement and materialism. The advent of electronic commuting makes this option, as it does several others, much easier to consider.

The trade-offs between satisfying material wants and following a dream deserve and receive separate treatment at the end of this chapter.

Try Flextime

One option is simply to negotiate with your employer to create employment hours that suit your overall needs. The total hours may be more or less, but in most cases are the same as a regular job. Flextime is an appealing alternative for people who have responsibilities such as child care or those who are involved with other activities, or who are making a transition to a new way of life.

Serve in Government or Charities

Public service as an employment alternative means not just nonpaying volunteer work, but elected or administrative jobs in local state or national government and administrative jobs in such organizations as the Red Cross. These paying jobs are still considered public service because people who seek them (claim to) want to accomplish something for the general welfare, and because the pay usually is less than that of comparable regular employment.

Work in Government

All levels of government afford employment opportunities, yet private-sector people know little about how to research and pursue these jobs. Research on federal employment opportunities can begin with the *U.S. Government Manual,* which is available in most libraries. If you want your own copy you can write to the U.S. Government Printing Office, Washington, DC 20402. The Manual lists contacts for employment in each department of the government. A separate section gives information on employment programs such as those for veterans.

You can also buy *Federal Career Opportunities,* which lists available federal jobs and gives application instructions. This publication can be purchased from Federal Research Services, Box 1059, Vienna, VA 22183. The cost is $38 for three months. State employment can be researched at your state employment office, and local government employment is probably best researched by visiting your city or town hall.

Work at Home

Each week, thousands of Americans decide to work in home-based settings. Some set up home-based businesses. Figure 6–1 lists 25 in-home businesses that require less than $500 to start. An established and very ex-

1. Residential cleaning service	14. Computer instruction
2. Auto detailing	15. Consultant
3. Pet sitting	16. Mobile bookkeeping
4. Take-out food delivery	17. Window washing service
5. Word processing service	18. Button and badge making
6. Mail order business	19. Tub and tile reglazing
7. Gift basket business	20. Errand service
8. Carpet cleaning	21. Novelty balloon sales
9. Bed and breakfast	22. Knife sharpening
10. Lawn/leaf/snow maintenance	23. Health claim management
11. Home handyman	24. House sitting and management
12. Home baking service	25. Laundry and tailoring
13. Catering service	

Figure 6–1. In-home businesses. (*Source: Small Business Opportunities,* Harris Publications Bimonthly).

tensive infrastructure now exists around the world of the small office/home office, called *so/ho* by those in the arena.

Here are some resources for your exploration of this exploding phenomenon.

Center for the New West
600 World Trade Way
1625 Broadway
Denver, CO 80202
(303) 572-5400

Rocky Mountain Home Based Business Association
9905 E. Colfax Avenue
Aurora, CO 80010
(303) 361-2953

The American Association of Home Based Businesses
P.O. Box 10023
Rockville, MD 20849
(202) 310-3130

The Oklahoma Home-Based Business Association
c/o Oklahoma State University
Stillwater, OK 74078
(405) 744-5776

Work on Contract

With the growth in "outsourcing," work on contract represents what many see as the biggest trend in employment for the future. As an independent contractor you are engaged by firms or individuals not as an employee, but as a supplier or vendor who works for a price under a contract for service. Two types of contract work are agency contracting and independent contracting.

Agency Contracting

Working through an agency for a company on a specific task under a defined contract is an increasingly popular way for people to work and for companies to keep down their permanent payrolls. Once confined to laborers, truckers, or technicians, contracting now enthusiastically embraces white-collar workers. Contract employment agencies, sometimes known as interim agencies, exist for the traditional kinds of contract work, and now some general employment agencies deal in contract labor.

Contract labor today includes computer programmers, charter flight crews, and nurses.

Independent Contracting

Working directly for a company as a contractor, not through an agency, provides companies with an alternative to regular employment. The arrangement can be attractive to companies because it frees them from paying Social Security and other benefits and exempts them from certain aspects of wages and hours laws. However, the rules defining what is independent contractor status are quite specific and are being enforced with more vigor than was once the case.

One well-known example of independent contracting is the real estate salesperson.

Advantages. Independent contracting offers several advantages to the employer, as mentioned above: The independent contractor receives no employee benefits and the employer incurs none of the potential liabilities that go along with the employer/employee relationship, though there are some obligations owed a contractor. Companies often put projects out for bid with several independent contractors, using their competition to get the best deal.

The employer has greater flexibility in dealing with an independent contractor. By making limited commitments to independent contractors, the employer can add or remove them from the workforce as needed. This flexibility, combined with the use of competitive bidding and the absence of long-term obligations makes the use of independent contractors a variable and more easily controlled cost. Companies that have suffered the trauma and cost of downsizing are often reluctant to restaff with permanent employees.

From your standpoint, status as an independent contractor means that you can, in theory, work for any of hundreds of employers, not just one. The opportunities for you to earn money from your skills and knowledge are far broader and can represent solid insurance against the vagaries of being tied into one economic unit.

If you have built your in-demand skills as advocated in this book, you will have the ability to select the contract assignments that best suit your criteria for income, content, hours, and other working conditions.

Disadvantages. You do need to know that there are disadvantages to independent contracting. If you have no abilities to market yourself or to be marketed by others, you run the risk of not working. Managing your own employment can take a lot of time and work. In hard times, competition can cause you to work at jobs for less than you might want, and to work harder to get even those jobs.

A very big difference for you as an independent contractor is that you must provide for your own financial security—medical insurance, disability income, life insurance, and retirement. These coverages can be costly and difficult to obtain.

Minor inconveniences arise from the need to keep records, do billing, and deal with added tax regulations, but for those who want to achieve self-reliance, independent contracting is an attractive option.

Moonlight

As the slang name indicates, moonlighting usually refers to a night job. More specifically, moonlighting is a night or day job held in addition to a regular job. Moonlighting can provide added income and added satisfaction, and it can be used as a stepping stone to a change in career.

Work Part Time

You can take on part-time work as an employee or as an independent contractor. Some of the employer motives of flexibility and cost apply to the increasing acceptance of part-time workers. Workers who have other obligations or who prefer to have time off make up the bulk of part-time workers, but when full-time jobs are scarce, people will take what's available. The part-time alternative can allow you to have more than one job for added income, variety, or other reasons.

Temporary employment agencies are booming as companies remain wary of rehiring full-time people. Your experience can be a plus.

Don't Shun Personal Service

Being a companion, caretaker, cook, maid, or servant for someone may be something you haven't considered. For certain people this alternative can provide a sense of satisfaction and security that is not provided by any other form of employment.

Personal service can also mean doing things for more than one person or family. Whatever your view of this alternative, it is one that is very difficult to ignore. Nearly everyone has the necessary skills. Figure 6–2 lists examples of personal service alternatives.

Baby sitter	Guy/gal Friday
Butler	Handyman
Caddy	House sitter
Caretaker	Interpreter
Companion	Maid
Cook	Masseuse/masseur
Dog walker	Personal trainer
Gardener	Shopper
Groom	Tutor or teacher
Groundskeeper	

Figure 6-2. Personal service jobs.

Contemplate Religious Service

It is not extraordinary for someone who has led a secular life to choose to make a change and take up a religious calling. Opportunities to serve one's religion are abundant.

Retire!

The picture of the elderly retiree quietly living out life's end is not today's picture. With good financial planning, proper habits of health and fitness, conscious career strategies, and a bit of luck, retirement is not an ending, but rather a transition from being in demand in one setting to being in demand in another. As such, retirement is an alternative.

Retirement was not a real alternative in years past. The company pretty much decided what the policies were and when the employee fit the rules, he or she was, with few exceptions, retired. Today there are a variety of retirement plans, and policies are as varied as employers care to make them. Be sure you know what your retirement alternatives are.

Unfortunately, the fact that you are entitled to retirement from one or more companies does not mean that you will receive any benefits. Some plans, companies, and even insurers have gone broke, leaving pensioners out in the cold.

Seek Seasonal Employment

Working in Florida for the winter and in Maine for the summer is a viable alternative if you have skills that are in demand. Skill at picking citrus fruit and blueberries can give you a Florida–Maine axis, and so can skills in the tourist and hospitality businesses. With the right language skills you might prefer to shuttle between Acapulco and the French Riviera.

Thousands of jobs open up every season somewhere in the world and possibly right in your part of the world. In colder climates winter brings ski business, snow clearance, firewood sales, and indoor sun tanning. In warmer regions agriculture, tourism, and summer recreation offer opportunities.

Become a Seminar Leader

Leading seminars and giving lectures on your own is a business and may be a high-demand business for you. However, you have the alternative of leading seminars for others. Geneva Corporation (financial services), Fred Pryor (sales training), and the American Management Association (management) are three organizations that engage people to conduct seminars and to lecture on their behalf. Outplacement companies use independent "stringers" to lead training seminars and workshops. Your experience at midcareer is a big plus.

For a thorough treatment of the seminar alternative, see Howard Shenson's *How to Develop and Promote Successful Seminars & Workshops* (John Wiley, New York, 1990).

Explore Teaching

Teaching as an alternative has lots of variations. Public and private education offer opportunities from preschool to postgraduate to special and continuing education. Requirements are very stringent for positions involving accreditation or other standards but are little more than practical and common sense for others.

Your business background may be all the qualification you need to teach an evening course in some aspect of your discipline. If you take courses in education you may be able to become qualified to teach in many settings, opening up rich alternatives as a teacher, professor, or education administrator.

Try Temporary Work

The concept of temporary work has changed. "Temping" once meant that a person would work temporarily at a job, often as a fill-in for a permanent employee. Today the jobs are temporary and the person can work full time if he or she chooses and has the in-demand skills. Adia, Kelly, Manpower, and Olsten are agencies that specialize in the temporary work alternative.

The ready availability, flexibility, and variety of temporary work make it the first-choice alternative for many people.

Volunteer

Although it is not a paying alternative, volunteerism does offer a wide range of work and a potential source of great satisfaction. It also represents a potential source of paying employment. A volunteer job can become a paying one if the need can be demonstrated and the funding can be established. Volunteering is certainly one way to stay in demand.

A Case Study in Alternatives

Finally, consider Steven and Gwen Lowe. The Lowes have availed themselves of nearly every alternative we have described.

An Army couple, the Lowes took early retirement last year, sold their big house in Washington, D.C., and now live in a sunny upstairs apartment in the home of an elderly couple in St. Petersburg, Florida. They pay no room or board; rather, in exchange Steven does errands for the couple and Gwen takes care of their landlords' medical regimen of pills and shots and does some minor cleaning. They found the couple by advertising in the classifieds.

Steve got some training, became a licensed livery, and formed his own company, contracting to work part time driving people to the airport. Gwen takes frequent temporary teaching assignments. They are active in their church choir.

The Lowes' experience demonstrates that you can combine just about any and all of the alternatives we have looked at to find employment, stay in demand, and keep your life rich and full of choices.

The key to success in alternative employment is your ability to provide yourself with in-demand skills and your willingness to exercise initiative to gain recognition for those skills. The result can be a lifetime of self-reliance.

Four Routes to Ownership: Buying a Business, Owning a Franchise, Starting a Business, Becoming a Consultant

Becoming a business owner does not begin with a business plan. Nor is it necessary to devote much time to what type of corporation to form. The sta-

(*Continued*)

(*Continued*)

tionery, the office furniture, the phone system, and other trappings contribute only peripherally to success.

As you will read, becoming a business owner does not depend on some special type of personality, family background, or childhood efforts at selling lemonade. I used to say that it takes three things to be a successful business owner:

1. *An idea.* It need not be a new idea, a great idea, an original idea, or even your own idea, but it has to be a marketable idea.
2. *A plan.* The idea is fine, but how will you implement it? What actions in what time frame will be needed?
3. *The resources.* You have the idea and you have the plan, but how can you execute the plan without the required resources?

I have since changed my mind. I now believe that you need only one thing to be successful—customers, people who will buy your products or services. If you have customers, the idea is marketable. If you have customers you can easily develop a plan, and you will be able to find the resources. Business ownership is about customers.

I have also changed my mind about one other matter. I now believe that one trait is required in a business owner: desire. To get you through all the challenges you will face, you must want to do this.

Business ownership today is probably only slightly riskier than a corporate job. The difference is that in your own business nothing happens unless you make it happen.

If you feel a strong desire to make things happen, read about the four routes to ownership:

1. Buying a business
2. Owning a franchise
3. Starting a business
4. Becoming a consultant

CHAPTER 7

Understanding the Background

Finding life beyond the corporation by starting your own business is not new, but it is a course of action that people now take for some new reasons. The long-standing American dream of independence is even more popular today because of changes in corporate America and new encouragement for entrepreneurship. We can add to this the explosive growth of franchising, which opens up business ownership to those who are not necessarily wealthy or experienced.

Changes in Corporate America

"Do a good job and you'll keep a good job." For most of modern industrial history, a long-service corporate employee, particularly a manager, could be assured of continued employment if he or she did a good job. This is no longer true.

Charles Handy, writing in *Hospitals and Health Networks* (August 1995), reveals the formula driving the corporate world today: "½ × 2 × 3— half as many people paid twice as much, producing three times as much." Handy points out that the only questions remaining are: "How long will it take to get there?" and "Which half will I be in?"

Management gurus urge us to live on the edge of chaos, constantly fluxing in virtual organizations, behaving like "tribeless warriors" without permanence or loyalties.

Corporate Cutbacks

Companies of all sizes are cutting back, laying off, and firing talented, productive people. The facts about de-jobbing are well known:

- Mergers of large companies result in duplicate staffs. Whether on the basis of performance or politics, cuts are made and productive people are let go.
- Foreign competition has caused many firms either to shift production overseas or to reduce costs of domestic operations. Either way, good performers are left without jobs.
- Technology has caused whole industries, such as steel, to be restructured.
- Cost-reduction programs now focus on eliminating jobs as a way to lower costs.

Even IBM and AT&T, traditionally considered "lifetime employers," have laid off tens of thousands of people.

The Baby Boomers

Another phenomenon affecting job security is the huge bulge in the population known as the "baby boom." The leading edge of the baby boom has turned 50 and reached the narrower parts of the corporate ladder. Competition is keener and promotional progress is becoming slower and less sure. With this excess of human talent, the individual has less power and leverage.

Whether it is called early retirement, voluntary severance, or a layoff, the result is the same: the previous, if unspoken, contract of continued employment in exchange for good work no longer exists. Hard work no longer equals job security. In a free economic system, these actions by companies are proper responses to markets and competition.

The individual faced with unemployment also has proper economic responses. He or she can seek another job in another company or industry and hope that this employment experience will not suffer the same fate as the last one. Or the individual can follow a path that has become increasingly viable and discover a new life and career beyond the corporation by owning a business.

Severance Programs

Corporations have made owning a business a more viable alternative by providing financial support. Severance payments and benefit coverage may run for several months or even a year or more. Pension service is often adjusted to "bridge" the time required to qualify for benefits.

The corporate action that contributes most to promoting entrepreneurship is the decline of job security as a reason to work for a company. If organizational employment cannot provide job security, one of the major arguments in favor or working for someone else no longer exists.

Encouragement for Entrepreneurship

Wanting to eliminate the vagaries of working for others is not the only reason entrepreneurship is becoming more popular. Today the corporate employee finds it easier to become an entrepreneur. In addition to corporate severance payments and benefits, three other factors encourage entrepreneurship: franchises, a new infrastructure, and the American drive for independence.

Franchises—Turnkey Entrepreneurship

Franchises offer some special appeals, particularly to the first-time business owner. Most franchises come with tested systems to help manage the business. From the sign over the front door to the payroll accounting system, the franchisee has the franchiser's experience and support available. Many established franchisers employ field consultants who visit the locations on a regular basis and who can be called on to help with problems.

"Be in business for yourself but not by yourself" describes franchise ownership. Owning a franchise can make the buyer instantly a part of a large organization with sophisticated advertising and strong market recognition.

Buying a franchise is a fairly straightforward proposition. Federal and state laws require the franchiser to disclose the material facts about the franchise and offer to sell. Little or no negotiating is required. This is considerably different from buying an established, nonfranchise business, for which financial data may be vague and the price is determined only after lengthy negotiations.

The franchise industry enjoys a better reputation now than in years past, and it is growing rapidly. The super successes in the field, such as McDonald's, coupled with tight government regulation, have raised the image of franchises. While there are still bad franchises and dishonorable franchisers, there is generally a more positive view toward franchise ownership.

Franchises are now available in a wide variety and price range. One recent collection of franchise offerings contained a $3,000 franchise to provide business education seminars and a $1 million top-name restaurant franchise. In between were franchises for instant printing ($35,000), hair styling ($75,000), automotive repair ($100,000), and even a minor league sports franchise for $250,000.

This variety gives people more chance to find opportunities that match their desires and their financial capabilities, making franchises attractive and affordable to more people who are seeking to become entrepreneurs.

We shall look in depth at franchises in Chapter 15.

An Infrastructure Now Exists to Support Entrepreneurship

Two new fixtures in American business, the personal computer and business networks, are good examples of the support infrastructure for entrepreneurs.

The personal computer allows individuals and smaller businesses to undertake projects, maintain controls, do analyses, and handle communications in ways formerly available only to larger firms. With a personal computer, a modem, a fax machine, and a few other accessories, a small business owner can have access to huge databases of information and to additional communications and computing power.

Business networks may constitute an even more important element of the new entrepreneurial infrastructure. These networks include venture capital groups in which people with ideas and a need for capital meet regularly with those who have capital to invest. Lots of other entrepreneurial activity goes on at these meetings as well; consulting arrangements are made, acquisitions and mergers are pursued, partnerships are conceived, and so on.

Another very effective and relatively new network phenomenon is the "tips club." This is typically a group of 10 to 30 people who represent noncompeting businesses. Meetings are most often weekly early-morning sessions over coffee, and they last about an hour. The club has only one purpose, and that is to generate business for its members. Members are expected to patronize each other as much as is practical, but the real objective is for members to bring business leads and tips to each meeting. Members often ask for help with special leads and introductions. Some clubs have tough requirements for continued membership. Really effective clubs have a waiting list for membership.

You can form a new club simply by getting a few business people together, as you learned in Chapter 4.

The Long-Standing American Admiration and Desire for Independence Still Lives

The spector of real or potential severance from employment, while a powerful motivator, represents only one reason to consider a business of your own. Owning a business can mean independence, the opportunity to excel, a chance to do what you want, a way to build for you and your family, and the satisfaction of setting and meeting your own goals. It can also be the best investment you can make under the new tax laws. Of course, owning a business does not lead automatically to wealth, happiness, and financial security.

Whether you see yourself standing among the plantings in your tree nursery, consulting with your staff in your electronics plant, winning a major client for your agency, or greeting guests in your restaurant, never forget that technology and competition can affect any business. Owning a business can mean long hours and high financial risk. Stress can affect the entrepreneur as much or more than it does the corporate employee.

Entrepreneurship brings an important difference, however. The entrepreneur has a high degree of personal control. Instead of the impotence often experienced as an employee, a business owner can take action and make choices and decisions. While the outcome may be no better, most competent productive people, if given a choice, would bet on themselves—not a corporation—to do the best job of looking out for their own interests.

Concerns about health and stress, a desire to be more involved with family, and a strong need to set one's own personal standards of conduct and performance can all potentially be satisfied by owning a business.

Before proceeding, you should take a moment to ask yourself why you want your own business. You may have lots of other alternatives: a different job, a different company, consulting, teaching, government service, or even retirement. While your reasons for pursuing business ownership may vary from seeking security to building wealth, and while there are no right or wrong reasons, you do need to understand clearly why you want your own business and what you want from ownership. Owning a business must satisfy your basic criteria for ownership or you will be no better off than you are now.

Worksheet 1, which follows, will help you focus on these fundamental criteria.

Worksheet 1
Why Do You Want to Own Your Own Business?

For each of the following statements, mark your degree of agreement; 0 equals no agreement at all and 5 equals complete agreement.

Statement of Reason	Degree of Agreement 0–5
I just can't stand to work for anyone anymore.	_____
I'm tired/bored doing what I'm doing.	_____
I want to get (very) rich.	_____
I feel insecure working for someone else.	_____
I want something I can really commit to.	_____
I have good reason to know that I can handle risk, especially personal risk.	_____
I don't like being around so many people.	_____
I want to work less (more).	_____
I want to travel less (more).	_____
I want to build something of my own.	_____
I can afford to fail.	_____
I would like the feeling of owning my own business.	_____
I want to move somewhere else.	_____
I can do without status symbols.	_____
I have an idea/a concept I want to pursue.	_____
I want to do something that can really grow.	_____
I want to stand out.	_____
I feel like a servant.	_____
I want to be properly rewarded for my efforts.	_____
I want to build something my family can get involved in.	_____
I don't like the politics and inefficiencies of corporate life.	_____
I want a lifestyle with more _____ and less _____.	_____
I have full family support in this effort.	_____
I don't like being so dependent on others.	_____
I've tried finding a job and can't find what I want.	_____
I'll never get promoted where I am.	_____
I'd gladly pinch pennies if I had to.	_____
I don't like all the organizational competition.	_____
I'm being held back working for someone else.	_____

Other: _____

The purpose of this worksheet is to help you articulate your feelings and to start you thinking about the benefits and drawbacks of owning your own business. Scoring your answers is simply a way to see which of them are most important to you. When you are done, complete these sentences:

I want my own business because _____
_____
_____

I think I can be successful in my own business because _____
_____
_____

CHAPTER 8

Preparing While You Are Still Employed

No matter what your reason for considering ownership—boredom, a dead-end job, corporate cutbacks, or just an unrelenting desire to be on your own—you can do a lot about owning your own business while you still have a job. You don't have to give up your salary and benefits because you don't have to give up working. You can do much of the preliminary work in your off-hours and spare time. Many people have gotten their own businesses up and running while still keeping their jobs. Others have completed major steps of the process before they resigned or before the severance clock started ticking. In his book, *Mail Order Moonlighting* (Ten Speed Press; Berkeley, CA, 1976), Cecil C. Hoge, Sr., offers a whole plan on how to start a mail-order business at home while keeping your job.

At the least, your analysis and fact finding can be done with less than full-time effort. Most of the time you will be making inquiries and waiting for responses. A good part of your time should be spent reflecting on your motivation and commitment and on determining the kind of business you want. You do not have to jump off an economic cliff just yet.

Maximize Your Severance Benefits

If you are employed or in the process of being separated, your first job must be to understand and lock in all the compensation and benefits your company policies and practices provide. Companies will sometimes bend these policies, and the practices can vary with circumstances. Terms of severance, early retirement, and even resignation can be subject to some degree of negotiation.*

An example of negotiated separation occurs when a company is planning a large-scale cutback. The cutback may be done all at once, or it may be spread over a long period. To minimize the impact on its people, the company may ask employees to volunteer to be separated. Although a general severance package is offered, companies typically offer variations to try and satisfy individual employees' needs. Older employees, minority employees, and those in other protected classes receive special attention. While the company is trying to ease the burden for its people, it is also, understandably, trying to limit its exposure to employee suits for discrimination or unlawful discharge.

The human resources or personnel department is typically the keeper of the general policies. In some companies, this department controls all policy exceptions. In others, department heads or other executives can influence severance policies.

Depending on your company and your personal situation and relationships, you may go directly to the human resources department or to a senior executive with whom you have a good relationship. If you know and can trust the discretion of anyone who has recently been subject to termination or severance, you might inquire about their experience to get a good fix on actual practices.

Some Considerations

- What is the length of the salary continuation period? Are exceptions being made? Can other elements of the package be traded for more time? A very easy way to lengthen the period is to negotiate a later date to start it. In some cases, employees can negotiate a lump-sum (though lower) payment.
- Which benefits and insurance are continued, and for how long? Some benefits, such as employee discounts, are relatively low in cost and might be easy to extend. Most insurance coverages run coincidental with employment. Some states have now passed laws requiring that terminated employees be provided the opportunity to obtain insurance coverage. You should check out this opportunity, but don't jump to buy it. The insurance offered may not be the same coverage your company had, and it may be very expensive. The purpose of the legislation was to ensure that people would not be left without any op-

---

*Negotiating a resignation may sound odd, but it is done. Whether out of conscience, fairness, guilt, or fear, employers will, on occasion, extend some form of severance benefits to a person who is resigning.

portunity to buy some coverage. When negotiating for extended insurance coverage, be sensitive to how the insurance carrier calculates coverage periods. One day's service in a month or quarter may extend coverage for the full period.

- How will your retirement credits be calculated, and what is the status of your pension? This item is subject to detailed regulations. Obtain copies of your company's pension plan and have it explained. Although the safety, administration, vesting, and payout schedules of your plan are narrowly prescribed, the calculation of length of service, credit for broken service, and so-called *bridging* or extending service in order to allow an employee to meet the threshold requirements of pension eligibility are subjects for negotiation.

- What happens to deferred compensation, stocks, options, and savings plans your company is holding for you? Regulations do apply, but practices vary, so check your firm's approach. Because your company may have recorded the liability of owing you these assets, they may be willing to ease the rules on how long they must be held. As with all of these compensation elements, you won't know if you don't ask.

- What happens to accrued vacation and sick days? What are the provisions for earned but unpaid bonuses and commissions? These are things within a company's control and are implemented through well-known and accepted practices. Be sure you understand how to use your vacation and sick days best to lengthen your salary continuation and benefits coverage.

- Are you entitled to relocation benefits? In some cases, employees who are transferred and then severed within a relatively short time or who are transferred under conditions considered to be temporary are entitled to be relocated back to their "home" location.

- Can you become a part-time consultant to your present company? Can you become an independent contractor or work on a special project? In addition to providing income, these arrangements might allow for benefits to be continued or for time to be credited toward retirement. These arrangements allow companies to technically achieve their goals of reducing employees while allowing them to get important work done by qualified people.

- Are you entitled to outplacement counseling? This fringe benefit can be very useful to you and very costly to your company. (Costs average 10 percent of your salary.) Most outplacement programs help individuals examine several alternatives for their future: retirement, a similar position in the same industry, a similar position in a different industry, a position in academia or in government, a consulting practice, and the alternative of starting or buying a business. If you are entitled to outplacement help, ask that your program include a full examination of the ownership alternatives.

- Are you entitled to any support services? Quite often a company will provide secretarial and phone service and the use of an office for some period of time. Ask about services that can be used in your search for a company. Think about things like the company's library, the use of a computer, an e-mail or Internet address, mailing privileges, use of financial reporting services such as Dun & Bradstreet, or even legal advice from the company's attorneys.

Guidelines

No matter which of the above elements you decide to pursue, there are three general guidelines to follow:

1. Understand the legal and personal tax implications of these compensation and benefit items. There may be large amounts of money involved. You need advice, so consult professionals in the field (more on professional advisors later in this chapter).
2. Be pleasant and businesslike in your dealings with your company, even if you feel bitter. You will get more help that way. You can always get angry or sue later, and you never know when you might want to use the company or some of the people in the company as references.
3. If you don't ask what exceptions or additions to policies and practices you can have, you will never know what extra help could have been yours. As you read on, you will see that some of this help can be very useful in your quest for ownership. Worksheet 2 at the end of this chapter will help you organize your benefit entitlements.

Select Advisors

Another step you can take while you are still employed is to select your advisors. Some key professionals you may need include:

- Accountant
- Appraiser
- Attorney
- Banker
- Business broker
- Consultants
- Financial planner
- Insurance agent
- Real estate broker
- Stockbroker

You may already have a relationship with some of these advisors. Others you may not need for some time. Whenever you make your choices, select these people on two criteria: competence and willingness.

Competence

Are these advisors competent in their field as it relates to what you want to do, which is to become a business owner? Almost all professional fields have special areas of interest. That means that the attorney who prepared your will may not be experienced in negotiating a purchase agreement for a business. Your accountant may do a great job on your personal taxes, but he or she may not know the first thing about "normalizing" a small business income statement. Your residential real estate broker may have no contacts in the commercial or industrial field, and your banker may be involved only in consumer services.

Ask what specific experience the advisor has in small business matters. In most cases, your advisors will be candid and, if they are not qualified, will refer you to someone who is.

Willingness

Do these advisors want to work with you in this effort? Not every qualified professional cares to work in this field. Business transfers are complicated, a high percentage of the transactions fall through, and the responsibility is significant. Be sure your advisors do want to work with you. Ideally, they should be enthusiastic and supportive while at the same time providing you with sound advice and protection.

After you have selected your advisors, record their names, addresses, and phone numbers (including home phone numbers) and have them handy at all times. It is normal to need advice in a hurry. Get them to know each other so that they can work for you as a team. Worksheet 3 at the end of this chapter will help you organize this information about your advisors.

Getting Ready

There are dozens of minor and not so minor steps involved in setting up to own your own business. Don't delay starting on them, because they do take time to complete. Following are some "generic" steps that will be applicable to almost any business venture.

Form a Corporation

The largest percentage of business purchase and sales transactions are technically asset purchases, not the purchase of stock in a corporation. The reasons will be discussed in Chapter 14, but the result is that whether you are buying or starting a business, you will probably need to form a corporation. Under some conditions, you may want to establish yourself as a sole proprietor or form a partnership rather than a corporation. Table 8–1 compares the three forms of organization in terms of a range of tax and expense considerations. Your attorney can show you how to provide for a corporate charter broad enough to conduct virtually any line of business. The process is simple, costs $1,000 or less, and can be fun as you pick out a name and become a corporate officer in your own company.

Establishing the form of your business is important because it permits you to apply for the proper state and federal identification numbers, which will be needed for other purposes as well.

Establish a Location

Eventually you will need a base of operations from which to conduct your search or start your business. There are lots of ways to establish a location, even a temporary one. At the top of the cost ladder is renting and furnishing an office. Next is renting space in a cooperative office. Under this arrangement, you have a furnished office and share reception and secretarial services with other tenants. You might share an office with someone you know who has space for you. Another level of service is one that will receive your mail and phone calls but may or may not actually have office space for you to use.

Of course, you can use your home as your location. You can augment your in-home location with a post office box, an answering service or answering machine, a fax machine, a separate phone line, and secretarial services purchased as necessary. At some point, you will probably want to consider a computer and all its peripherals. A visit to a computer store will be an important part of your plan.

Order Business Cards and Stationery

Whether you use your new company name or just your own name, you will need business cards and stationery. Establishing credibility with sellers, financial sources, and others can be a critical factor, and your use of proper business cards and stationery can help.

Open a Bank Account

You will need a bank account for your company, and the cost to set one up is low. Be sure the bank you choose wants your type of account. A corporate account will require a corporate resolution, and the bank can show you how to prepare one.

Table 8-1. Legal Forms of Organization

Consideration	Sole Proprietorship	LLC	Partnership General	Partnership Limited	Corporation C Corp.	Corporation S Corp.
Complexity of formation and operation	Simple	More complex than limited partnership or C Corp.[a]	Relatively simple most of the time	More complex, requires written agreement and state filing	Most complex, requires state charter, election of officers, and directors, etc.	Same as C Corp. in legal operation and formation
Limits on number of owners or shareholders	One	Unlimited members[a]	Unlimited	Unlimited	Unlimited	Limited to 35 shareholders
Owner's personal liability for business debts and claims of litigation	Unlimited personal liability	Same as C Corp., limited to investment[a]	Unlimited personal liability	Generally limited to amount of investment	Generally not liable for corporate debts, with a potential exception for federal withholding taxes	Same as C Corp.
Federal income taxation of business profits	Tax paid by owner at individual rates	Same as partnership[a]	Tax paid by partners at individual rates	Tax paid by partners at individual rates	Tax paid by corporation at corporation rates	Tax paid by shareholders at individual rates

(Continued)

97

Table 8-1. (Continued)

Consideration	Sole Proprietorship	LLC	Partnership		Corporation	
			General	Limited	C Corp.	S Corp.
Deduction of business losses by owners	Yes, provided active participation by owner	Same as limited partnership[a]	Yes, but limited to amounts personally at risk and passive loan rates	Yes, but limited to amounts personally at risk and passive loan rates	No	Yes, but limited to investment in stock and loans to the corporation; also subject to passive loan rates
Taxation of dividends or other withdrawals of profits	No	No[a]	No	No	Yes	Yes
Social Security tax on owner's earnings	13.02% up to $48,000 of earnings (with scheduled annual increases)	For managing members, same as partnership; for nonmanaging members, same as limited partnership	Same as sole proprietorship	No	15.02% of shareholder/employee earnings up to $48,000 (with scheduled annual increases); 50% paid by corporation, 50% paid by employee	Same as C Corp. for salaries

98

Unemployment taxes	No	No	No	No	Yes, both federal and state generally	Yes, both federal and state generally
Availability of deductible qualified deferred compensation plans for retirement	Yes, however, borrowing prohibited	Same as partnership	Yes, however, borrowing prohibited	No	Yes, including the ability to borrow	Yes, however, borrowing prohibited by 5% shareholder/employee
Medical, disability, and group term life insurance on owners	Generally not deductible; however, 25% of medical insurance	Same as partnership	Same as sole proprietorship	Same as sole proprietorship	Corporation deduction generally not taxable to employee under certain conditions	Generally not deductible if paid for by a 2% or more shareholder
Available options of reporting year	Limited to calendar year	Calendar year	Must conform to year end of majority partners	Same as general partnership	Any 12-month period, except for personal service corporations	Must conform to year end of majority shareholders (exception provided for natural business year)
Ability to allocate income among several owners	No	Yes	Yes	Yes	No	Yes

(Continued)

99

Table 8-1. (Continued)

Consideration	Sole Proprietorship	LLC	Partnership		Corporation	
			General	Limited	C Corp.	S Corp.
Automobile expenses	Deductible to extent of business use; maintain records	Same as sole proprietorship	Same as sole proprietorship	No	Same as sole proprietorship	Same as C Corp.
Business meals and entertaining	Deductible to the extent of 80% of ordinary and necessary expenses of carrying on a trade or business; maintain adequate records	Same as sole proprietorship	Same as sole proprietorship	No	Same as sole proprietorship	Same as C Corp.

[a]From C. D. Peterson, *Introduction to Business Brokerage*, John Wiley & Sons, New York, 1991.

Apply for a Home Equity Credit Line

A home equity credit line, a flexible, low-cost line of credit, can be a cornerstone of your financial strategy. The psychological hurdle of obtaining what is essentially a second mortgage on your home can be overcome if you consider how useful it may be. At some time in the process of buying a business, you will be asked to personally guarantee your borrowings. Lenders will want your personal guarantee for security and as a demonstration that you believe in your venture and are fully committed to it. A home equity type of loan can actually give you more control over the results.

There are three important considerations with home equity loans:

1. The interest rate, terms, and charges vary considerably from institution to institution, so shop carefully.
2. Even though you may have substantial equity in your home, most lenders will still require evidence of your ability to repay the loan. You stand a better chance of being approved if you can substantiate a steady income.
3. Home equity loans can take a long time to obtain. Because they are a form of mortgage, you will have to go through all the steps of application, including obtaining an appraisal. Further delays can be expected because recent changes in the tax laws favor this type of credit and many people are submitting applications, which lengthens the processing time.

Special Preparation: Learn about Personal Selling

No matter what route to ownership you take, your ability to sell can make the difference between success and failure. To convince investors or bankers to back you, you need to sell your idea. To hire people for your fledgling company, you need to sell your company's prospects. You may need to sell vendors on the soundness of granting you credit, or a landlord on the value of giving you a break on the rent. Most certainly, you will need to sell customers or clients on why they should give you their business.

Chapter 17, "Forming a Consulting Practice," discusses personal selling at length; here we give only a preview.

There is a well-known model of selling that describes the sales process. It is based on a theory of how the change process occurs. After all, selling is a change event; someone does something differently.

To summarize, this theory of change says that uncoerced change occurs *only* when the following conditions exist:

- A perceived need to change
- A readiness to change
- A willingness to change
- An ability to change
- An expectation that change is possible and positive

The selling model recognizes the elements of change in an order of its own, as shown in Figure 8–1. Let us look briefly at each of these elements.

Getting *permission to proceed* does two things: It ensures that you are going to be heard, and it should ensure that you are talking to the right person.

As obvious as it sounds, the biggest mistake in selling comes from not *understanding what is needed.* Need is a complicated idea. The market's needs are not as simple to ascertain as the name might imply. The problem stems from the fact that the people you will deal with in companies also have their own needs, and those needs may or may not be the same as the company's needs. The company may need your consulting service, but the purchasing agent may need to buy from another consultant to satisfy old loyalties.

More complications arise when different people in the same company have different needs. The purchasing agent wants the lowest-cost consulting service, but the manufacturing boss wants the consulting service with the broadest range of skills and experience.

Also, we need to accept that the customer's perceived needs, right or wrong, are the customer's present needs. If you are selling what the company truly needs to someone who perceives those needs differently, you won't sell much.

Finally, some people don't know what they need. They may know their problem but not the solution. Some people will lie, perhaps because they are embarrassed or perhaps because they don't want to deal with you. Most will change. Needs can change rapidly, and you might be responding to a need that no longer exists.

A good salesperson knows that the customer is always right, because the customer's perception of reality *is* the customer's reality. If the customer's perception is faulty, the good salesperson works as an agent to change it. Before any selling can begin, there must be an *agreement on need.*

Permission to proceed	Tentative close
Need identification	Overcome objections
Agreement on needs	Restate
Present features and benefits	Close

Figure 8–1. The selling model.

Once you are in front of the right person and the needs are agreed upon, you can begin presenting the *features and benefits* of your offering. Features are what you have or can do; benefits are what they mean to the buyer.

The difference between features and benefits is extremely important. It is easier, more common, and tempting to talk about the features of your product and service. You know them and you know how hard you have worked to develop them into your offering. The fact is that customers and clients don't buy your features; they buy the benefits they perceive your product or service gives them.

Before you shrug off the difference as being semantic, be aware that converting a feature to a benefit is not always easy. For example, most consultants spend a majority of their selling activity touting their service's special process of fact finding, analysis, and recommendation. But those features are not what the client needs. They may be important to know to build your credibility, but they are of no direct benefit to the client. Examples of the differences between features and benefits are given in Figure 8–2. Benefits are what people buy. Features are what the salesperson offers as the "what, how, and why" you can fill the needs.

After presenting the features and benefits of your offering *ask for the business.* (May I begin on Monday?) This is the "temporary close." If you are refused, find out exactly what the objections are.

The next step is to *overcome the objections.* The methods depend on the objection, but one rule is irrefutable: Listen to and understand the objection very carefully. Probe for the real reason. Restate the objection as merely something to be resolved. Here is an example dealing with price.

Objection: "I'm afraid your price is too high."
Restatement: "I understand that price is an important consideration. Why do you feel the price is too high?"

Check to see if you are being compared to a competitor. Find out the basis for the price objection. It may be simply an attempt to pressure you for a reduction, or it may be that the client has not really understood the value of your offering.

Features:	**Benefits:**
All steel construction	Will last longer and save money
20 years of experience	Will perform better for you
50% stronger	Will be trouble free
On-time delivery	Will serve you faster
The largest	Will give you the means to perform

Figure 8–2. Features versus benefits.

To save time	To save effort
To feel good	To be popular
To win praise	To gain recognition
To conserve possessions	To increase well-being
To be in style	To copy others
To protect a reputation	To avoid criticism
To avoid trouble	To profit from opportunities
To gain control over his or her life	To solve a problem
	To please someone important
To be safe and secure	To end confrontation or sales pressure
To obey the law	
To be different	

Figure 8-3. Why clients hire consultants.

Once you have responded to objections, *reposition your selling proposal*, based on the response to your questions, and focus on the value of your services.

Clients may have many reasons to use your services. Figure 8–3 presents a partial list. This long list contains subtleties, but you can do only two things of real value for the customer: add to revenue or reduce costs.

Finally, you must *ask for the business* ("close").

The model for selling shows the need for both knowledge and skill. In order to sell well you need knowledge about your service, your customer, the market, competition, needs, and more. You obtain knowledge through study and experience.

The skills in selling include listening, thinking on your feet, speaking, persuading, building trust, and so on. You obtain skills through practice and feedback. Unless you are already a skilled salesperson, reading books on selling and attending sales training programs should be part of your personal preparation.

Other Personal Preparation

If you believe you will need a special license or permit, get started now. Read books and attend seminars that you feel will help you. Talk with consultants and industry people.

Above all, talk with people who have done what you are planning to do. Find business owners who made the transition from employee to entrepreneur. Not all entrepreneurs will have relevant experience, but they can provide interesting, first-hand insight, and most like to talk about their transition.

Keep track of all your expenses as you go through this process. Many of them are allowable business expenses. Worksheet 4 at the end of the chapter can help you manage these necessary setup steps that could cause critical delays later.

Deciding what else can be done while you are still employed is a matter of your personal situation, your relationship with your company, and other factors. The important things are to be aware of how much can be done and to consciously manage this important time of transition.

Worksheet 2
Locking in Your Compensation and Benefits

Compensation or Benefit Item	Company Policy or Practice*	Your Objective	Contact Person in the Company	Status
Salary continuation start date				
Length of salary continuation ($ _____)				
Insurance:				
1. Health				
2. Life				
3. Dental				
4. _____				
Retirement:				
1. Length of service credits				
2. Bridging				
3. Payments				
4. Vesting				
5. _____				
Deferred compensation:				
1. Stock				
2. Savings				
3. _____				
4. _____				
Accrued compensation:				
1. Vacation				
2. Sick days				
3. Commissions/bonuses				
4. _____				
5. _____				
Relocation services				
Outplacement				
Support services:				
1. Secretarial				
2. Office space				
3. Computer usage				
4. _____				
5. _____				
Part-time employment				

*If you are resigning or otherwise have the option of deciding when you will leave, check to make sure you are not leaving just short of some date that would qualify you for extra benefits.

Worksheet 3
Your Personal Advisors

Consider accountants, attorneys, appraisers, bankers, brokers, consultants, financial planners, insurance agents, and anyone else you will be using to help you.

Competence relates to the advisor's experience and knowledge in the purchase/sale of businesses.

Willingness relates to the advisor's desire to work on your business buying activities.

Name/ Profession/	Business Phone/ Address	Home Phone/ Address	Competence	Willingness	Comments

Worksheet 4
Getting Set Up

Item	Estimated $	Action Planned	Date of Next Step	Status
Establish a location	_____	_____	_____	_____
Business cards/stationery	_____	_____	_____	_____
Open a bank account	_____	_____	_____	_____
Apply for a home equity credit line	_____	_____	_____	_____
Personal preparation:				
Reduce expenses	_____	_____	_____	_____
Save	_____	_____	_____	_____
Attend classes/read	_____	_____	_____	_____
Obtain license	_____	_____	_____	_____
Second job	_____	_____	_____	_____
Spouse's job	_____	_____	_____	_____
Join network	_____	_____	_____	_____
_____	_____	_____	_____	_____
_____	_____	_____	_____	_____
_____	_____	_____	_____	_____
Form a corporation, partnership, or proprietorship	_____	_____	_____	_____

CHAPTER 9

Deciding What You Want

You have reached the most crucial decision point in the whole process of making the transition from an employee to an owner. Now it is time to ask whether ownership is right for you, and if it is, what kind of business you want.

First, let's separate the concept of "entrepreneur" from that of "owner." Dozens of entrepreneurs exist in such companies as 3M and Rubbermaid. They create new products and innovate services but they have little ownership risk. Owners of tightly structured franchises such as McDonald's or Subway do little that is entrepreneurial, following detailed and proven practices. However, they do endure the risks of ownership. And while Bill Gates is still entrepreneurial at Microsoft, his ability to shift and hedge his enormous wealth makes his personal ownership risk practically nil.

An *entrepreneur* invests, allocates, or reallocates resources to create an improved or new product, service, or business entity. The resources can include all kinds of things—money, manufacturing capacity, time, creative skills, or any useful good or service.

An *owner* bears the risks and rewards of property ownership. The property can be as tangible as a factory or as intangible as a list of customers. The degree of ownership and its risks and rewards can be total or as small as those connected with 1 share of stock.

Entrepreneurs are defined by behaviors, owners by rights and obligations; neither is defined by personal traits. That understanding is the key to making the right decision.

109

The Myth of the Entrepreneurial Type

Now, a few words about comparing yourself with your image of an entre-preneur. You have probably heard the stereotypical descriptions of entre-preneurs, descriptions so exaggerated you would bet you could recognize one of these superhumans on sight (most likely by the glint in the eye and the brash, self-assured walk).

Beware of "entrepreneurial tests." Most are based on clichés and anec-dotes, asking questions about your father's self-employment, your interest in paper routes at an early age, and similar apparently associative ques-tions. Some tests claim that they can compare you to the profile of a suc-cessful entrepreneur—a profile of desire, good work habits, tenacity, a solid sense of self, and reasonable risk taking. The fact is that the entre-preneurial profile exhibits a remarkable similarity to the profile of *any* suc-cessful business person. That shouldn't be surprising. Whether you work for yourself or for others, good work habits, tenacity, a solid sense of self, and reasonable risk taking are always valuable traits, and little is ever ac-complished without strong desire. The following fictitious display ad shows that the traits of entrepreneurs are often the same as the traits of corporate executives (and vice versa).

Immediate Opportunity for Seasoned Executive
Must be innovative and willing to take thoughtful risks. Experience in our industry preferred, but results-oriented per-son with strong desire to achieve goals should apply. Must be a self-starter with good work habits and confidence.

Excellent compensation for the highly motivated performer.

Like any successful group of people, entrepreneurs have traits that range from shy to pugnacious, from workaholic to sloth, and from vi-vacious to dull as a stone. Some were previously failures, and some have been winners at everything they have tried. Some are driven by in-security and others cannot even imagine failure. Reflect on the situa-tions described in the box on page 111.

These examples point out that the keys to success are so multivariate as to be beyond correlation with personal traits. Obviously, a failed, lazy, un-ambitious, nonentrepreneurial employee stands a good chance of exhibit-ing the same traits when becoming an owner. Just as obviously, a person

> Think about what kind of person would succeed as a fund-
> raising consultant. Now think about what kind of person
> would succeed as the owner of a locksmith business. These
> are two different kinds of people, but both are successful en-
> trepreneur owners.
>
> *   *   *
>
> Think about a small town where one person owns the only
> computer services and supply store. Now think about a large
> market, where one person owns one of 15 competing stores.
> These similar entrepreneurial businesses require two differ-
> ent kinds of people.

with limited physical strength would be unwise to take on a business that
requires long hours of physical labor.

Forget Checklists and Lists of Entrepreneurial Traits

Some extreme definitions of entrepreneurs restrict the term to the creators
of new enterprises. Other definitions are broad enough to include anyone
who bears the ultimate risk of a business. It is important to put the idea of
the successful entrepreneurial type in perspective. There are no easy
checklists that can eliminate or excuse you from considering your own
business or that can guarantee you have the "right stuff." Other than strong
desire, there is no special common denominator.

Before looking at the ownership option, it is important to forget the
myth of the "entrepreneurial type" or personality. There is no entrepreneurial personality, no special set of traits that ensures success or guarantees failure. *You are as able as the next person to explore the entrepreneurial alternative.*

Tests show it: Entrepreneurs are as varied as any of us. The only trait
that is absolutely required is *desire*—you must really want to own your
own business.

As we pointed out in Chapter 1, if you happen to be an experienced executive at midcareer, you may have an advantage in trying to become an
owner. To reiterate, your experience translates into more confidence, better judgment, and more realistic objectivity. If you are at midcareer, your
status brings with it your established reputation and, most likely, measures

of resiliency and resourcefulness. Experienced people may have fewer financial commitments and more useful business contacts.

The Three Real Questions to Ask

While questions about your traits are vaguely interesting, they lead nowhere. To really dig into the possibility of becoming a business owner you need to answer these three questions:

- Can I run it?
- Will I like it?
- Should I do it?

"Can I Run It?"

"Can I run it?" asks simply whether you have the knowledge, skills, and traits to make the business a success. You have a pretty good grasp of your personal inventory. A tougher task will be to determine what the business requires.

Analyzing the requirements of a business you might own presents the midcareer person with a unique challenge. The business requirement and your background may look superficially the same. Both may include "financial management," for example. However, your financial management function may be compiling and analyzing financial information, and the business may require someone who knows how to keep its banker happy when cash is short.

"Sales management" to you may mean conducting research, setting annual goals, building a national plan, and implementing a sales compensation program. To the small company, sales management may mean personally accompanying salespeople on calls to learn what the market wants and what the salespeople need. In a small company you may *be* the salesforce.

The same consideration applies to manufacturing. You may be able to devise complex productivity improvement programs, whereas the business may need a practicing engineer.

These examples have two interesting dimensions. First, most younger corporate managers are experienced in only one or a few disciplines. Business ownership usually requires broader expertise in all basic disciplines. That gives the midcareer manager an advantage.

On the other hand, midcareer corporate managers experienced enough to be thinking about their own businesses are probably senior enough that they have for some time been able to delegate detailed tasks. Tasks such as approving individual customer credit and devising equitable weekend work schedules may be trivial to the senior corporate executive, but they could be important in a small business, and the owner-manager will be required to do them.

You need to understand in detail what it's really going to take to run the business. Later in this book you will learn the best way to find out what a business requires.

Right now you probably don't have to have all the knowledge and skills the business requires. You can try to acquire them later, or you can plan to hire someone else who has them, but you should be mindful of the potential for problems.

You may not be able to master certain skills or knowledge, leaving yourself very vulnerable to failure. Hiring can incur a high cost in a small business and, by hiring for a key skill, you may become dependent on or even hostage to someone else.

As a midcareer person you once again have an advantage. You most likely have a business network broad enough and trusted enough to call on for help.

Taking Your Personal Inventory

Even before you begin your search, start to answer the question "Can I run it?" by taking a personal inventory. Use Worksheet 5 at the end of the chapter to take your personal inventory. The inventory is divided into three parts: knowledge, skills, and traits.

Knowledge is a thing you know. As a midcareer individual, don't restrict this to things from your work experience. Your family, sports, hobbies, vacations, or other interests have all provided things you know. Ask yourself this question: "What five things do I know more about than almost anybody else?" Rank them. While you are at it, list five things you know almost nothing about. (Most of us find this an easy list to develop.)

Skills are things you can do. The same ground rules apply to skills as to knowledge. The question this time is "What five things can I do better than almost anybody else?" Also make up a list of things you do poorly. This is not as easy an exercise as you might think, and it will be helpful later on to recognize deficiencies as well as your skills.

Traits are things you are. Complete this sentence five times: "I am . . . ." Concentrate on your physical and mental attributes.

Separating knowledge, skills, and traits establishes the differences among them. Knowledge can usually be acquired by study. If you want to see whether you have some particular knowledge, you can take a test or answer some questions.

Skills, on the other hand, are things you do. Skills come from practice. While most people can reasonably expect to acquire knowledge by studying, not everyone can acquire skills by practicing. For example, you can study and learn all there is to know about juggling, but you may never have the skill to do it well no matter how much you practice. You may improve with practice, but you might remain relatively unskilled.

This distinction becomes important when we look at the essential requirements of a business. If you are deficient in knowledge (say, knowledge of the product line in a distribution business), you can probably overcome it. If you are deficient in a skill (say, selling in a retail business), it may be a real cause for concern.

As a midcareer manager you have a big edge, not only because you have had more time to acquire your basket of knowledge and skill, but because you have had the experience to assess it.

And what about traits? Traits are things you *are* as opposed to things you know or can do. Traits are usually described in clichés: people-oriented, self-starter, highly motivated, and so on. (These clichés are found regularly in the display ads for executive jobs.) As mentioned earlier, I am not sure they apply to entrepreneurs, who are often described as eccentric. In any event, there is little you can do about traits, and only two kinds seem essential to success:

Physical traits. You will need whatever level of health and energy the business and your objectives require. You will be the engine that drives the business, and without you the business will come to a halt.

Mental traits. Most businesses don't require superintelligence, but you should be alert for special mental requirements such as the creativity needed in an advertising agency or the fashion sense essential in a business involving style or design.

What It All Means

In order to answer Key Question # 1, "Can I run it?", you first need to understand thoroughly your knowledge, skills, and traits. Reflect on your analysis in Worksheet 5. How do you look on paper? The answer should matter only to you; after all, there is no right way to look on paper. Remember, too, that your knowledge, skills, and traits are only one side of the equation. You won't really know how you stack up until you see what the business requires.

Successful entrepreneurs probably have no more *total* knowledge and skill than you do; what they do have is very relevant to their business. Besides, as we have noted, you can almost certainly acquire any needed knowledge, and most skills are not as hard to master as juggling.

In summary, get a good feel for your knowledge and skills. Be prepared to rule out businesses that are obviously outside your competence, but keep the gates as wide open as possible for now.

This inventory of knowledge, skills, and traits represents a starting point to determine what kind of business you should buy. Any business description based on these elements will directly reflect your past experience and will be very general. That's fine for the moment. Whatever business definition you have formed has properly eliminated some extremes and is based on a degree of logic.

"Will I Like It?"

"Will I like it?" relates to the obvious fact that there are more considerations to business ownership than having the competence to run it. Enjoyment and satisfaction depend on other things. Figure 9–1 lists some criteria to explore that bear on whether or not you will like having your own business.

Let's look carefully at the criteria shown in Figure 9–1, which can truly trigger a positive or negative response to a business opportunity. These are the things we really think about when we evaluate a business. Use Worksheet 6 at the end of the chapter to help you establish your criteria for a business. Keep in mind that you still have four routes to ownership: buying a business, taking a franchise, starting a business, or forming a consulting practice.

How Much Money You Need

It is time to look at how much money you need and want. First understand clearly the difference between how much money you need and how much money you want.

Don't be tempted to add up how much you are spending and say that's how much you need. The fact is, you can always cut back. Cutting back can vary from eliminating some luxury to completely reshaping your lifestyle.

1. How much money you need to earn	6. Growth potential
2. How much money you want to earn	7. Physical working conditions and hours
3. Location	8. Status and image
4. Risk	9. People intensity
5. Liquidity	10. Competition
	11. Content of the business

Figure 9–1. Criteria for enjoyment.

As a midcareer manager you have, at some time, had to do a zero-based budget. Examine everything from the private schools to how often you go to the movies. Only you can say whether you really need something. You may find it useful to prepare two budgets, one you would like to have and one that represents an absolute minimum.

Some business buyers have had such a strong desire and commitment that they have sold everything and lived with just the barest essentials in order to keep their needs for money low.

You should also know that when you own your own business, there are ways to shift certain insurance, automobile, legal, accounting, and other expenses to the business. If the business is successful, it can provide employment and perks for family members.

Speaking of family members and money, this is a good place to bring up the subject of how your family fits into this entire process of leaving employment for the risks and rewards of ownership.

This book is not intended to be a text on family relations, but this advice is offered. You can understand that your family is going to react with some surprise and anxiety when you tell them what you are considering. If you are the principal wage earner, their concerns will be heightened.

When you explain your desire and explain that this is what you want, their self-concerns can become touched with guilt. You need to help them open up about their concerns. To the extent you honestly can, involve them in the decision. Have them participate in completing the worksheets. Share with them your expectations about how all of you, and your lifestyle, are going to be affected. Talk with them about money, family time, and the stresses to be expected. Share your vision of the opportunity and what it could mean to all of you.

Above all, explain the risks as you see them. If you want their support and help, ask for it, particularly if this is the first time they have been involved in your business dealings. You should pay attention to their concerns, and they should pay attention to how much you want to do this.

Be as accurate as you can in deciding how much money you need. It is a critical factor in the final decision to become an owner. If you have overstated how much you need, you may miss a great opportunity. If you understate your needs, you could start or buy a business and end up in financial distress. Use Worksheet 6A.

How Much Money You Want

How much money you want can be your most definitive screening criterion. For example, if you want a business that earns a minimum of $500,000 today, you have eliminated all but a few individual retail businesses and nearly any business that you could buy for less than $2 million.

How much money you want to earn has the added dimension of time and cannot be entirely separated from your other criteria. Here are four examples demonstrating how the criteria are interrelated.

1. You just want to find a company that will provide you with a nice living, year after year. If the business does well, you will probably trade off any higher earnings to work less instead.
2. You want a company with a present cash flow adequate to cover your needs, but it has to be able to grow. Your targets are $100,000 in three years and $200,000 in five years. After that, who knows?
3. You don't even care if the business is losing money right now. What you want is a business that can grow into a multimillion dollar enterprise. Without that potential, you aren't going to give up your present situation.
4. It really depends on what you are doing. If you can find a business in the perfect location, involved in your favorite area of interest, or one that satisfies your criteria for status, travel, and so on, the money you make will be relatively unimportant.

At midcareer, you probably fall somewhere among all these examples.

What is important right now is to convert your income desires into a useful criterion so that you can measure it against the business you are going to consider. Use Worksheet 6B.

Now that you have set criteria to cover how much money you need and want, let's look at other criteria.

Location

Location, once the simplest of criteria, now needs to be considered in two ways to determine whether the location suits you (personal criterion) and whether it suits the business (business criterion).

Personal Criteria. Think here about where *you* want to be located. The three general models are:

1. You want businesses only within a reasonable commute of your present home.
2. You are willing to relocate anywhere (or somewhere) for the right business.
3. You want to relocate to some specific area.

People buying a business or franchise are tempted to look at every good opportunity, no matter where it is. You might ask what the harm is in doing so. The harm comes from the time and effort expended by you, the seller, and your advisors. Good brokers, for example, will be less inclined to bring opportunities to you if they feel you waste their time by looking at businesses you will never really pursue.

People starting businesses or practices would seem to be able to locate anywhere, but they may not be able to satisfy the business criterion.

Business Criteria. Here we are concerned about whether the business is or will be in the right place to succeed. Does the location represent a plus or a minus for the specific business you are considering? Each business has different needs for street visibility, traffic, parking, ease of access, neighborhood surroundings, proximity of competition, and labor availability.

Mention should be made here about the risk of moving an established business that you buy. This is a potentially costly proposition. You may lose key employees, customers, vendors, and community relationships. The new buyer of a business has plenty to contend with already. Some businesses can be moved and others should be moved, but most should be left where they are, at least until you have established yourself in the business.

You can find exceptions to this rule in a newsletter called *Relocatable Businesses*, available from Business Listing Services, Inc., Box 1248, Highland Park, IL 60035, (800) 927-1310.

Location as a Goal, Not a Criterion. So/ho, the small office-home office phenomenon, is not new as a place to start a business. Many small and large businesses started in a home or in a small office or garage. Ford, Disney, and both Microsoft and Apple are examples. But so/ho has added a totally new dimension to considerations about location. Before faxes, modems, telecommuting, and the Internet, only a few smaller businesses could be permanently located in small or home offices. Now these settings can accommodate you and a wide variety of businesses in almost any location. Where once someone chose a business and then located it where it best belonged, today people first choose where they want to be. Chapter 6 has more about the booming home business phenomenon.

A flock of people, many of them at midcareer, have turned this criterion upside down, picking location first and business second. Philip Burgess and Colleen Boggs Murphy of the Center for the New West call them Lone Eagles, mostly midcareer knowledge workers, for whom location is a goal. Boggs and Burgess see a variety of Lone Eagles, as shown in Figure 9–2.

Most midcareer people, with children grown or nearly so, face an exciting array of options for location. Use Worksheet 6C to set your location criteria.

Payrollers, who work off-site from their salary-paying employers
Freelancers, who are independent contractors or consultants
Planters, who select a specific location to start or move their
business
Trustfunders, who live off investments
Gardeners, who are former employees still contracting with their old
firms
Country hawks, who are motivated to live in a specific location,
usually rural, and are challenged to find a way to make a living
there

Figure 9-2. Types of Lone Eagles.

Risk

Risk represents the most complex of the criteria to establish. Risk has
many dimensions, one of which, risk preference, needs special explanation. This dimension of risk reflects your attitude toward *magnitude* of
risk, not the risk itself. Here is a classic example.

The Gambler's Risk Preference

You are a gambler who bets on coin flipping. The odds when
flipping a coin are 50/50. No matter how much you bet, you
have an equal chance to win or lose, and the 2-to-1 reward is
in line with the risk. You might be comfortable betting a dollar or two, but would you bet $1,000? Or $10,000? For most of
us, our *risk preference* is not to risk that much, even though
the risk odds remain the same 50/50 and we might still double
our money.

Some people prefer to invest very little in high-risk/high-return ventures; others prefer these types of ventures as investments. Any investment
has this phenomenon attached to it, and unless you are aware of it, you
might not be able to articulate your criteria of risk. At midcareer, a riskier
venture requiring little investment may be preferable to one that provides
less risk but takes all of your retirement fund.

Risk of Loss. The more well-known dimensions of risk involve the risk of
losing your investment and the risk of not earning a return on your investment. (*Return* is not only the earnings on the investment but the appreciation in value of the investment as well.)

Loss of Investment. Buying a business with lots of readily salable assets, such as a machine shop outfitted with standard equipment or a liquor store filled with normal inventory, provides a lower risk of losing your investment: You could sell the assets to recover a portion of your investment. Businesses such as advertising agencies or consulting firms have few salable assets and carry a higher risk of losing your investment.

Loss of Return. However, while the machine shop and the liquor store have assets, they are rather fixed in the ways they can generate the business required to earn a return on your investment and therefore are more risky in this dimension than the advertising agency and consulting firm. With an advertising agency that has a few thousand dollars in furniture as its assets, a small profit could be a good return on investment. These service firms have wider ranges of earning behavior and less fixed expense to carry.

Consider one more thing when thinking about risk. If you plan to manage the business you are going to start or buy, you are also risking your time. Your salary represented a return on your time, which you will need to replace. Realize, too, that the time you spend on your new venture risks your present contacts and networks. If you spend a year or two on an entrepreneurial venture away from your network of contacts, you may find, if you try to return, that they have changed so much that you have lost those resources.

Remember, we are not yet calculating rates of return or computing your probability of success in a specific business; we are establishing your criteria regarding risk. Even assuming that you and your advisors will structure the start-up or purchase in the best way you can to limit risks, you must prepare yourself to take some degree of risk.

In summary, then, you have *assets* and *time* you are preparing to invest for a *return*. There is no mathematical formula to set this criterion, but you should develop qualitative descriptions of the degree of risk you are prepared to take. Use Worksheet 6D.

Liquidity

Unlike risk, liquidity is a straightforward issue. How quickly could the business be converted to cash? No business provides the liquidity of stocks, bonds, or other similar investments, but some businesses, such as one with inventory being held on consignment, can be converted to cash easily; a business such as a rental apartment complex, on the other hand, may require many months or even years to liquidate.

Once again, we are not yet evaluating businesses, just establishing your criteria for liquidity. You should determine if you are liable to face any sudden obligations or investment opportunities requiring cash. If you don't provide for your cash needs, you could be forced to sell assets or your entire company under "fire sale" conditions.

Because you will probably be personally guaranteeing any debt, lack of liquidity in a business could force you to liquidate some of your retirement investments.

Use Worksheet 6E to set your criteria for liquidity.

Growth Potential

Growth potential is a very useful criterion because it provides an effective screen. If you require a "sky's-the-limit" type of growth business, you are not going to want a historic bed-and-breakfast inn on the sea coast of Maine. This is not to say that a business that is small today cannot be expanded. Many businesses can be expanded physically, geographically, and conceptually. In fact, almost any business can grow to some extent.

The practical facts are that some businesses lend themselves to growth through easy replication, fast-growing markets, or competitive advantage, whereas others do not. Your task is to decide what you need at this stage of your career for growth potential in the business you are going to own. Use Worksheet 6F.

Physical Working Conditions and Hours

Most of us can be somewhat flexible about working conditions and hours, but be sure you know your limits. A screw machine shop can require 12 hours a day in the factory, a wine distributorship can mean 5 days a week on the road, and owning a company that consults on fund raising could easily lead to 4 nights a week attending meetings.

To some, predictable hours that allow for family or hobbies is an important criterion. Some, often those at midcareer, feel they are at a stage where comfortable surroundings do matter. On the other hand, you may be willing to work nights and weekends or out of a briefcase in the corner of a warehouse.

One aspect of working conditions can be quantified. You can calculate what a luxurious office suite, plush furniture, and a private secretary cost. In metropolitan centers, the costs could exceed $50,000 per year:

800 square feet at $25 per square foot	$20,000
Private secretary	40,000
$10,000 furnishings (5-year life)	2,000
Total	$62,000

No matter where you are on the scale, the physical environment and working conditions of your new company and the hours you will work are important components of your future satisfaction. Use Worksheet 6G to set your criteria for physical working conditions.

Status and Image

Status and image are very personal matters. When considering a business, you should be excited about seeing yourself as the owner. Some people would rather own a break-even newspaper than a very profitable, high-volume gas station/convenience store. For some people, the business will have to be large; for others it will need to be glamorous.

Don't look for right or wrong in such a personal arena. Just be sure you honestly match the business to your needs for status and image. Use Worksheet 6H.

People Intensity

"The more people, the more problems," say many business owners. People problems can result from the difficulty in managing a large workforce. (Just ask the owner of a big real estate agency or the night-shift manager of an industrial cleaning business.)

But people problems can also result from a lack of workers to fill job openings. A few years ago, in fashionable Fairfield County, Connecticut, for example, workers for fast-food stores, supermarkets, and shopping centers were being bussed in from surrounding counties. A lack of afford-able housing perpetuated this situation for some time.

Even in the time of highest unemployment, some types of workers, such as physical therapists, can be hard to find. Recruiting and retaining hard-to-find workers can require a significant amount of time, which you might prefer to spend on some other aspect of making and selling your product or service.

By midcareer you have learned the axiom, "Get the people right and everything else will work out." Unless you are a solo performer in your business, you will still need to hire, train, compensate, discipline, motivate, and otherwise manage people.

If the business is dependent on the number and quality of the people you can attract and retain, you need to be comfortable managing people. To some buyers, this is an important criterion of the business. Use Worksheet 6I to set your criteria.

Competitive Environment

No business exists completely without competition, but there are ex-tremes. At one end we find businesses in large markets facing competition everywhere. Food service is an example. Almost every market hosts restaurants, fast-food franchises, delicatessens, and even supermarkets, all competing for business. At the other extreme we find special-niche businesses in relatively small markets. A company that makes turntables for revolving restaurants is an example of this kind of business.

Either competitive choice carries risk. Your risk in a large competitive market is that competitors will find better ways to meet the needs of the market. Your risk in the special-niche business is that the market will dry up, adopt a new technology, or become oversold, and you will have no place to sell your specialized product.

If the extent of competition is important to you, make it a part of your search criteria. Use Worksheet 6J.

Specific Business Content

The final criterion eclipses all others in determining what kind of business you want. Spend a lot of time on it. It is going to be the key starting point in your search for a business to buy or start. The work you do to establish this criterion will help you answer not only the question "Will I like it?" but also the previous question, "Can I run it?"

You may have special requirements for your business. Perhaps it has to be involved in some specific field so that you can capitalize on your experience. Maybe it has to serve some social goal. You may want a manufacturing business, or you may want to exclude restaurants. You might want to be involved in or avoid high technology, international dealings, or some other special element of business. The point is, if something is important to you, make it a part of your business criteria.

On the other hand, many midcareer people have no idea about the specific business they want. Some have an idealized image of independence, whereas others hold a vague vision of wealth.

You may find difficulty making a connection between your life's work and a business you might own. Corporate job titles don't match cleanly with business opportunities. You may try some elaborate system of analysis to equate details of your job experiences with the underlying requirements of a business. This popular exercise presupposes that you know the inner workings of business opportunities in some detail.

A more logical (and easier) way to explore specific business content is to begin with the knowledge, skills, and traits you have already examined and expand outward to the system. You can creatively leverage your corporate experience, experience that comes from being at midcareer.

Customer knowledge is an easy example. Let's say your career involves selling building maintenance products. You began as a salesperson and progressed up through to sales management. You have met and now know a great many people involved in building maintenance, probably hundreds. Because you are good at your job, you have built good relationships with them.

Now you find yourself not wanting (or not able) to find another sales job in your field. What are your possibilities? An obvious business opportunity is to start your own sales firm as an independent rep to the maintenance industry.

Perhaps a little less obvious opportunity comes from your industry knowledge and relationships to solve other problems that these customers have.

- Help them solve their peak workload problems by creating a temporary employment agency.
- Create a newsletter or on-line computer service that will let them share information.
- Learn lease financing and become an independent broker specializing in leasing maintenance equipment.

And so it goes. If you have some special skill or knowledge such as fluency in another language, your possibilities increase. Your years of in-depth knowledge of your customers affords many opportunities to create a business.

The same can be said for knowing suppliers, regulators, clients, a country or a special population, "key players," auditors, financial sources, unions, contractors, consultants, inspectors, and other components. Use your experience and think about these people in two ways:

1. What do they need?
2. Who else would like to reach them?

You need to explore the same thing relative to the considerable skills you have acquired at this stage of your career. Sales skills can be used to raise funds; financial skills often meld with computer skills and can be the basis for a business. Mature skill in a language or culture can easily lead to a business opportunity.

Don't be afraid to dream. Martha Sinetar in *Do What You Love, the Money Will Follow* (Dell, New York, 1987), urges readers to find what she calls their "right livelihood"—the work that will bring them true satisfaction and thus genuine wealth. If you are like most people, your early career may have come about by accident, the advice of others, or casual happenstance. It may have been nurtured simply by your inertia or by a lack of opportunity elsewhere. At midcareer, it is time to consider what you really want to do with your life outside the corporation. Your decision about what kind of business you want should provide a resounding "Yes!" to the question, "Will I like it?"

Owning a business in a field you love is no guarantee you will be good at it, but the added enthusiasm that comes from doing something you thoroughly enjoy can help you succeed.

Case Study—Building on Experience

Tom C. had worked for a major publisher, traveling the Far East while opening and developing distribution outlets for his company's books and magazines. A new, small, but growing part of the business was Tom's volume in mainland China. Conducting business in China was difficult; regulations, politics and, most of all, unique cultural behaviors and customs required patience and sensitivity.

Tom learned the market and its complex dynamics. He enjoyed China and patiently developed solid contacts and earned the trust of those he dealt with. Unfortunately, Tom's company had far less patience than he and terminated Tom as part of an early-1980s downsizing. During outplacement he was encouraged to at least explore building on his experience. The logical option of finding a job with another publisher seeking the Chinese market was exhausted early on. While publishers recognized the potential in China, none wanted to invest the substantial money it would take to develop the market for their publications.

Tom had accepted an assignment from his old employer to make one more trip to China to wrap up some lose ends. On a hunch, he called two other publishers and asked if they would like him to do some research for their products while he was in China. Tom was able to price his services low, thanks to his old employer, and he got the assignments.

His contacts provided research suggesting what we all know now, that demand for Western goods in China was about to explode. Tom reported back to his clients and then reflected on his situation. He was in a perfect position to help publishers enter the Chinese market. While no one of them could afford his salary and expenses, the could share his costs and gain his ability to develop their business. He then contacted several other publishers and offered them his services on a contract basis. By spreading his expenses among several firms he offered them all a cost-effective strategy.

Tom now has more than a dozen clients and enjoys a new life beyond the corporation.

Don't be too rigid. At this stage, you aren't even aware of the many kinds of businesses that exist and might really make you happy.

If you have never worked with the Standard Industrial Classification (SIC) system, you should review the descriptions in this most widely used method of classifying businesses. Just reviewing the names of these business types can spark ideas.

Going Beyond the Obvious . . .

- A midlevel executive who loves to cook might make a lousy restaurateur but might publish a great newsletter on kitchen appliances and utensils.
- A pet fancier might never be able to become a veterinarian but could own a boarding kennel or grooming salon or a chain of them.
- If the outdoor life is for you, you don't have to become a forest ranger. There are tree service companies, fishing lodges, lawn, landscaping and yard-care firms, fencing companies, and many others.
- If sports are important in your life, you can look for a sporting goods store to buy, but how about a small magazine that caters to some special sports niche?
- If you want world travel, owning a travel agency will do it, but why not look for an import/export business?

A big-city Yellow Pages is another source of ideas. Flip through them and keep imagining yourself owning this business or that. You may begin to find that certain businesses hold an attraction while others are clearly of no interest.

Don't think you have to get what you want all at once. If you want to own a large commercial printing firm, you might start off by owning a small quick-print shop. You may want a telecommunications company, and you could get started by buying a small interconnect business or an answering service.

The important thing is to get into the arena you want; then you can get familiar with the market, the suppliers, the competitors, and the customers. This is how you will find the next opportunity and build the base to take advantage of it. Use Worksheet 9K to analyze your specific business content criteria.

"Should I Do It?"

"Should I do it?" examines the universal aspects of ownership, which are inescapable no matter what the business.

Risk is the best-known of these universal considerations. Even though corporate employment has become more risky, business ownership still represents a higher and more total risk. Failure as a business owner can result in loss of wealth and savings, self-esteem, business reputation, and personal happiness. You will almost certainly be asked to personally guarantee or secure any money you borrow, so all your wealth may be on the line. The loss of time that could have been spent in another endeavor may represent a major cost. The losses may even strip away the resources needed for future opportunities. Can you withstand this nearly total risk?

Loneliness can certainly be expected. There may be many things wrong with corporations and corporate employment, but they can provide support, both psychological and physical. The infrastructure of a corporation usually provides employees with plenty of feedback and reinforcement. Not so for the business owner. The loneliness of ownership can sometimes play tricks on the imagination. With no equal co-workers to provide a peer frame of reference, the owner can easily magnify successes and failures out of proportion. A strong sense of self and personal confidence are needed to handle the loneliness. Have you any experience to indicate that you can handle prolonged loneliness?

Pervasiveness constitutes the least-known aspect of business ownership. Stated simply, your business can come to affect every part of your life. Employment may let you compartmentalize your life and keep your job separate from personal and family matters. However, the time and emotional demands of business ownership can invade any safe haven a person might have. The responsibilities are yours, and they are there 24 hours a day. Can you live with a 24-hour day of obligations, responsibilities, liabilities, and calls on your time?

Although these generalized universal considerations about becoming an owner have been presented last, they should be examined first. They apply to *all* business ownership.

But How Can I Know What the Business Is Really Like?

Nothing in this book or any other book on becoming a business owner will offer any statement worth more than this: *Before you decide to become a business owner, spend time in the kind of business you think you want to own.*

In case after case where I have seen new owners fail or become terribly unhappy, I could trace the cause to the owner having little or no idea what the business was truly like. They often didn't know about the hours. Seldom did they know how difficult it was to get customers. The regulation and paperwork turned out to be a surprise.

One classic and common example is the buyer who wants to own a restaurant. "I love to cook!" the buyer says. "I just know I'll love it!" Unfortunately, restaurant ownership isn't just about cooking. It's about how to get customers in the door. It's about how to hire people and how to get them to come to work. It's about suppliers wanting to be paid. It's about cash flow. It's about the health department inspector. One week in a restaurant will educate most potential buyers. If he or she still wants a restaurant after that, it may be right.

How can you get the experience? Sometimes it's as simple as asking. Many small business owners are willing to share their experiences, often letting someone with a genuine interest spend time in the business. In order to avoid a situation where a business owner might view you as a potential competitor, you may need to go outside your own market area.

If you feel strongly that a specific kind of business might be right for you, you could invest some time working in that business, perhaps part time or on a temporary assignment.

Reading affords a way to learn. A literature search will turn up books, periodicals, and articles. The business you are considering may have an industry association. If it does, the association certainly has literature and statistics. It probably has a newsletter that discusses issues, problems, and opportunities.

Many business associations offer training programs, seminars, and conferences. Not only will you learn, but you will meet people you can talk to and question.

Former owners, suppliers, financial and other advisors, bankers, and anyone else close to the business can be sources of information. At mid-career, you have lots of contacts who should be able to help you get inside or get close to the kind of business you want.

No matter how you do it, get to know the business you are considering owning. This will give you the best way to answer the three essential questions:

"Can I run it?"
"Will I like it?"
"Should I do it?"

Worksheet 5
Personal Inventory

A. KNOWLEDGE: THINGS YOU KNOW

What five things do you know more about than almost anybody else?

1.
2.
3.
4.
5.

And less about?

1.
2.
3.
4.
5.

B. SKILLS: THINGS YOU CAN DO

What five things can you do better than almost anybody else?

1.
2.
3.
4.
5.

And less well?

1.
2.
3.
4.
5.

C. TRAITS: THINGS YOU ARE

I am . . .

1.
2.
3.
4.
5.

I am not . . .

1.
2.
3.
4.
5.

(Continued)

Worksheet 5 *(Continued)*

D. WHAT THE INVENTORY MEANS

The inventory suggests I should consider these kinds of businesses/situations:

1.
2.
3.

And avoid these:

1.
2.
3.

N.B. If your spouse or other family member will be a part of this effort at business ownership, repeat the form for him or her.

Worksheet 6
Setting Your Criteria

Complete the top portion of each section in Worksheet 6 now and save it. Complete the bottom portion, which rates your candidate company, after you find one.

6A. HOW MUCH MONEY YOU NEED

Item	Minimum Amount	Desired Amount
Housing (primary home)	$ _____	$ _____
Utilities	_____	_____
Transportation	_____	_____
Food (in home)	_____	_____
Meals (outside of home)	_____	_____
Clothing	_____	_____
Education	_____	_____
Entertainment/vacations	_____	_____
Medical and hygiene expenses (est.)	_____	_____
Life insurance	_____	_____
Health insurance	_____	_____
Other insurance	_____	_____
Dues, memberships, donations	_____	_____
Maintenance, cleaning, laundry	_____	_____
Debt repayments	_____	_____
Savings	_____	_____
Other	_____	_____
Other	_____	_____
TOTAL	$ _____	$ _____

Rating

Your candidate company has an estimated cash flow available to an owner of $ _____. Your candidate company rates _____ (1 to 10).

N.B.   Be sure you are comparing your needs and the candidate's cash flow on the same tax basis.

6B. HOW MUCH MONEY YOU WANT

Consider amount, growth, and risk.

Year 1 $ _____   Year 3 $ _____   Year 5 $ _____
Year 2 $ _____   Year 4 $ _____

Rating

You estimate that your candidate company can provide:

Year 1 $ _____   Year 3 $ _____   Year 5 $ _____
Year 2 $ _____   Year 4 $ _____

Your candidate company rates _____ (1 to 10).

(Continued)

Worksheet 6 *(Continued)*

6C. LOCATION

Search Criteria

1. Must be within _____ miles.
2. Can be in _____ or _____.
3. Can be anywhere; I will move.
4. I am prepared to relocate the business if I have to.

Evaluation Criteria

Consider visibility, traffic, parking, ease of access, neighborhood surroundings, proximity of competition, and labor availability.

Rating

Your candidate company location is _____.

Your candidate company rates _____ (1 to 10).

6D. RISK PREFERENCE

For an acceptable opportunity:

I am prepared to risk $ _____ in total, with $ _____ down payment and _____ years of work.

For an excellent opportunity:

I am prepared to risk $ _____ in total, with $ _____ down payment and _____ years of work.

Assuming a typical business opportunity with a normal degree of risk, I can mark myself on this scale:

I will risk some of my savings but not my house or other possessions.	I will risk it all to have my own business.

Rating

Your candidate company requires $ _____ in total, with $ _____ down payment and a potential commitment of _____ years.

Your candidate company rates _____ (1 to 10).

6E. LIQUIDITY

Year	Annual Cash Requirements		
	known*	Probable	Possible
1	$ _____	$ _____	$ _____
2	_____	_____	_____
3	_____	_____	_____
4	_____	_____	_____
5	_____	_____	_____

*This amount can come from Worksheet 6A, "How Much Money You Need."

Worksheet 6 *(Continued)*

If you could face sudden requirements for cash, your business needs to be easily able to be converted to cash or to be sold.

Rating

Year	Estimated Cash Flow From Normal Operations	Estimated Additional Cash Available Through Liquidation of Assets	Total
Historical average	$ _____	N/A	$ _____
1	_____	$ _____	_____
2	_____	$ _____	_____
3	_____	$ _____	_____
4	_____	$ _____	_____
5	_____	$ _____	_____

Your candidate company rates _____ (1 to 10).

6F. GROWTH POTENTIAL

My basic objective is to live well. If (when) the business has sales of $ _____ and an owner's cash flow of $ _____, all I will want is enough growth to keep the business healthy.

I eventually want a business with sales of approximately $ _____ and an owner's cash flow of about $ _____. The business I buy needs to be capable of reaching that level in _____ years.

My objective is to build a very large company very quickly. Any business I buy must have at least $ _____ in sales and $ _____ in owner's cash flow now, and in five years should have $ _____ in sales and $ _____ in owner's cash flow.

Rating

Your candidate company is estimated to have this growth potential:

	Sales	Owner's Cash Flow
Present Level	$ _____	$ _____
Year 1	_____	_____
Year 2	_____	_____
Year 3	_____	_____
Year 4	_____	_____
Year 5	_____	_____

Your candidate company rates _____ (1 to 10).

6G. PHYSICAL WORKING CONDITIONS

Hours per week I want to work:_____.
Number of days a month I want to travel:_____.
The type of office or surroundings I want can best be described as _____ .
It is _____ or is not _____ important that I avoid certain hazardous or physical conditions.

(Continued)

Worksheet 6 *(Continued)*

Rating

Your candidate company has these characteristics:

Working hours per week: _____ .
Day travel per month: _____ .
Clothing requirements: _____ .
Office/surroundings that can be described as: _____ .
Hazardous or dangerous conditions that include: _____ .
Your candidate company rates _____ (1 to 10).

6H. STATUS AND IMAGE

	No	Doesn't Matter	Yes
I want:			
A business that will give me high visibility	_____	_____	_____
A business that is considered large or substantial	_____	_____	_____
A business that is more knowledge based (white collar) than skill based (blue collar)	_____	_____	_____
A business involved in a sophisticated or glamorous field	_____	_____	_____
A business on the cutting edge of innovation	_____	_____	_____
A business that provides a service to the community and its people	_____	_____	_____

Rating

	Yes	No
Your candidate company:		
Will give you high visibility	_____	_____
Is considered large or substantial	_____	_____
Is a "white-collar" business	_____	_____
Is sophisticated/glamorous	_____	_____
Is on the cutting edge of innovation	_____	_____
Provides community or other service	_____	_____

Your candidate company rates _____ (1 to 10).

6I. PEOPLE INTENSITY

	My Degree of Comfort	
People Issues	Low	High
Recruiting, interviewing, hiring, training	_____	_____
Specialized skills supervision	_____	_____
Wage and salary administration	_____	_____
Union (labor) relations	_____	_____

Worksheet 6 *(Continued)*

	My Degree of Comfort	
People Issues	Low	High
Personnel policy development and administration	_____	_____
Motivation, discipline, firing	_____	_____
Organization design and development	_____	_____
Conflict resolution, counseling	_____	_____
Recognition and incentives	_____	_____
High turnover, morale problems	_____	_____
OSHA, ERISA, etc.	_____	_____

Rating

Your candidate company:

	Required Degree of Intensity	
People Issues	Low	High
Recruiting, interviewing, hiring, training	_____	_____
Specialized skills supervision	_____	_____
Wage and salary administration	_____	_____
Union (labor) relations	_____	_____
Personnel policy development and administration	_____	_____
Motivation, discipline, firing	_____	_____
Organization design and development	_____	_____
Conflict resolution, counseling	_____	_____
Recognition and incentives	_____	_____
High turnover, morale problems	_____	_____
OSHA, ERISA, etc.	_____	_____

Your candidate company rates _____ (1 to 10).

6J. COMPETITIVE ENVIRONMENT

It is important that the business I buy
is the only (or one of the only) businesses
of its type in the market area.   Yes _____   No _____

The business I buy must be the market share
leader or near leader in its field.   Yes _____   No _____

I want a business with high barriers to entry
for potential competitors.   Yes _____   No _____

I especially want protections such as patents
and licenses.   Yes _____   No _____

The business should not be subject to
inordinate foreign competition.   Yes _____   No _____

The business must measure up to its competitors
in terms of margins, productivity, modern
equipment, etc.   Yes _____   No _____

(Continued)

Worksheet 6   *(Continued)*

Rating

Your candidate company:

Has _____ competitors in its market.
Has _____ percent market share and ranks #_____.
Is in a field with high _____ low _____ barriers to entry.
Has patents or licenses: Yes _____ No _____
Is subject to inordinate foreign competition: Yes _____ No _____
Has competitive margins, productivity,
   equipment, etc.   Yes _____ No _____

Your candidate company ranks _____ (1 to 10).

6K.   SPECIFIC BUSINESS CONTENT

The three things I have most enjoyed doing

In my business career:

1.
2.
3.

As family or recreational activities:

1.
2.
3.

In academic pursuits:

1.
2.
3.

In community or public service:

1.
2.
3.

As fantasies:
1.
2.
3.

Based on these most-enjoyed activities and on my knowledge, skills, and traits, here are some kinds of businesses that either make, service, sell, consult, or are in some way a possible fit for me:

My "perfect company" would be:

Worksheet 6   *(Continued)*

Rating

What your candidate company does:

What it could do:

Your candidate company rates _____ (1 to 10).

N.B.   If your spouse or other family member will be a part of this effort at business ownership, repeat the form for him or her.

CHAPTER 10

Determining What You Can Afford

Before you begin your business start-up plan or your search for a business to buy, you need an idea of what you can afford. You don't want to waste your time pursuing businesses that are beyond your means or miss out on businesses that you can afford.

Unfortunately, you will only have a general idea of what you can afford at the outset, because so much will depend on the specific opportunity or company and on the final terms of the purchase. What you can afford depends on four things:

1. How much money you have or can borrow
2. Your ability to persuade lenders or investors
3. The value (price) of the business you plan to buy and the terms of sale
4. The capacity of the business to support itself, support you, and repay its debt

You may be surprised at what you can afford.

How Much Money You Have or Can Borrow

Worksheet 7 can help you organize all the possible sources of money. Begin with the wealth you may be surprised to know you already have.

What You Have

Cash and the near cash available from publicly traded stocks and bonds are the easiest to calculate.

Investments of other types, such as rental real estate, represent another source of money.

Assignable assets, including notes due you or a time-sharing contract, can be converted to cash.

Partnership interests may allow for you to cash in or sell out.

Personal property may represent considerable value you can convert to cash. Some determined people have sold almost everything they own in order to buy or start a business.

A second job is another source of cash used by determined people.

Overtime, freelancing, and moonlighting might provide substantial cash in some cases.

A working spouse, in addition to contributing money, may also be able to provide medical and insurance coverage.

Insurance policies can be a surprising source of cash, particularly if they are older policies. Often they can be liquidated and replaced with new insurance products, giving you cash to invest.

Deferred compensation can mean cash in one of two ways. As mentioned in Chapter 2, you may be able to have your deferred compensation awarded early as part of your severance. If this is not possible, the cash will at least be realized later.

Retirement accounts, whether they are company managed, your own IRA or Keogh, or any other type, may have rules that allow you to convert them to cash. Penalties may be assessed, but you should at least know the potential availability.

Income from trusts and annuities is an obvious source of cash, but less obvious is the fact this stream of income may be able to be capitalized and sold, thus giving you a lump sum of cash to invest.

The equity in their homes is a significant cash-yielding asset for most people. Past inflation in home values and the eagerness of financial institutions to lend against home equity have made cash readily available to home owners in the form of equity credit lines, a refinanced first mortgage, or a second mortgage.

What you save is the final source of money you already have. Cutting back on club memberships, entertaining, and other luxuries is a first step, but if you are really committed to raising cash, you should consider a complete reevaluation of your lifestyle.

Once you have added up all the money you already (could) have, it is time to see where you can borrow more.

Where You Can Borrow Personally

First we shall consider your opportunities to borrow money personally.

Friends and family represent a common (if sometimes contentious) source of money. In addition to lending money, friends and family can provide financial support by guaranteeing your borrowings from some other source. Co-signing an auto loan is an example familiar to most of us. In business transactions, your co-signer may have to pledge some specific asset such as the equity in a house. Because you are, in effect, "renting" someone else's wealth to be pledged for you, you should be prepared to pay for this financial support.

Your *bank* or *credit union* may extend a personal line of credit, and you may have a *margin* or *borrowing account* with your stock brokerage firm. You may also be able to borrow against *insurance policies.*

A newly recognized source of borrowing is the *credit card.* Some people receive dozens of unsolicited, preapproved credit card applications. With credit limits ranging from $1,000 to $10,000, this can represent significant credit. One Hollywood producer claims that he produced an Academy Award-winning film with the help of nearly $1 million in credit he had amassed from credit cards.

The midcareer person may have a special source of personal borrowing, the funds in a 401K or similar retirement account. These funds may be available and substantial, but you should carefully consider the risks in drawing from them. Think through what will happen if you risk the funds and lose them? Can you withstand the loss? Do you have enough earning power to replace them?

Another special source for the midcareer borrower might be the separation package provided by an employer. Once again, think through your financial condition. If the package is a substitute for your planned retirement from the company, you may not want to risk the funds. But if the money in the separation package is more than you expected to have, you may feel you can risk it in a new venture.

Although there are relatively few sources for personal borrowing, there are a tremendous number of sources of money for businesses.

Where You Can Borrow through the Business

Banks are the most visible source of money. They lend money directly and indirectly through various guarantee programs. Any bank will provide you with a description of its loan types and can tell you the criteria of the business borrower it considers to be its market.

Asset lenders and factors provide money against specific assets of the business. They may take a mortgage or lien on the asset, buy it outright at a discount (accounts receivable), or buy it and lease it back to the company.

The *Small Business Administration* (SBA) is an institution that everyone in or considering a small business should understand. It provides loans, loan guarantees, participation loans, and financial assistance. It assists state and local government programs to aid small businesses. It offers special programs to aid minorities. It also provides consulting services, training, government contract assistance, and a library of publications for little or no cost.

Other federal agencies, such as the Veterans Administration, the Department of Housing and Urban Development, and the U.S. Department of Agriculture, offer a variety of programs.

Many *states and some cities* also offer loans, guarantees, and other assistance to small business. The departments responsible for these programs usually come under the heading of economic development, small business development, or commerce. Some states and cities offer special grants or tax consideration to companies that participate in programs to create jobs, provide training, or assist minorities.

Partners are another source of money. Your advisors should carefully review any decision on partnerships.

If you own or are buying a franchise, the *franchiser* is a potential lender.

A company's *suppliers*, if they sell on credit, are already lenders in a way. Extending the payment terms can generate money. Some suppliers can offer leases in place of sales as a way to reduce large cash requirements. Regular suppliers may be able to provide inventory on a consignment basis; you receive an invoice only when you replace sold stock.

Even *customers* can be sources of money. They can place orders early, which might serve as collateral. They can lend money and accept repayment in goods and services.

A *landlord* might be a source of money. Deferring or forgiving some of your rent may be agreeable if the landlord's alternative is empty space. You may be able to renegotiate the lease to provide for lower rent now during your critical period but higher rent later when you believe you will better be able to afford it. A variation on this idea is a lease tied to some percentage of your sales. Your base rent is lower than it would otherwise be, but if you are successful, the landlord can receive much more than the regular market rent rate. This is common in a shopping center tenant lease.

Insurance companies, foundations, and the use of *barter* are less common sources of money but may be available if your intended business has the characteristics to use them.

Venture capitalists and *investment bankers* are major sources of money. They most often lend and invest in companies that may have a relatively high degree of risk so they can earn a higher-than-average rate of return. Their return may be in the form of interest, stock ownership, or consulting fees, but for many venture capital firms, the objective is to take the venture public. Most of them issue a published statement of their objectives and investment criteria.

In addition, there are *venture groups* around the country that exist to bring investors together with investment opportunities. Some of these groups sponsor monthly luncheons where they use an open microphone to help investors and those seeking funds to find each other.

The *seller* is the most common source of money for buying a business. Estimates are that 75 to 80 percent of business sales are seller financed, and the percentage financed is between one-half and two-thirds of the selling price. Borrowing from the seller is easier, cheaper, and can often be for a longer term than from other sources.

Sellers are willing to finance sales partly because they understand and trust the collateral for the loan, which is the business being sold. Another reason for their willingness is the fact that right now all their investment is tied up in the business. Your purchase down payment will be some cash in hand. However, the major reason sellers provide financing is to help sell the business and to sell it for more than they would get in an all-cash transaction. Sellers know there are more potential buyers who can operate the business successfully and pay off a loan than there are potential buyers with resources to pay all cash.

How to Persuade Lenders or Investors

An axiom in negotiating and selling says "Find out what the other party wants." Common sense says that you are more likely to get what you want if the other party gets what it wants. You are also more able to develop alternatives the more fully you understand someone's true desires. The following list explains some common investment and lending objectives.

Return on investment. Lenders and investors want to earn a return on their investment. Investors may be satisfied with little or no immediate return because their objective is long-term gain. Lenders usually want an immediate schedule of returns that will cover their cost of money and the risk premium of your loan.

Repayment of principle (investment). Both lenders' and investors' objectives vary here. Some will want scheduled repayment much like a mortgage, while some will leave their money in your company indefinitely, content with the return they are (or will be) receiving, similar to your credit card lender.

Security. Security can be specific, such as a piece of machinery or accounts receivable, or it can be general, such as a corporate or personal guarantee. Large, long-established businesses can borrow on a general line of credit, whereas smaller and less creditworthy companies are required to provide more specific security. It is this fact that severely limits a buyer's ability to borrow money from a bank to finance the purchase of a small company that has few real assets to secure the loan.

Equity participation. Most lenders don't want stock in the companies they finance. They are in the business of lending money. Investors by definition do own stock and are motivated to provide money, whether debt or equity, to increase the total value of their investment.

Your task is to learn from your targeted sources what they want for each of these objectives and to select those that match your objectives and capabilities. Once you know what your sources want, you can develop your presentation to address the issues of ability to repay and the provision of security.

---

1. A summary of the present situation
   a. The market(s)
   b. Competition
   c. The economy
   d. Current financial performance
2. An analysis of company strengths and weaknesses
   a. Management/people
   b. Products and services
   c. Facilities and equipment
   d. Financial resources
   e. Market position
   f. Technology
3. A description of what needs to be done
   a. Opportunities
   b. Threats
   c. Barriers
   d. Resources
4. A plan of action
   a. What will be done
   b. When
   c. By whom
5. Financial projections
   a. Income and expenses
   b. Balance sheet
   c. Sources and applications of cash
6. Measurement
   a. How you will measure results
   b. When
   c. What are the criteria for success

Figure 10–1. The business plan.

The Application Presentation

Your application for financing may be an informal meeting with the seller or a full business plan presentation to a venture capital firm or bank. In all cases you will need to cover what you plan to do with the business and why you are qualified to do it. Figure 10-1 is a sample business plan.

Your Personal Qualifications to Succeed

Lenders maintain that they lend to people, not to deals—that the borrower's reputation and qualifications determine the lending decision. Those lenders may be underplaying somewhat their desire for collateral, but your qualifications to succeed are important. Submit a resume of your education, knowledge, skills, and experience. Point out where your abilities match the needs of the business plan. Prepare a list of references that will be meaningful. List people who can comment favorably on your business judgment, work habits, and reputation. If you can, list people known to your lenders or investors.

Your Commitment to Succeed

One element essential to earn financiers' confidence is your own commitment. You will need to submit a personal financial statement that shows both your financial status and how much of it you are directing to the venture. Lenders and investors want to see that you believe strongly enough in yourself and your venture that you will commit yourself to it fully.

One Man's Commitment

Jack C. had worked for IBM for 18 years. He and his family lived a comfortable upper-middle-class lifestyle. Jack recognized earlier than most that his job had lost its security. A talented engineer, Jack looked for and found a company to buy that matched his skills. The specialized engineering construction company was fairly priced, but the price and terms of sale appeared to require more resources than Jack had.

Jack decided to make the commitment. The decision involved tough choices. He and his wife sold their house and all but a few pieces of furniture and moved into a small apartment near the factory. They sold both late-model cars and bought a used small truck. Food, clothing, and all other expenses were slashed. The three children were told that college wasn't guaranteed, and the one child already in college was urged to find a job and seek financial aid.

Jack believed that he could make the business succeed and was willing to commit everything to it. He got his financing and was eventually very successful. Today he would say he paid a big personal price, risking his family's security, but he would do it again if he had to.

Worksheet 7
Sources of Money

7A. WHAT YOU HAVE

Source	On Hand	Available
Cash, stocks, bonds	$ _____	$ _____
Other investments	_____	_____
Assignable assets	_____	_____
Partnership interests	_____	_____
Pesonal property	_____	_____
Second job income (annualized)	_____	_____
Spouse income	_____	_____
Insurance policies	_____	_____
Deferred compensation	_____	_____
Retirement accounts	_____	_____
Trusts and annuities	_____	_____
Equity in your home	_____	_____
What you can save (annualized)	_____	_____
Total	$ _____	$ _____

7B. WHERE YOU CAN BORROW

Source	Specific Contact	Potential Funds Available
Friends and family	_____	$ _____
	_____	_____
	_____	_____
Banks or credit union	_____	_____
	_____	_____
	_____	_____
Margin/borrowing account	_____	_____
Insurance policies	_____	_____
	_____	_____
	_____	_____
Credit cards	_____	_____
	_____	_____
	_____	_____
	_____	_____
Asset lenders/factors	_____	_____
	_____	_____
	_____	_____
SBA	_____	_____

Worksheet 7   *(Continued)*

Source	Specific Contact	Potential Funds Available
Other federal agencies	_____	_____
	_____	_____
	_____	_____
State and local agencies	_____	_____
	_____	_____
Partners	_____	_____
	_____	_____
Suppliers	_____	_____
	_____	_____
Customers	_____	_____
	_____	_____
Landlord	_____	_____
Insurance companies/foundations	_____	_____
	_____	_____
	_____	_____
Barter opportunities	_____	_____
Venture capitalists	_____	_____
	_____	_____
	_____	_____
Venture groups	_____	_____
	_____	_____
The seller	_____	_____

CHAPTER 11

Finding the Business

Finding the business, now that you have defined it, involves an orderly process of investigation, contact, and follow-through. It takes time, but you will be able to generate a sizable pool of candidates. Table 11–1 gives an overview of a business search. Your success will depend on how well you manage the search process.

Managing the Search

Your search will involve contact with a great number of potential sellers, intermediaries, advisors, and others. Because you are not the only person looking for a business, you will need to establish your credibility. You will want recognition as a serious buyer and a business person of substance.

Establish Credibility

You can establish credibility in a direct way by preparing a printed statement of your objectives and criteria and a summary of your qualifications. The objectives and criteria should be specific enough to give the reader a clear idea of what you want, but not so detailed or rigorous that they discourage response. Indirect ways to establish credibility involve the use of quality stationery, business cards, and businesslike telephone and office procedures. These items are discussed in Chapter 8.

Table 11-1. The Business Search

Preparation	
Set up to manage the search	Print copies of your objectives, criteria, and background.
	Obtain stationery and business cards. Establish clerical and phone resources.
Develop a list of contact sources	Consider newpapers, newletters, trade magazines, business brokers, business owners, lawyers, accountants, bankers, friends, venture capitalists, networks, vendors and suppliers, customers, trade associations, and others.

The Active Search	

Targeted direct marketing
  Direct mail
  Telephone solicitation
  Personal contact
	Set objectives, develop key questions for each criterion.

	Define your targets for each source.
	Develop lists, select desired format.
	Develop messages for mail, phone, and personal contact.
	Execute direct marketing search, Mail the letters, make the phone calls, and knock on the doors. Follow up.
	Evaluate and develop your pool of candidates.
Advertising (print is suggested)	Decide which of your contact sources can be reached through advertising.
	Determine how best to reach them.
	Develop messages(s).
	Place advertising. Follow up. Evaluate and develop your pool of candidates.

Your search needs to be executed crisply and with control. The easiest way to stay in control is to organize your activities into manageable segments. Direct-mail programs should be large enough to be economical but small enough to permit telephone follow-up. A mailing of 250, with a 5 percent response, would produce 12 to 13 responses. Personal contacts should be staggered far enough apart to allow for rescheduling and also to allow ample time to pursue any opportunity that might develop.

If you have a computer or your own office services, you can set up planned cycles of contact, follow-up, and follow-through. If you do not have your own facilities, you can buy the services you need. In almost every city and town you can now find service companies that will type and mail to your mailing list. Most of them can maintain your mailing list and handle responses according to your instructions.

Conducting your search in a businesslike manner also means that you handle any contact, correspondence, follow-through, or rejection with courtesy and professionalism. Your search may take a long while. View it as a process of building a network of relationships that you will maintain.

Develop Contacts and Sources

Newspapers are the easiest place to start looking for a business. The heading most commonly used in the classified section is "Business Opportunities." Most of the advertisements will be for small businesses, but occasionally large opportunities will be offered. The *Wall Street Journal,* in its "Mart" section on Wednesdays and Thursdays, lists opportunities of all sizes. The *New York Times* Sunday "Business Opportunities" section runs several pages and contains a very diverse range of opportunities.

Specialized business opportunity newspapers are now being published. Some are national, such as the *Business Opportunity Journal;* some, such as the *New England Business Opportunity Review*, are regional.

New on the Internet!

Now you can search for—or sell—a business on the Internet. The service is offered by Meyers Internet Service, 1590 Oakland Road, San Jose, CA 95131, Internet address http:/www.dirs.com.

Industry trade magazines sometimes contain a classified section with business opportunities. *Restaurant Exchange News*, a regional trade magazine, has extensive offerings. If you have narrowed your search to a particular industry, get copies of industry trade papers and magazines.

Business opportunity ads are usually very cryptic. Only general descriptions are given; names and location are almost never provided. Sellers employ such anonymity to protect their businesses. Severe harm could be

---

Answering Ads

When you answer advertisements, whether by mail or phone, you are trying to do one thing: obtain information to determine if the business might meet your criteria. When responding by mail, the approach should be to present yourself as being as fully qualified as you can, so the advertiser will want to contact you. If you do receive a return contact or you answer the ad by phone, you are beginning your active contact, which is discussed later in this chapter.

When you respond to an advertisement, you may be responding directly to the seller or to an intermediary, typically a business broker. Your approach to a broker should be the same as to the seller, but most likely you will be asked some qualifying questions and then be asked to meet with the broker to continue the process.

---

done if customers, employees, suppliers, or competitors knew the business was for sale.

Business brokers offer the next easiest method to explore available business opportunities. Business brokers function much like real estate brokers. They are engaged by the business owner and paid a commission to market and sell the business. In that situation the broker is the seller's agent and should be acting in the seller's best interest at all times.

You can engage a broker under a buyer-broker agreement in which the broker agrees to seek out companies for you and to work in your best interests. A business broker may have many businesses listed, but few brokers have any cooperative or multiple list arrangements. This means you will need to contact nearly all the business brokers in an area to learn of all the businesses listed with them.

Make building good relationships with business brokers an early step in your search. Business brokers have an extensive inventory of businesses listed for sale. They have experience that can help you. If you can get brokers to share their listings and their experience with you, you have a valuable resource at no cost. The courtesies you owe the brokers are to deal with them honestly and to remember that their time is the way they earn their money.

You can learn the names of business brokers from reading the advertisements or from the Yellow Pages. You can obtain a list of the brokers who belong to the International Association of Business Brokers by contacting the IBBA:

International Business Brokers Association
11250 Roger Bacon Drive
Suite 8
Reston, VA 22090
(703) 437-4377

Evaluate business brokers as you would any advisor. Try to obtain information on the competence and reputation of anyone whose advice you will be using, by talking to others who have used that advisor. Ask the broker for names of former buyers and sellers.

Business owners are excellent contacts for you. Even if their businesses are not for sale, they can often tell you who might be selling. They can pass your name along to others. If they ever do decide to sell, your past contact may get you an early look at the business.

Lawyers, accountants, and other personal advisors are sources. They are properly protective of their clients' interests and may be difficult to contact, but they will respond to a professional inquiry if they have a client who may be selling.

Bankers can be helpful in your search. Take the time to meet bankers and find out who handles business accounts. Become known to them. Present your objectives and your background. You may someday be asking the bank to help you finance your start-up or your purchase, so your contact work can be doubly valuable.

Your friends have wide networks of contacts. If you let your friends know your objectives and give them some idea of the kind of company you are seeking, they can be alert for opportunities.

Venture capitalists, merger and acquisition specialists, and corporate development executives all live in worlds in which you may find your business. These people may function independently or inside other companies. Most will be interested only in large transactions. A worthwhile long shot is a call to the corporate development executive or merger and acquisition specialist inside a large company to see if the company may have a small product line or division it wants to sell.

Networks that exist not as part of a club or civic group but solely to be sources of business are a relatively new phenomenon. They are mentioned throughout this book as a basic part of today's entrepreneurship. Some network groups may require that you represent a company, but many are much more informal and hold meetings that are more like mixers. Locating these groups takes some work. Start with your Chamber of Commerce and then check places where such meetings might be held, such as hotels or restaurants. (If no such networks exist in your area, you may want to start one. See Chapter 4.)

Vendors and suppliers can be good sources of leads. If you know you want to buy a restaurant, find the salespeople for restaurant paper supplies, meats and provisions, equipment, and so on. They have several motives for helping you. Most salespeople pride themselves in knowing what is going on in their market, and that pride is satisfied by displaying their knowledge to you.

Salespeople search for ways to help their customers, and bringing news that you are looking to buy into their industry might be very helpful. Finally, if your are successful in buying a business in the industry, a salesperson will hope that by helping you, your appreciation will be reflected in orders.

If you do know the exact type of business you want, vendors and suppliers can be a source of contacts that will put you way ahead of others who are looking for similar companies. Not only will you know about companies sooner, your initiative and determination will be recognized by a seller as signs of your seriousness.

Customers have fewer motives to help you and may be harder to locate, but they still represent a source to find companies for sale.

Industry trade associations are worthwhile contacts for many reasons. They are repositories of membership lists, statistics, and other information about the industry and the people in it. You can learn a great deal about what you are getting into by contacting or possibly joining a trade association for your target industry. Your efforts will have both present and future benefit.

This list of sources is by no means exhaustive. Real estate and stock brokers, civic groups, and various state development agencies are additional sources you might use. There are a great many sources for the determined business seeker. Worksheet 8 at the end of this chapter can help you organize your contacts.

Of course, just compiling a long list of contact sources won't produce a pool of candidates. You have to actively work these contacts.

Provide Incentives to Leads

Because you are asking people to do something for your economic benefit, you should be willing to compensate them. Compensation for brokers may be regulated in some states, but in your contacts with others you can offer a finder's fee to those who bring you opportunities. You may want to pay the fee only if you actually purchase the business, or you may want to encourage leads and be willing to pay if the lead simply meets your criteria. The payment just for providing a lead would be relatively small, but the payment for a lead that results in the purchase of a business can be several thousand dollars, depending on the size of the business.

Meaningful incentives will get people to make efforts they would not have otherwise, and will cause them to remember you when they otherwise might have forgotten. Paying people for their time and effort is not only fair, it is good business.

Get Help with Your Business Search

$1,000 Reward!
Help me find a wholesale distribution business.
If I buy it, I'll pay you $1,000
Contact Nicholas Riley (212) 555-1111

The Active Search Program

Answering newspaper ads, contacting brokers, and responding to business opportunity offerings represent activities you should conduct, but they are a passive approach to finding a business: You are looking only at businesses that someone else has already put up for sale. An *active search program* will lead you to businesses before other buyers find them.

Once you have provided for your clerical and administrative needs and have generated an extensive stock of contacts, you can devise an active search program (see Table 11–1). You will be able to find businesses that owners have not actively tried to sell but that are available if an offer is made. Your active inquiry may be the event that initiates an owner's interest in selling.

An active search program uses targeted direct marketing techniques and well-planned advertising.

Targeted Direct Marketing

Targeted direct marketing, as the name implies, involves direct solicitation of specific contacts. *Direct mail* is the easiest and broadest reaching of the direct marketing techniques. *Telephone solicitation* is an effective method for a smaller and more qualified list of contacts. *Personal contact* and canvassing is the most powerful but most time-consuming direct marketing activity. These three techniques are most often combined to achieve maximum effectiveness. The steps involved in targeted direct marketing are:

Setting objectives
Defining the target
Developing lists
Creating the message
Executing the search
Following up and evaluating results

Setting Objectives

The objectives you establish for your direct marketing contacts will depend on the type of contact.

Objectives with Advisors and Others. With accountants, attorneys, vendors, trade associations, friends, and other business people who are indirectly involved, your primary objective is to learn the name of a company that may be for sale. If you can get an introduction, that's a big plus.

Another objective is to use the occasion of the contact to network to others who may be helpful. The question, "Do you know anyone who . . ." is a good network builder.

A third objective is to leave a clear, positive impression with the contact so that he or she will remember to call you when a company meeting your general criteria becomes available.

Objectives with Intermediaries. The objective for direct contact with brokers and other intermediaries differs from the objectives with advisors. Here you want to build a more substantive relationship. We mentioned earlier that brokers can be a major resource in your efforts to buy a business. You want to convince intermediaries that you are a serious, qualified buyer, who will act quickly and professionally when they present opportunities which meet your criteria.

Objectives with Targeted Business Owners. There are special objectives for your direct contacts with owners of businesses who might be candidates for your pool of opportunities. The overriding objective is to determine whether the company is for you and whether it is, or could be, for sale.

View your efforts with these business owners as a series of contacts. Owners are cautious when answering questions about their business. You will need to earn their confidence. Earlier in this chapter we presented ways to help establish credibility (written objectives, a personal summary, business cards, etc.). Use these tools in a well-organized, professional way in your contacts with business owners.

An objective for any contact you make should be to learn as much as you can about the industry and the companies in it.

Defining the Target

The key to success in direct marketing is the quality of your target list, and the key to the quality of your list is how well you define your target. Defining some targets is easy. All accountants in your geographic area are target contacts. The same may be true for attorneys, bankers, and brokers.

Some contacts may need to be defined more narrowly. Using our previous example of vendors as contacts to learn about restaurants, you would need to identify the vendor type (i.e., paper supplier) and the industry being served (restaurants). Consultants, venture capitalists, customers, and trade associations all need this kind of refinement to be worthwhile contacts.

Most often you will initially define the companies you want to contact in three dimensions. Your definition will involve the type of business, the location, and the size—perhaps in sales, earnings, or number of employees. Fortunately, you have already defined the kinds of companies you want to target. In Chapter 9 you established explicit criteria for the company you want. In Chapter 10 you developed a working approximation of what you can afford. The better job you do in refining your list, the better will be the results of your search.

Developing Lists

The next step in an active search is to convert these defined contact targets into real names, addresses, and phone numbers. You need to develop your list.

Working with lists has become an easier task now that computers are commonplace. Directories of thousands of companies are available on CD ROM disks. These lists usually contain very detailed information about company size, products, and services, and even contact names.

Readily available software permits easy construction of a database of the names on your list. Word processing software can generate letters, envelopes, and labels. Service companies in your area can perform all of these tasks, usually on a per-name price basis.

Buying Lists. The easiest way to develop a list is to buy one. List companies and brokers can supply lists of all the target contacts we have used as examples. Some lists can be refined to your specifications. The cost and quality of lists varies greatly. Prices ranges from $20 per 1,000 names to several hundred dollars per thousand. Some lists are well maintained and accurate, whereas others are not. The list provider should advise you of the "percent deliverable" for any list you buy.

A good source of help in locating and dealing with list companies is an advertising agency that is active in the field of direct mail.

Compiling Lists. You may prefer to compile your own list. Getting the names, addresses, and phone numbers of most of your contacts may be as simple as looking in the Yellow Pages or buying a membership directory. Your network of friends and personal contacts is probably already compiled into a list.

Your list of target companies will take some effort to compile, but not as much as you might think. There are directories for almost every industry segment imaginable. There are even directories of directories. These directories can often help you key in on such specific criteria as size, location, number of employees, and years in business. Some may even provide the names of the owners or chief executives.

Directories can be expensive to buy. Some sources that may permit you to use their directories include:

College or large community libraries
Chambers of Commerce
Trade associations
Advertising agencies
Marketing departments of companies that sell to your target companies

In addition, there are full directory services that operate across all industries. Two of the most well known are Dun & Bradstreet and Thomas Publishing Company, publishers of *Thomas' Register.* Dun's Marketing Services, a Dun & Bradstreet division, provides standard or customized directory listings, on hard copy, disk or CD ROM, and they will produce mailing labels if you order them.

Obtaining lists of businesses, then, can be as easy as looking in the Yellow Pages or as involved as getting the attendance list for a conference your targets might have attended.

List Formats. The last thing you need to know about ordering lists is that you must specify the format you want. If the list is on a CD ROM disk, you will need word processing software to convert the names to printable labels.

Lists also come on magnetic (computer) tape, pressure-sensitive (peel-and-stick) labels, and Cheshire (machine-applied) labels. You will want magnetic tape if you are working with a service firm which uses it. Cheshire labels are usually cheaper, but they require a printer or mailer to apply them, sometimes at an extra cost. They are not economical for short runs. Pressure-sensitive labels cost more but are easy to apply. If you are doing the mailing yourself, this is the format to order.

Creating the Message

Once you have a well-defined and usable list of contacts, you can turn to the second most important element in your direct marketing program: the message you send. The purpose of your message is to get a response. Whether you are using mail, the telephone, or personal canvassing, you will need to convey enough in your message to trigger the desired response from the desired target.

Messages for Direct Mail. Some sample letters for the mail segment of your direct marketing program are shown in Figure 11–1, a sample letter to an advisor, Figure 11–2, a sample letter to a trade association, and Figure 11–3, a sample letter directly to a business owner.

Mr. James Stevens, Esq.

Stevens and Jones, Attorneys

37 Arch Street

St. Petersburg, Florida 33705

Dear Attorney Stevens:

I am interested in buying a business in the Tampa/St. Petersburg area.

I would especially like to find a lumberyard or building supply center where my 20 years of building products experience would be applicable. Garden centers, landscaping companies, and specialty contractors, such as swimming pool or tennis court installers, would also be of interest. I have substantial cash on hand and an excellent credit standing. Bank references are available. I will move quickly and professionally to evaluate any candidate you may bring forward.

If you know of an opportunity or if you would like to discuss my objectives, please call or write.

OR

Figure 11–1. Sample letter to an advisor.

I will take the liberty of calling you to explain my objectives and to learn whether you have any clients who might be candidates.

Thank you for your consideration.

Yours truly,

Christopher Cronin

Telephone (813) 555-1111

Figure 11-1. *(Continued)*

Ms. Stephanie Davis

Membership Director

Florida Building Products Association

211 Main Street

Tampa, Florida 33615

Dear Ms. Davis:

I am interested in buying a business in the Tampa/St. Petersburg area. Garden centers, landscaping companies, and specialty contractors, such as swimming pool or tennis court installers, would also be of interest.

Figure 11-2. Sample letter to a trade association. *(Continued)*

I have over 20 years experience in the industry and I am prepared to move quickly and professionally to evaluate any opportunity. I have substantial cash on hand and an excellent credit standing.

Because you are a key part of the industry, I would especially appreciate any help and advice you could give me. Please be assured that I will comply with any requirements for confidentiality or anonymity that you may suggest.

I will take the opportunity of calling you to more fully explain my objectives and to ask your advice on how to proceed.

Thank you for your consideration.

Yours truly,

Christopher Cronin
Telephone (813) 555-1111

Figure 11-2. *(Continued)*

Mr. Fred Steck

Steck's Lumber

11277 Bayside

St. Petersburg, Florida 33705

Dear Mr. Steck:

I am interested in buying a lumberyard in the Tampa/St. Petersburg area. Although I have not heard that your business is for sale, I decided to approach you directly in the event that you may have a desire to sell.

I have over 20 years experience in lumber and building products. My financial situation is solid, and I have cash available.

If your business is not for sale, perhaps you could forward this letter to another business owner who may be interested in selling. Garden centers, landscaping companies, and specialty contractors, such as swimming pool or tennis court installers, would also be of interest to me.

If you would like to know more about me and my objectives, please write or call.

OR

Figure 11-3. Sample letter directly to a business owner. *(Continued)*

I will take the liberty of calling you to explain more fully my objectives and to learn whether you or someone you know may have an interest in selling.

Thank you for your consideration.

Yours truly,

Christopher Cronin

Telephone (813) 555-1111

Figure 11–3. *(Continued)*

Messages for Telephone Solicitation. Making "cold" telephone calls is a stomach-churning experience for some people. The prospect of personal rejection is both probable and unappealing. Two things can help you overcome the apprehension you may have. One is simply experience. People who were frightened to call strangers learn through experience that success can be achieved and failure is anonymous. A well-rehearsed opening script can also help with cold calls. Experts in the field of telemarketing advise newcomers and old pros to do lots of rehearsing. Rehearsing instills confidence and makes you more comfortable and natural with your script and your presentation.

Scripts for contacting accountants, attorneys, brokers, trade associations, vendors, and other nonowners can be paraphrases of the direct mail letters shown in Figures 11–1 and 11–2. Scripts for owners require one major revision. Unless the owner answers the phone, you may have trouble getting through to talk with the owner. Here are some approaches that assume you do not have the advantage of the owner's name:

Approaches for Telephone Contact with Owners

"Hello, my name is Chris Cronin. Who am I talking with, please?"

("This is Bob.")

"I'm trying to locate the owner of Steck's Lumberyard. Are you the owner?"

(If the answer is "yes," use the letter to owners as a script. If the answer is "no," continue.)

"Oh. May I ask who the owner is?"

(If you get the name, ask to speak to him or her. If you are asked to give your reason for wanting to know, continue.)

"Bob, I'm interested in buying a lumberyard in this area and I thought the owner of Steck's might know if any are for sale. I'm sure the owner would be interested in hearing about my plans."

(If you are still refused the name, continue.)

"Say, I can understand the owner's desire to keep a low profile. But would you please do this, Bob? Would you give the owner my name and phone number and explain that I am looking to buy a lumberyard and I would really appreciate some advice? The name is Chris Cronin, and the number is (813) 555-1641. Thanks for your help, Bob."

(Optional)

"I'd like to call you later to find out the owner's reaction. Thank you. Good-bye."

Other variations are required when you are told the owner is out or unavailable. Emphasize to the person you are talking to that it is important to the owner to know that a potential lumberyard buyer is seeking advice. When you do get a business owner on the phone, the questions presented in Table 11–2 can get you started.

Messages When Using Personal Contact. Personal contact and canvassing is the most time-consuming direct marketing technique, but it is also the most powerful. Personal contact allows you to make a strong impression. Whether you are contacting business owners by telephone or in person, you will need some special techniques to get information from these cautious people.

Getting permission to ask questions is the first step. Phrases such as "May I ask . . ." or "Would you allow me . . ." help lower owners' concerns by giving them control over the conversation. Another device to gain permission is to ask "How would I find out . . ." or "How would you suggest that I . . . ."

Having good questions to ask is the second step. You have your criteria, including some financial parameters, already established. You can convert these criteria into specific opening questions you can ask, either over the telephone or during personal contact, to see if this business might satisfy them.

Your personal presence emphasizes your determination. Being face to face allows you to do a better job establishing rapport and getting information.

Prepare for personal contact by typing or printing copies of your objectives and background summary. Business cards are a must. The message for personal contact is a variation of your direct mail letter. If you are making cold canvassing calls on businesses, the telephone script and the questions presented in Table 11–2 are both relevant.

If personal contact is a follow-up to your mail and telephone work, or if you have otherwise made appointments for personal contact, you are set to conduct this part of your active search. If you plan to do cold calls, that is, calls without an appointment, plan on doing a lot of call-backs to contact the people who will not or cannot meet with you when you make your call. Your call-back can be another personal visit or a contact by mail or phone. If you cannot make a personal contact, do the next best thing and try to get your printed material to the targeted contact.

The targeted direct marketing portion of your active search is now ready to go. You have your list of contacts, your messages, and their style of presentation.

Table 11–2. Sample Opening Questions

Factor	Opening Questions
Business factors	
History	When and how did the company start? What has been its history of ownership and activity? Who owns the company now, and in what form is the ownership?
Purpose	What is the fundamental nature of the business? What does it do? Why does it exist? Does it have a plan or direction?
People	Who are the people? How many are there? How long have they been there? What do they do? Are they competent? Are they satisfied? Are any of them critical to success? Is here a union? How well are they paid? Are there enough of them? Is there a manager other than the owner? Will key people leave if a sale takes place?

Table 11–2. *(Continued)*

Factor	Opening Questions
Organization	What is the company organization? Does it work well? What function does the owner play? Are there organizational policies and practices? Is there depth in the organization?
Facilities	What are the facilities? Is the size right? Are the facilities owned or leased? What are the terms and length of the lease? Is it assumable? Is the facility where it should be? What is the condition of the facility? What would it take to relocate?
Equipment	What type of equipment is there? Is it modern? Is it well kept? What is the percent utilization? Is there enough/not enough? Who supplies it? Who maintains it? Could it be sold easily?
Technology	Are company methods and techniques modern? Are products and services modern? How does the company provide for innovation? Does technology change rapidly? What computer systems does the company use?
Market	What/who is the company's market? How large is it? Is it growing or declining? Is it concentrated on a few customers or spread broadly? Is it style or fad based?
Competition	Who are the competitors? Is competition increasing? Do competitors have any special advantages? Who has what share of the market, and how is that changing? Are any competitors for sale?
Company operations (as appropriate)	
Manufacturing	What is the manufacturing process? What is the total capacity? How much is available? What would it cost to expand? How is productivity measured? Any special skills required? Is there any special dependence on suppliers? Are there any problems with the EPA or OSHA? Are there any labor problems?
Legal	Is the company involved in litigation? Is there some exposure? What contracts or obligations does the company have? Who is the company's attorney? Does the company require licenses to operate, or is it otherwise regulated? Does it have any patents? To what associations does the company belong? Does the company have adequate insurance?
Marketing and sales	What are the key marketing activities and techniques? How many people do what tasks? How are the products and services perceived in the marketplace? What have been the trends in sales volume and prices? How are prices set? How are salespeople hired, trained, and compensated? How many customers does the company have? Are sales concentrated among a few customers? How spread out are the customers geographically? Has the company lost any customers? Are customers long established? Do they sign contracts? Will they stay on after the sale?

(Continued)

Table 11–2. *(Continued)*

Factor	Opening Questions
Accounting/finance	How is the accounting and/or financial function organized? Is it adequate for the company's needs? Are systems and reports satisfactory? Who is the company's outside accountant? Who is the company's banker? Are adequate lines of credit established? Does the company pay its bills on a schedule?
General	What are the strengths and weaknesses of the company? What area needs the most immediate improvement? Where does the company's greatest potential lie? What is the biggest threat to the company?
Outside factors	Are there any special problems or opportunities relating to general economic conditions, world trade, governmental agencies, or other outside factors?
Financial factors	
Financial performance	Is the company profitable? How profitable? Is it growing? Is enough cash being generated to operate the business and support its growth? What adjustments are needed to get from the accountant's reported profit to the real cash flow?
	(Before you ask these questions, determine if the information you have is accurate and complete. Study the trends. Get three to five years of data if you can.)
Balance sheet	What has been the trend of inventory? How much is finished goods, how much is raw material, how much is work-in-progress? Is the inventory worth the value? Has the level of accounts receivable varied? How old are they? Are they owed by a few or many customers? What are the fixed and other assets? How have fixed assets been valued and depreciated? What market value do they have? Has the level of accounts payable varied? To whom are they owed? Are they current? Identify the debt and each creditor. How much is it? What is the trend? How old is it?
Income (P&L) statement	What have been the trends in sales? In costs? Have any expense items changed significantly? Is adequate money being spent on repairs (or any other item)?
Ratios	If you can, determine the following ratios and percentages: return on investment, return on sales, individual expense items to sales, costs to sales, current assets to current liabilities, income (cash) to debt payments, receivable turns per year, inventory turns per year, salaries and benefits as a percent of total expenses (see Chapter 12).

Advertising

The advertising portion of an active search requires you to reach the right people with the right message so that they will respond and contact you.

The Right People

The right people to target with advertising are business owners, business brokers, and other intermediaries. It is unlikely that any of the other contacts we have discussed will take action on your advertisement.

The Right Method

Having decided who the right people are, you need to decide the best method of reaching them. Although other media may be interesting to consider, we are going to assume that print advertising is the best method for reaching our targets.

Newspapers are the best print medium with which to reach brokers and intermediaries, who regularly read the "Business Opportunities" section of newspapers. Which newspapers you use will depend on the business you are seeking. If you are looking for a small or locally oriented business, the local newspaper may be all you need. If the business is large or specialized, you may want to add the *Wall Street Journal* or one of the specialized business opportunity newspapers. Newspaper classified advertising will reach business owners who read the business opportunities, but those are a small percentage of the owners you want to reach.

Deciding where to advertise to reach business owners takes some analysis of what these business owners read. Trade papers and magazines are good prospects. If the business has a special focus such as sports, you may want to use that section of your local newspaper.

If the business you want has no trade publications or special focus, accept the fact that advertising to these business owners probably will not work, and that any advertising will be useful only with intermediaries. After you select the publications you are going to use, call to find out the procedures and rates for advertising.

The Right Message

The next step is to write an advertisement based on the rate information you obtained and the message you want to send. The objective of your ad is to get a response from your target. If you put yourself in the target's shoes, you can pretty much determine what will trigger a response:

You are a potential buyer.
You are qualified.
You have money.

Here are two sample ads of average length. The first assumes that you have a specific kind of company in mind.

WANTED TO BUY
LUMBERYARD/BUILDING CENTER

20-year industry exec seeks lumberyard, building, or garden center or similar business in Tampa/St. Petersburg. Cash available. Will structure deal to meet seller's objectives. Replies held confidential. C. Cronin (813) 555-1111.

Any lumberyard owner or business broker will understand that ad and will respond if appropriate.

Here is an ad to use when you don't know exactly what you want for a business:

BUSINESS WANTED
TO BUY

Business exec with $200,000 cash plus strong credit seeks distribution or manufacturing company in Tampa/St. Petersburg. Will structure deal to meet seller's objectives. Replies held confidential. C. Cronin (813) 555-1111.

Note that in the first ad there is no mention of the amount of cash available, but in the second ad we declared the amount. The first ad has such a narrow target that we want to find every and any lumberyard opportunity. In the second ad our specifications are so broad that we need to include some kind of filter in the ad. The ad presumes that we don't care how small the business is, but we do have some upper limit.

You may want to run your ad several times. Owners might need to see the ad a few times for the idea of selling their business to develop into the action of calling you. Every response generated by your search activities needs to be evaluated and followed through. If a lead or candidate is generated that is outside your criteria, thank the source and encourage more appropriate leads.

A Disadvantage of the Active Search

The active search does have one disadvantage when compared to reading ads or talking with brokers. The active search will bring you in contact with business owners who may not want to sell but who are curious about what their business is worth. The expression you might hear is "every business is for sale if the price is high enough." You can waste lots of time with these owners unless you can determine quickly whether they are potential sellers.

You can ask straight out what the price is, but most sellers can't and won't answer. Unless they have had their business on the market, they really don't know what their business is worth. They will want you to tell them what you think it's worth—you represent a free "wealth check."

If and when you are asked to offer a price, you have your chance to determine if the seller might be serious. The opportunity usually comes when the owner says something like "Take a look around and tell me what you think the place is worth." Point out that you are more than willing to make an offer but that surely the business is worth more than the equipment (or fixtures or inventory) that one can see. Much of the value has to come from the financial strength and you will, of course, need to see the financial records to be able to work up a price that is fair. If the owner refuses to let you see the books, ask him or her for an alternative way to proceed. Perhaps your accountant can talk with his or her accountant. Offer to sign a confidentiality agreement. If no alternative is satisfactory, you can assume that the seller is not serious and move on to another business.

Follow-up and Evaluation

Follow up on every lead you get from your active search and your advertising. Even if the lead is a poor one, it may be a connection to one that is worthwhile. Another reason for following up on all leads is to reinforce your reputation as a competent business person.

Evaluate your leads by comparing them to your criteria. If the lead or candidate is within your criteria, set up an information file and a schedule of contacts.

Summary

You are now able to generate a pool of candidate companies. You know how to identify sources and contacts. You know how to develop lists of contact names and how to implement an active search. You know how to use direct marketing techniques and advertising to get the response you want. Worksheet 8 and Table 11–1 will help you organize your search.

Worksheet 8
Sources and Contacts for Locating Businesses

Source	Specific Contact/Comments
Newspapers	
Newsletters	
Trade magazines	
Business brokers	
Business owners	
Other business people	
Lawyers, accountants, other advisors	
Bankers	
Friends	
Venture capitalists, merger and acquisition specialists, corporate development executives	
Networks	
Vendors and suppliers	
Customers	
Industry trade associations	

CHAPTER 12

Analyzing the Business

When your pool of candidates produces a company that seems to meet your criteria, you can begin the work of analyzing the business. During this phase, you will rely increasingly on your advisors.

Managing Your Advisors

The three advisors most involved are intermediaries, accountants, and attorneys. If there is an intermediary, you need to be certain of his or her loyalty and responsibility. Most intermediaries work for the seller, not the buyer. Get a clear definition of the intermediary's function.

Intermediaries

Some brokers and other intermediaries have full power to negotiate on behalf of their seller clients, whereas others act only as communication conduits. Some are active and creative in structuring deals, and some only transmit offers. Levels of skill and experience vary. Ask how the intermediary operates.

Find out how the seller wants the chain of events to proceed. Setting expectations about how information will be exchanged and especially about the timeline for events will keep unnecessary tensions to a minimum. Intermediaries are paid to complete transactions and are normally very helpful in the process. However, you cannot rely solely on the intermediary, who is the seller's agent, for your information and advice. You need to manage the intermediary as a part of managing this phase of your purchase.

Accountants

Managing your accountant begins with the kind of financial arrangement you have with him or her regarding the kinds of services you want and the payment your accountant expects. We covered the selection of an accountant earlier in Chapter 8, so by this time, your accountant should be well aware of your objectives and your resources.

The two of you should discuss one very important subject relating to the purchase of a small business: the condition of the financial information. For most small businesses the standard accounting statement and tax return information will be limited by the owners' accounting acumen and their attitude and honesty regarding tax obligations. You will learn later in this chapter how to adjust financial information to make it meaningful to you.

Some accountants are not comfortable with the risks of using adjusted information, so the two of you need to agree on how to deal with small business financial data. As we suggested earlier, pick an accountant who is thoroughly familiar with small businesses and their accounting practices.

Unless you are secure about your own accounting skills, you will want your accountant to perform tests and analyses and provide you with recommendations. You may want your accountant to advise you on how to structure your transaction.

You should know, too, that accountants can face a special dilemma when advising on the purchase of a business. If a buyer relies heavily on an accountant and buys a business on which the accountant has advised favorably and then has trouble with that business (even of the buyer's own making), he or she might be the kind of buyer to hold the accountant liable, and initiate a lawsuit. If, on the other hand, the accountant advises against buying a business and the client proceeds and is successful, the accountant has avoided risk and has only to be happy for the client's success.

So the accountant may feel pressure to avoid positive recommendations. You can help allay that pressure by letting your accountant know you will welcome advice, but you will accept responsibility for your own judgment in making the final decision.

Attorneys

Managing your attorney involves much of the same discipline as managing your accountant. Have a discussion about how you will work together. You may want your attorney just to review the contract and closing documents, or you may want him or her to handle all the negotiations. In between these extremes is advice and counsel on the purchase transaction.

If you have already selected the company you are going after, your attorney might be able to estimate the complexity of the transaction and thus the time and charges you might budget.

The last step in managing your accountant and your attorney is to develop them into a team. Their work is interrelated. At midcareer you need to examine closely how this purchase will affect your overall tax situation, and that requires their coordination. Estate planning is another area of common interest. These two advisors may be excellent resources in your negotiating tactics. You want your objective—buying a business—to become their objective.

With your team in place, you can begin your evaluation.

Evaluating the Business

Gathering information and analyzing all the factors about a business may seem like an overwhelming task. Just remember at all times that you do *not* have to buy *this* business. Most assuredly, you do not have to buy it in a hurry. Although you should conduct your analysis with consideration for the time of others, this does not mean that you should rush.

You have an accountant and an attorney as advisors, and you can hire specialized advisors such as machinery appraisers if you need them. Yet, with all this help, you will make any final decision on imperfect and incomplete information, because there is no other way. Buying a business is a risk. The challenge is to minimize the risk as best you can.

An important constraint in your evaluation activities is the need for confidentiality. We mentioned in Chapter 11 that the seller's concern for confidentiality is genuine. It should be your concern, too. If knowledge of the potential sale of the business upsets customers, employees, the landlord, or others, you may be the one who suffers. Telling a friend or neighbor about your plan may spread it to the entire community. If you breech confidentiality, you may spark interest in your candidate company by another buyer and face the not-uncommon prospect of having the business bought out from under you. This requirement for confidentiality means that extra care should be taken when gathering information.

The complex task of evaluation can be broken into steps. First, we shall decide *what* information we need to have. Then we will develop a list of all the sources *where* the information might be found. Finally, we shall work on *how* to analyze the information you uncover.

What: The Information Needed

You need and want considerable information about the company and its environment. Figure 12–1 lists some of the information you will need. You will need one vital piece of information about the owner: You need to find out *why* the owner is selling. The seller's motives can be an important clue to the condition of the business. Unfortunately, when you ask the owner you may get acceptable-sounding answers such as "other business interests" or "retirement," when the real reason is "I can't hire any help" or "competition is killing me." You need to probe any reason you are given. Ask to know more about the other business interest or the retirement. If you ask in several ways about the owner's future plans, you may get some insights.

Developing company information involves considering a list of business factors and asking questions. The opening questions are designed to get you into the topic. Your direction after that will be governed by the answers you get and the importance of the factor to this particular company. Table 11–2 lists opening questions to a business owner. These questions can be used as a guide in developing company information. Many more

```
The owner's reason for selling
Company history
Purpose
People
Markets
Competition
Organization
Facilities
Equipment
Technology
General conditions
Outside factors
Company operations:
    Marketing
    Manufacturing
    Legal
    Finance
Financial factors:
    Financial status
    Balance sheet
    Income (profit and loss) statement
    Ratios
```

Figure 12–1. What information is needed?

questions can and will be generated as you actually dig out the information.

Finding the information is our next task.

Where: The Information Sources

The seller and the intermediary will be your primary sources of information, but you do not have to rely on these sources alone. Figure 12–2 lists various sources of information. Not all will be relevant to your company, but you may find some surprisingly good sources in the list.

You can locate all but a few of these sources on your own. The rest you can reach by working with your advisors. The contacts you have built over the years can be a big help in digging out information. Hard detective work should yield the information you were seeking (and more).

Now that you have it, you need to decide what the information means.

How: Analyzing the Information

You are first faced with the task of sorting through all the data you have gathered and organizing it. The *qualitative* process of analysis we will use is called *forced rating*. It is simply a 1-to-10 scale that makes you rate your findings explicitly. The *quantitative* portion of the process will be conventional financial analysis.

Associations	Landlords
Banks	Library
Better Business Bureau	Neighboring businesses
Bonding company	Newspapers and magazines
Chamber of Commerce	Patent office
Company records	Personal observation
Competitors	Private investigator
Consultants	Real estate broker
Court/land records	Seller
Credit reporting companies	Seller's advisors
Employees (and former employees)	Stockbroker
Franchise records	Suppliers
Government records	Tax returns
Insurance policies	Unions
Intermediary	Your advisors
	Your networks

Figure 12–2. Sources of information.

Help Available

You have several sources of help in analyzing the information you have gathered. We have mentioned your advisors, industry statistics and standards, and company history. Real estate appraisers, inventory appraisal companies, specialized equipment appraisers, and dealers are others who can help.

The Seller's Advisors

You can also use the seller and the seller's advisors. No one knows more about the business than they. Often there is no other way to understand some fact or figure but to ask the seller. Some sellers are candid to the point of total disclosure. The obvious risk in asking these sources is that they are selling a business and want to present the best picture of it possible.

The offset against the risk is the fact that the seller is probably going to finance your purchase. The seller knows that if you discover you have been deceived, you are going to be less than cooperative in repaying your debt. Do as you would with any advice, and evaluate the source as well as the information.

One source of help may take some selling on your part, but it is worth the effort. The seller's banker will know more about the business than almost anyone else. If you have the choice of selecting the seller's banker to be your banker, your motive to work with this source of help will be even greater. The seller's banker will be less likely to use "puffery" to help the sale, but rather will be interested in seeing a well-executed transaction.

Computer-Assisted Analysis

A ready source of help is computer-assisted analysis. Several software programs on the market can calculate ratios, construct comparative tables, and provide projections of sales, profit, and cash flow based on your plans.

This software is most helpful in doing sensitivity analyses. These are the analyses that pose "what if" questions. The software programs have the ability to calculate the total impact which results from changes in the company ("What if sales increase or decrease by 5 percent?"). The calculations are done so quickly, you can probe nearly every variable of interest.

Qualitative Analysis

You have gathered information on some or all 17 business factors. As a summary and reminder, they are history, purpose, people, market(s), competition, organization, facilities, equipment, technology, general, outside factors, marketing, manufacturing, legal, finance, reason for selling, and financial performance.

Worksheet 9 at the end of the chapter can be used to rate the combined weight of your evaluation of these factors against each of your criteria and risk elements. The rating process does two things:

1. It forms an integrated idea of desirability;
2. It points out extremes and suggests areas for further investigation.

The rating is imperfect because it assumes an equal value for each criterion and for each risk factor. Nonetheless, you have followed a logical path to this point, and you can now make your first judgments about whether this business is for you. If the business is far outside your preferred degree of risk or does not at all satisfy your criteria, there is no need to analyze the quantitative data. If your judgment does not eliminate the candidate, you can move on to the numbers.

Quantitative Analysis

What follows is an overview of fairly conventional financial analysis. The degree of your own skills in this area and the complexity of the data will dictate the extent to which you involve your accountant.

Before you begin, remind yourself of the well-known fact that many small business owners keep their financial records (if they have them) in ways to "minimize taxes and maximize lifestyle." Records may be imprecise or just plain false. We will see how to adjust for this in the next chapter, on pricing the business. This chapter focuses on analysis.

Comparative analysis is one kind of quantitative analysis. Facts, figures, and ratios developed for the business you are considering are compared with standards of some kind. The most readily available standards can be found in the company's previous financial statements. Comparing current operations to historical financial performance will give you a sure way to spot significant deviations in current performance.

Comparisons can also use more or less generally accepted benchmarks such as a 2-to-1 ratio of current assets to current liabilities. Your accountant or banker can provide you with these interesting but very imprecise rules of thumb.

Other comparisons can be made with industry norms. Basic financial figures and ratios are available for many kinds and sizes of business. Industry trade associations may publish them. Trade papers and magazines sometimes publish an annual edition of financial performance ratios. Your stockbroker has access to performance statistics for many kinds of businesses. The federal government offers industry financial statistics through the Small Business Administration and the Department of Commerce. Two comprehensive sources of ratios are the *Almanac of Business and Industrial Ratios* and *Financial Studies of the Small Business.**

Financial statement analysis is a second kind of quantitative analysis, which involves the interpretation of the financial statement contents. Here we are not trying to compare but rather to understand and evaluate.

Both comparative analysis and financial statement analysis are based on ratio analysis, cost and expense analysis, sensitivity analysis, breakeven analysis, and an analysis of the sources and applications of funds (cash).

Ratio Analysis. Ratio analysis is a common quantitative technique. The relationship between two financial statement items can be reduced to a simple standardized ratio that is easy to compare and understand. Here are some common ratios and their implications:

Current Ratio. This is the ratio of current assets to current liabilities. This is an indicator of a company's ability to meet its short-term obligations. It is an indicator of liquid strength, at least in the short term.

Acid-Test Ratio. This is an even more stringent liquidity measure. It, too, uses the ratio between current assets and current liabilities, but inventory and other nonliquid assets are not included in current assets.

Fixed Assets to Long-Term Liabilities. Although this test is not much used in small businesses, it does show the degree of security behind long-term debt.

Turnover. The two common turnover ratios are inventory and accounts receivable. They are good comparative measures to help analyze how well a candidate company does in managing these two asset investments. Inventory turnover is typically calculated by dividing the cost of goods by the average inventory (year-beginning inventory plus year-ending inventory divided by 2). Accounts receivable turnover is determined by dividing net sales by average receivables (year-beginning receivables plus year-end receivables divided by 2).

Return on Investment (ROI). In this book, we compute return on investment using the adjusted owner's cash flow as the return figure and the net market value of the investment as the investment figure. We use these measures because they produce information useful in making an investment decision. However, to be able to compare a candidate company to conventional standards of ROI, you will need

---

* Leo Troy, *Almanac of Business and Industrial Financial Ratios*, Ingram Price; Englewood Cliffs, NJ, 1996; Financial Research Associates, *Financial Studies of the Small Business*, Winter Haven, FL, 1976.

to use conventional measures. The conventional measures do vary from industry to industry, and it is vital that you understand them.

ROI in industries with large capital investments will be no comparison to returns in certain service industries. For example, when analyzing residential real estate companies that have little investment in assets, return on investment is a secondary measure. Analyses are more often expressed in terms of percent of net revenue (company dollars). Just determine how your standard is derived and use the same method of calculation.

Return percentages form a critical part of your analysis because they reduce all of the financial data to one key number. Because of the apparent precision employed in computing the return percentage, people tend to misuse it. It is a good comparative measure (if your standard of comparison is valid) but not a good valuative measure. The percent return on investment is not a measure of return on your *actual cash* investment unless you invest all cash.

Return on investment has one other practical shortcoming in that it does not measure any appreciation the investment may have enjoyed. The following real estate investment example can demonstrate these shortcomings. Ignore any tax implications.

If you bought a small shopping center for $1 million and received income after all expenses of $25,000, you would have a gross ROI of 2½ percent. But if you put only $100,000 in cash as a down payment, you could view your cash-on-cash ROI as 25 percent.

Now assume that you sell the shopping center after a year for $1,100,000. Does that $100,000 profit represent a 10 percent return on the $1 million, or does it represent a 100 percent return on the $100,000 cash you actually invested? In fact, it can mean both things. Remember that the actual amount of $100,000 is the same—only your definition of "investment" (the degree of financing) changed.

Be aware of two principles that apply to this return-on-investment analysis:

1. A high level of financing can make a bad business affordable, but it does not make it a good business.
2. A basic rule of financing is that you should borrow only if you can earn more than it costs you to borrow—that is, your return exceeds the interest you pay.

If you put down very little cash and borrow a great deal, you may end up using all your income for debt repayments. Your very important analysis of return on investment needs to involve not only the historic rates of return on the financial statement, but your projections of returns based on your own financing plan.

Cost and Expense Ratio Analysis. Cost and expense ratio analysis can be very enlightening because it allows you to compare your target company with others, with its own history, and with your own judgment. The ratio analysis is done by dividing sales by the individual cost and expense items. Table 12–1 shows a simplified example.

You should be alert for changes in trends and for numbers that seem outside the normal standards and outside your common-sense idea of what is normal.

Sensitivity Analysis. As the name suggests, sensitivity analysis is a quantitative analysis to determine how sensitive the company's performance is to changes in income, costs, and expenses. The analysis is accomplished by posing "what if" questions:

- What if the rent doubles?
- What if I add two people?
- What if sales go up/down 5 percent?
- What if I raise prices 10 percent and lose 1 percent in volume?

Your objective should be to get a feel for where the business is most vulnerable and where it has the most potential. Financial analysis software makes sensitivity analysis easy to do.

Breakeven Analysis. Breakeven analysis is a special form of sensitivity analysis that allows you to understand the relationships among sales, fixed costs, variable costs, and profit. It assumes that some costs, such as rent,

Table 12–1. Example Cost and Expense Ratio Analysis

Item	Amount	Percent of Sales
Sales	$700,000	100
Cost of goods sold	315,000	45
Gross profit	$385,000	55
Salaries	84,000	12
Rent	35,000	5
Utilities	14,000	2
Interest	21,000	3
Selling expenses	35,000	5
Administration	42,000	6
Transportation	14,000	2
Total expenses	$245,000	35
Pre-tax profit	$140,000	20

administration, and insurance, are more or less fixed in the short term, while other costs, such as the cost of materials and selling commissions, vary with volume. After deciding whether the cost or expense is fixed or variable, you can construct a chart similar to the one in Figure 12–3.

This is a particularly useful analysis to test or verify a seller's claims. For example, if a seller claims that all a business needs is a little attention to sales, when in fact the problem is high fixed overhead, this type of analysis can be very revealing. It will show just how much of an increase in sales will be needed to improve profitability.

Sources and Applications of Funds. Analysis will show, for a specific period of time, whether the company being considered consumed more or less cash than it generated. The analysis uses a comparison of the balance sheets for two periods, and information from the income (P&L) statement. The income statement includes two items that affect the analysis: profit (or loss) and noncash expenditures such as depreciation. Profit and depreciation are sources of funds. Four simple rules to follow with the balance sheet are:

1. An increase in assets is a use of funds.
2. A decrease in assets is a source of funds.
3. An increase in liabilities is a source of funds.
4. A decrease in liabilities is a use of funds.

If the company you are considering has professionally prepared statements, they will normally include a statement of sources and applications of funds.

Worksheets 10, 11, and 12 at the end of the chapter can help you capture data for your analyses.

At some point, you will decide that you have enough knowledge to make a decision about whether to reject the candidate or proceed to make an offer. Before going on, it may be helpful to review all your work so far.

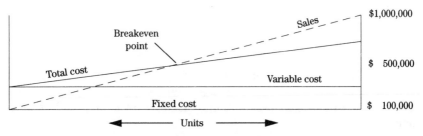

Figure 12–3. Breakeven analysis. (*Source:* C. D. Peterson, *Introduction to Business Brokerage,* John Wiley & Sons, New York, 1991, page 184.)

A Recap

Review

In Chapter 8, you took care of your benefits, selected your advisors, and did your preparation. Then, in Chapter 9, you took a personal inventory and established the criteria for your business. You made a tentative decision about what you can afford in Chapter 10, where you worked on how to value the business and how and where to get the money to buy it. Armed with all this, you went and found the business in Chapter 11. In this chapter you have done a great deal of analysis and, we will presume, you are ready to proceed to make an offer and negotiate the purchase.

Reconsider

Before you proceed, take the time to reconsider the whole idea of owning a business. Go back to Worksheet 1 and see whether your level of satisfaction will be significantly improved if you buy the business you are considering. Compare your life's situation under two assumptions: You either own this business, or you have a realistic job. Use a "plus and minus" list. If appropriate, involve your spouse.

If you have alternatives other than owning a business or having a job, such as retirement or public service, include these alternatives in this reconsideration.

Compare Income

Comparing the income from a job with the income from the business requires you to make some assumptions about the perquisites you will afford yourself. Any generous fringe benefits that might come from employment need to be evaluated carefully. Pension considerations may be important. Employment of family members and your personal tax situation will influence this comparison.

Compare Wealth

At midcareer, projecting your wealth may be difficult, but your situation makes it important to do. You are going to compare your personal balance sheet under two sets of assumptions, business ownership and employment.

1. Prepare a personal balance sheet that reflects your present situation.
2. Then prepare a balance sheet that projects your total assets and lia-

bilities, business and personal, under the most probable assumptions about the performance of the business. Try to do the projection for one year and for five years.

3. Repeat the projection of your present balance sheet assuming that you have a job instead of the business.

Compare Satisfaction

You can only imagine some of the satisfactions and frustrations that will come to you from owning the business, so the comparison of ownership with employment, while necessary, will be very subjective. Make your comparison by thinking through the things that affect satisfaction: family considerations, freedom, stress, risk, independence, working hours and conditions, intellectual stimulation, status and image, security (both short-term and long-term), recognition, accomplishment, and the special element of obligation.

The obligations that come with business ownership might be viewed as a weight to be placed on the balance scale opposite the feelings of impotence you feel working for others. When working for others you are, de facto, subordinate. No matter how subtle or how abusive your treatment, you are subject to being told what to do and you are directly dependent on people you cannot avoid. Not so in your own business. When you own a business, however, you automatically incur obligations. The obligations are legal, financial, and in some cases, psychological. They exist 24 hours a day and are unavoidable—you can't just quit. Sometimes you can't even take a day off.

Consider, too, that owning your own business will still mean that you are working for others—in this case, customers, who can be more demanding than any corporate boss. Of course, little can compare with the satisfaction of building something of your own, something of value—possibly growing value—for you and your family.

Worksheet 9

Comparing the Business to Your Criteria

Rating criteria. (See Chapter 9 for review.) Use a scale of 1 to 10, where 10 is best.

Cash flow	_____	Status and image	_____
Location	_____	People intensity	_____
Liquidity	_____	Competition	_____
Growth potential	_____	Overall risk	_____
Working conditions	_____	Content of the business	_____

Total _____ ÷ 10 = _____ Rating

Worksheet 10

Income Statement (P&L) for the Period _____ to _____

Sales	$_____	
Cost of sales	_____	
Gross profit	$_____	
Expenses:		
Owner's salary	$_____	
Owner's benefits and taxes		$ _____
Employee salaries (No. of people _____)	_____	
Employee benefits and taxes	_____	
Rent	_____	
Utilities	_____	
Travel and entertainment	_____	
Selling expenses	_____	
Depreciation	_____	
Insurance	_____	
Supplies	_____	
Interest	_____	
Automobile	_____	
Dues, licenses, subscriptions	_____	
Legal and accounting	_____	
Other _____	_____	
Other _____	_____	
Other _____	_____	
Total expenses		$ _____
Pre-tax profit	$_____	

Worksheet 11
Balance Sheet as of ____

Current assets:
Cash $ _____
Accounts receivable   _____
Notes receivable   _____
Inventory   _____
Prepaid expenses   _____
Other   _____

   Total current assets $ _____

Fixed assets:
Furniture, fixtures, machinery, and equipment $ _____
Less: Accumulated depreciation _____ $ _____
Land and buildings $ _____
Less: Accumulated depreciation _____ $ _____
Other assets _____   _____

   Total fixed assets $ _____

   Total assets $ _____

LIABILITIES AND OWNER'S EQUITY

Current liabilities:
Accounts payable $ _____
Wages payable   _____
Taxes payable   _____
Interest payable   _____
Notes/leases (current portion)   _____
Services or products owed to customers   _____
Other liabilities   _____

   Total current liabilities $ _____

Long-term liabilities:
Notes $ _____
Mortgages   _____
Other _____   _____

   Total long-term liabilities $ _____
Owner's equity:
Capital stock $ _____
Retained earnings   _____

   Total liabilities and owner's equity $ _____

Worksheet 12

Sources and Applications of Funds

Funds received from:
Profits $ _____
Noncash expenses (depreciation)   _____
Increases in liabilities   _____
Decreases in assets (other than depreciation)   _____

   Total funds received $ _____

Funds applied to:
Losses $ _____
Increases in assets   _____
Decreases in liabilities   _____
Payout of profit (dividends)   _____

   Total funds applied $ _____

CHAPTER 13

Pricing the Business

Valuing and Pricing Businesses

The *price* you will eventually pay for a business will depend on its *value* and *affordability*. Each of these terms deserves an explanation.

Value is what something is worth. It may be an objective measure against something similar with a known value, or it can be a subjective feeling of worth.

Price is what a buyer pays for something. The distinction between value and price becomes clear if you think about how often people pay more or less than something is worth.

Affordability is what a buyer is able to pay. A seller may value a business at a level that matches his or her idea of a fair price. But if the buyer can't afford to pay it, any efforts to attract and interest that buyer are wasted.

This chapter explores how these three factors work together.

Valuation

Valuing businesses employs methods ranging from crude rules of thumb, such as multiples of cash flow, to exotic and intricate mathematical models. The organizations listed on page 188 have members who specialize in valuing businesses:

The Institute of Business Appraisers, Inc.
P.O. Box 1447
Boynton Beach, FL 33435

The Business Valuation Committee of the American Society of
   Appraisers
(Publishers of *Business Valuation Review*)
P.O. Box 24222
Denver, CO 80224

Many groups and individuals offer to do business valuations. Some may
have other motives, such as obtaining the right to sell the business or gaining a consulting contract to prepare the business for sale.

Individual appraisers specializing in machinery, professional practices,
real estate, and other classifications can be found in most Yellow Pages. In
addition, many books have been published on the subject of appraisal and
valuation of businesses. You can also choose from several valuation software packages, including *Value Express 4.0* and *Biz Comps.**

The degree and depth of your evaluation will depend on how much you
feel you need. If you are buying a large company with substantial assets
and real estate, you may want a professional evaluation. The purchase of a
small service or retail company may require no more than a common-sense
idea of value.

The Variables

Valuing and pricing businesses is not an exact science. A great many factors go into business evaluation, many of them subjective. Figure 13–1 lists
more than 40 variables that can affect price. These variables can be
weighted and combined in an almost infinite number of ways to produce
an infinite number of prices.

Problems in Valuing and Pricing

The large number of variables represents only one problem of evaluation.
Lack of objectivity is another. Many special business situations require
unique valuation approaches.

The Reason for the Evaluation. One problem arises at the very beginning of an evaluation. Over a dozen different kinds of values can be placed
on a business. Your first task is to select the right one, and that depends on
the reason for the evaluation.   \

Value Express 4.0 is available from Wiley-Valuesource, 7222 Commerce Center Drive,
Colorado Springs, CO 80919. *Biz Comps* is available from Jack Sanders, CBA, Box 71777, San
Diego, CA 92171.

Ability to influence cost	Location
Ability to influence customers	Management competency
Ability to influence prices	Market share
Affordability	Operating performance and ratios
Alternative opportunities	Physical appearance
Asset value	Political outlook
Barriers to entry	Potential
Borrowing capacity	Production
Cash flow	Projected cash flow
Company history	Projected growth
Company reputation	Quality and competitiveness of products/services
Comparable businesses	
Condition of books and records	Real estate/lease situation
Cost competitiveness	Risk of return of investment
Desirability of the industry	Risk of return on investment
Ease to run	Special licenses, patents, franchises
Economic outlook	
Employee competency	Superiority
Goodwill	Tax considerations
Growth	Technology
Intangibles	Vulnerability
Legal situation or encumbrances	Working conditions

Figure 13-1. Variables that affect valuation. Any of these variables may have an influence at some time. Other variables, such as terms of sale and supply and demand, are treated separately because they directly affect the price of the business, not its value.

First, be sure of the reason for the evaluation. Here is a partial list of values for a business:

- Insurable value
- Book value
- Liquidation value
- Fair market/stock market value
- Replacement value
- Reproduction value
- Asset value
- Discounted future earnings value
- Capitalized earnings value
- Goodwill value
- Going concern value
- Cost savings value
- Expected value
- Conditional value

Each of these values, under the appropriate circumstances, suits certain kinds of evaluations. The reason for the evaluation determines which measure will be used. For example, if the purpose of the evaluation is to purchase proper insurance coverage, the value developed will be based on the cost of replacing the tangible assets; if the purpose is to borrow money, banks will be interested in collateral, so asset values will be key.

Our reason for evaluating the business is to establish a selling price. Selling price is based on what the business owns, what it earns, and what makes it unique, and so it is possible that all these listed values will be important to us.

Lack of Objectivity. This significant problem results from the lack of objective measures for so many of the variables. Projections are estimates. Assessments of employees are never precise. Risk is subjective. Even the appraisal of assets can produce wide variations. And who can measure goodwill or the political outlook?

External Influences. The external environment of economics, regulation, international affairs, and so on, influences value independent of the company itself. If times are good and predicted to get better, risk is perceived to be lower and value therefore higher. The same influences can come from interest rates, exchange rates, and more.

Invalid Comparisons. One method of valuation that is *not* available to you as a business buyer is comparison of one business with others. Real estate appraisers commonly compare the prices of residential real estate sales where recent selling prices on nearly identical houses in similar locations are known. Houses are similar and prices are recorded on the deed.

Businesses are not similar enough to compare this way, and selling prices are not published as are prices for real property. In addition, buyers are all different and may evaluate even similar businesses differently, making any comparisons invalid.

Buyer and Seller Have Different Viewpoints. The seller has built his or her idea of the value of the business on intimate knowledge gained over considerable time. The buyer will be working with what amounts to a set of snapshots that the seller or others will provide.

No matter what valuation methods you use or how certain you are of how much the company is worth, you will have to understand the company from the viewpoint of the other party. To make a deal happen, both parties have to feel that the price is right.

Special Business Situations. One problem of valuing and pricing businesses arises because there are certain special cases for which there are special rules.

New businesses. New businesses are typically valued by comparing them to the alternative of starting a similar business. The *duplication cost* pricing method, discussed later in this chapter, fills the function.

High technology. High-technology companies may require a separate evaluation of the technology employed. Evaluators are particularly interested in the level of development of the technology. Whether there is much or little research and development left will affect value. They are also interested in the vulnerability of the technology. It may be vulnerable to becoming outdated or to a lack of availability of specialized labor. Most important are the applications for the technology. The value of technology rests in its application, and that can require speculation.

Professional practices. Professional practices (medicine, accounting, etc.) are valued with an eye to the cash stream from the patients or clients. They are priced and sold with terms contingent on some continuation of the patient/client base. Value is highly related to the reputation of the individual practitioners.

Cost-saving value. When one business buys another, particularly if the result is a merger, the effect may be substantial cost savings by eliminating duplication, optimization of resources, and reduced price competition. These values are in addition to those intrinsic to the business otherwise.

The Impact of Price on Selling the Business

The emphasis given to pricing in this book results from the importance of price in buying or selling businesses. Poorly established values and prices for businesses create major difficulties in negotiations and produce a high failure rate in business buying transactions. (It is estimated that only 20 percent of businesses on the market actually sell.) A price that is too low can cost the seller money. A price that is too high can turn off a buyer and kill the sale of the company.

Prices have another impact on the selling process. Because, as you will see, the price of a business cannot be verified objectively, the two parties may continue to worry that they are making a bad bargain. This worry can infect all parts of the negotiations.

Establishing Value

Businesses are valued by methods ranging from crude rules of thumb to exotic and intricate mathematical models. Older texts on pricing and brokers from past generations quoted such rules of thumb as "Restaurants sell for 10 times a month's sales," and "A machine shop should be priced at asset

value plus one year's cash flow." The fact that the restaurant is not profitable would be overlooked by such a rule. If the machine shop has labor
problems, this simple rule would give a very misleading price. All rules of
thumb have these flaws.

At the other extreme, for the intricate mathematical models we encounter the problem of subjectivity masquerading as fact. We have a ten-
dency to believe that because something is computerized and printed on
green-and-white striped paper, it is accurate. Most of these computerized
pricing models require you to make assumptions about growth or to evaluate such things as risk or location, or the quality of the company's organization. Added to that, some predictions about interest rates or discount
rates are usually included in these models. These very subjective variables
have a substantial impact on the computerized price. In other words, the
use of the model does not eliminate the subjectivity, it just hides it.

Working through all the steps of evaluating and pricing a business may
become confusing, much like missing the forest for the trees. To help avoid
that, here is a plan for the rest of the chapter. We will begin by finding the
value of the business. Then we will convert the value to price using several
pricing models. We shall review some tests that you as a buyer can use on
the price. Figure 13–2 summarizes the pricing models and tests. All of the
work on evaluation and pricing will be pulled together in a case study, the
Hillcrest Corporation.

The second part of the chapter deals with determining what the buyer
can afford. Contrary to what some sellers believe, what the buyer can afford will be shown to depend to some extent on the seller and the terms of
sale he or she is willing to provide. Worksheet 13 at the end of this chapter
will help you value and then price the business.

The Three Components of Value

The degree and depth of your evaluation will depend on how much you
feel you need. If you are buying a large company with substantial assets
and real estate, you may need a professional appraisal and evaluation. The
purchase of a small service or retail company may require no more than a
common-sense idea of value. Whether your evaluation is highly detailed or
very basic, it involves three elements:

What the business owns—though not what's usually found on the bal-
ance sheet.
What the business earns—the profit, or more correctly, the cash flow.
What makes the business unique—the degree of risk and desirability.

Each of these elements provides a value, and the three can be combined in
some very surprising ways. On page 194 is one example.

1. Price based on assets (book value method)

Uses: Used most often as a minimum price, because a business should be worth at least the value of its assets. Exceptions might occur when a company is losing money.

Steps: Determine the market value of the assets being sold. Deduct the value of any liabilities being assumed by the buyer.

2. Price based on cash flow (capitalization method)

Uses: Used when a business has few assets. The buyer is buying the stream of cash flow. The buyer bases the price on the return on investment the cash flow represents.

Steps: Adjust the profit-and-loss statement to reflect the true expenses of the business. Calculate the owner's adjusted cash flow. Decide, based on risk and desirability, the desired rate of return (the cap rate). Divide the cash flow by the cap rate.

3. Price based on the integrated method (excess earnings method)

Uses: Used when a company has both assets and cash flow. This method accounts for the value of the assets and then capitalizes the cash flow, but only after reducing the cash flow by the cost of carrying the assets.

Steps: Determine the market value of the assets. Multiply the value of the assets by the interest rate the company pays to borrow money to get the cost of carrying the assets. Adjust the profit-and-loss statement to reflect the true expenses of the business. Calculate the owner's adjusted cash flow. Subtract the cost of carrying the assets to get the excess earnings. Decide, based on risk and desirability, the desired rate of return (the cap rate). Divide the excess earnings by the cap rate to get the value of the excess earnings. Add the value of the excess earnings to the value of the assets and subtract the value of any liabilities being assumed by the buyer.

4. Price based on duplication cost (replacement cost method)

Uses: Used to compare the buyer's alternative of starting a business.

Steps: Determine the market value of the assets, and the cost to install them. Estimate the number of years it will take for the new business to reach the level of profitability of the business for sale. (Remember that the existing business may be competition for the new business.) For each of those years, compute the cash requirements, the profits and losses from the business, the lost wages of the owner, and the interest that could have been earned on any investment.

5. Price based on net present value of future earnings

Uses: Used as a method to sell the value of a projected future stream of earnings as a discount. Used mainly with larger, well-documented companies, for which the future is somewhat more predictable.

Figure 13-2. Overview of pricing methods and tests. *(Continued)*

> Steps: Adjust profit-and-loss statement to reflect the true expenses of the business. Calculate the adjusted actual cash flow. Based on supportable plans, project financial statements for five years. Determine cumulative cash flow for the five years and discount it to establish the net present value.
>
> **6. Pricing tests**
>
> **(a) Alternative investment test**
>
> Uses: Used to compare the returns from buying the business with the returns from a safe alternative.
>
> Steps: Adjust the profit-and-loss statement to reflect the true expenses of the business. Calculate the adjusted owner's cash flow. Divide the cash flow by the purchase price to get the return on investment. (If the purchase price is being paid over several years, do a calculation for all the years cumulatively.) Compare this return from the business with the return from safe alternative investments. Compare the salary and benefits the business will provide to the salary and benefits the buyer could earn at a job. Note that risk of capital gain or loss is ignored.
>
> **(b) Testing the purchase for reasonableness**
>
> Uses: Used to test whether the business earns enough in cash flow to support its purchase price. It is a test of affordability.
>
> Steps: Adjust the profit-and-loss statement to reflect the true expenses of the business. Calculate the adjusted owner's cash flow. Deduct repayment of debt and interest. Deduct any required reinvestment. Deduct an amount equal to the reasonable return the buyer would have earned on the down payment (cash) invested in the business. Provide for a reasonable salary for the buyer's work in the business if not already provided in the true expenses. Provide a safety margin.

Figure 13–2. *(Continued)*

A company with a factory full of equipment makes something the market no longer wants, and the cost of retooling is prohibitive. It has $10 million in sales, but it had to cut prices to get the volume and it lost $1 million last year. So far we have a company with lots of assets and $10 million in sales, but the assets are outdated and the cash flow from the sales is negative. There is not much value here. *If, however, the company is your only competitor, its value to you could be very high.*

An example of the reverse situation might be a gas station that has few assets and rather modest sales but earns its owner over $250,000 a year because its prices reflect the fact that it is the only station on the road between two towns. Unfortunately, a new superhighway that will connect the two towns is being built 3 miles east of the present road, after which there will be no traffic for this station.

There are two points to these examples:

1. Relying on just the quantitative value of each element can be misleading.
2. Relying on less than all the elements can be misleading.

Professional appraisers have extensive formal training, but the following material should provide you with some useful knowledge of the concepts of value and price. As a reminder, the case study at the end of the chapter integrates all the ideas.

What the Business Owns

The balance sheet provides a useful indicator of value, but it distorts the real value of the business. The balance sheet generally states assets at historical cost less allowances for depreciation, not at their current fair market value. Replacement values may be higher or lower than the stated values. Table 13–1 demonstrates the limitations of the balance sheet by comparing two companies, A and B. Company A would seem a much stronger and more valuable company until we apply the two tests that are important to the buyer:

Test 1. What are the assets really worth at fair market value? The buyer, lender, or investor is really interested in the market value of the assets. Cash, accounts receivable, inventory, and other current assets are relatively easy to test for market value, but the fixed assets can present a problem.

In our example, Company A rents its facility and has all new equipment, which could be sold to others for about what is shown on the balance sheet. The actual market value of Company A's nearly new fixed assets matches closely the depreciated book value shown on the balance sheet. Company B, on the other hand, has older equipment that has been depreciated, and it owns its own factory. The equipment has been well maintained and is worth more than its depreciated value. More important, Company B's real estate, which is on the books for the original cost of the land plus the depreciated cost of the building, is in a high-value area and is worth $2 million on today's market.

The point to remember is that the balance sheet alone is not enough to determine the real value of the assets. Beware of any advisor who does not fully understand the important fact that net worth shown on the balance sheet of a small company is of little consequence.

Test 2. What do these assets earn for the business? Some assets, such as specialized machinery, may have little market value but might

Table 13–1. Comparison of Company A and Company B

	Company A	Company B
Cash	$ 20,000	$ 15,000
Accounts receivable	85,000	40,000
Inventory	100,000	65,000
Total current assets	$205,000	$120,000
Property, plant, equipment	600,000	750,000
Less depreciation	(100,000)	(500,000)
Net fixed assets	$500,000	$250,000
Total assets	705,000	370,000
Accounts payable	65,000	60,000
Short-term note	50,000	40,000
Total current liabilities	$115,000	$100,000
Long-term debt	290,000	170,000
Total liabilities	$405,000	$270,000
Simple net worth	$300,000	$100,000

produce products that earn high profit. Excess inventory, on the other hand, may technically have market value but may cost a company more in interest costs and spoilage to carry than it will earn when it eventually sells. In our example, let's assume that Company A operates at a substantial loss. This means that even though the assets on the balance sheet are valuable, they are not doing Company A any good and might better be liquidated.

The point here is that for assets to have value to a business and to a buyer, they must earn money, or be salable.

What the Business Earns

Profit and cash performance provide the second key indicator of a company's value and another example of how isolated analysis misleads. The profit on the accounting statement must first be adjusted to reflect the owner's real cash flow. Then the adjusted cash flow can be measured as a return on the investment tied up in the business.

As a buyer, you should know that business owners, particularly those who run small businesses, often treat income and expenses in ways that minimize their total taxes. "Minimize taxes and maximize lifestyle" is a well-known maxim for many small (and not-so-small) business owners. They may overpay themselves or take no salary at all. They may lavish perquisites on themselves and their families, or everyone may work for nothing. They may make substantial reinvestments in the business, but treat them as expenses.

Further adjustments need to be made for extraordinary items, both good and bad. The impact of past events such as strikes and fires as well as any special gains on the sale of assets needs to be disclosed.

Profits must be adjusted in order to show a true picture of the business' performance. The rule to follow when adjusting financial statements is simply to determine the true required cost and adjust accordingly.

Adjusted Owner's Cash Flow. Our definition of *adjusted owner's cash flow* is the cash available to an owner after adjusting expenses to the level actually required for the business, and after allowing an appropriate salary for the owner's effort in the business. This adjusted owner's cash flow includes no allowance for interest* or depreciation; that is, any interest or depreciation is added back as a plus to cash flow. The result yields cash available to the owner (or the buyer) for reinvestment, growth, taxes, debt repayment, or dividends. Here are two examples of income statements that have been adjusted.

The adjusted income statement for Company X, Table 13–2, presents a fairly typical example of a small business in which the owner has taken a larger salary and more benefits than would be truly required if a paid manager were hired. Several other items were higher than the business really required:

- Travel and entertainment were excessive.
- Household utilities were charged to the business, as was personal insurance.
- The automobile was completely unnecessary in this business, so its cost should be removed.
- Half of the legal and accounting expenses were non-business-related.
- Donations can always be deleted, because by definition they are not required expenses.

The happy outcome here is an adjusted cash flow of $82,000 in excess of the stated profit.

At the other extreme is Company Y, shown in Table 13–3. A major adjustment ($36,000) was required because the owner chose improperly to treat the employees as "independent contractors" and did not provide proper withholding and insurance.

---

* The seller's interest is removed as an expense because the buyer will not have that interest expense. The buyer's interest expense will depend on how much the buyer borrows to buy the business.

Table 13-2. Adjusted Income Statement for Company X

	Per Financials	True Required Cost	Adjustment
Sales	$500,000	$500,000	0
Cost of goods sold	200,000	200,000	0
Gross profit	$300,000	$300,000	0
Employee salaries	100,000	100,000	0
Employee benefits	25,000	25,000	0
Owner/manager's salaries	75,000	30,000	+$45,000
Owner/managers benefits	11,000	5,000	+6,000
Travel/entertainment	15,000	5,000	+10,000
Rent	15,000	15,000	0
Utilities and telephone	12,000	10,000	+2,000
Selling expenses	5,000	5,000	0
Insurance	8,000	7,000	+1,000
Automobile	9,000	0+	9,000
Legal/accounting	12,000	6,000	+6,000
Donations	3,000	0+	3,000
Total expenses	$290,000	$208,000	+$82,000
Income per statement	$10,000		
Adjustments	+$82,000		
Cash available after adjustments	$92,000		

Table 13-3. Adjusted Income Statement for Company Y

	Per Statement	True Required Cost	Adjustment
Sales	$750,000	$750,000	0
Cost of goods sold	450,000	450,000	0
Gross profit	$300,000	$300,000	0
Expenses:			
Employee salaries	$150,000	$150,000	0
Employee benefits	0	36,000	-$36,000
Owner/manager's salaries	0	30,000	-30,000
Owner/managers benefits	0	6,000	-6,000
Travel/entertainment	8,000	7,000	+1,000
Rent	12,000	32,000	20,000
Utilities and telephone	12,000	12,000	0
Selling expenses	0	12,000	-12,000
Insurance	7,000	7,000	0
Automobile	0	0	0
Legal/accounting	8,000	8,000	0
Donations	0	0	0
Total expenses	$197,000	$300,000	-$103,000
Income per statement	-$103,000		
Adjustments	-$103,000		
Cash available after adjustments	0		

It often happens that the owner of a small business takes no salary even though he or she may work full time at it. Table 13–3 shows the adjustment required to provide a fair salary and benefits.

In this case the owner also owns the building and charges the business less than fair-market rent.

Some adjustments require judgment. In this case the owner is spending nothing on sales and marketing and an adjustment was made to provide $12,000. The only minor positive adjustment was for slightly excessive travel and entertainment expense. *What initially appeared to be $103,000 in profit is really a breakeven in cash flow.*

Making Adjustments. Adjusting the income statement forces you to learn the important operating facts of the business. For you to know whether the employee salaries are realistic, you will first need to know how many employees are really needed, and then find out what salaries are appropriate for those people. You can't judge the insurance expense if you don't know the proper levels of coverage and costs. The same applies to the cost and use of materials. *If you don't know these key facts, you shouldn't be buying the business.*

Of course you can get help to learn them. Insurance coverage is a good example. Good insurance brokers can audit and evaluate appropriate coverage and costs for you and will probably be willing to do so as an inducement to get your business once you become the owner. To assess the employee situation, you can talk with owners of similar businesses, seek out trade association data, or do your own analysis. Ask the present owner to detail the hours and tasks of all employees and make a judgment about how you would staff the business. You can learn comparable wage and salary rates by talking to employment agencies, including your state employment service.

Examine phone bills. Verify the market rate for rent. Be as certain as you can that your adjusted income statement reflects expenses as realistically as possible.

Sales Figures—A Special Problem. Nothing presents more common or important adjustment problems than the sales figures reported on smaller business income statements. In an effort to avoid taxes, some business owners fail to record sales. The action breaks the law and lowers the value of the business. Nonetheless, it happens, and you need to decide how to deal with it.

One way is simply to give unreported sales no value. Banks and other lenders will do exactly that. Your position might be that if the sales are not on the income statement, they don't exist. Unfortunately, this may cause you to come up with a value that is far below the true worth of the business and one that can't satisfy the owner.

You can try to verify the real sales by examining cash register receipts, deposit slips, or using some other such method. You can observe or work in the business for some time to sample the level of sales. These methods are risky because they can all be manipulated by the seller, someone you already know to be less than honest. They also make you party to knowledge of tax fraud, something you should discuss with your attorney.

The most often used technique to deal with a seller's claim that sales are higher than reported, whether they were just withheld or are the result of some other phenomenon, is to make your purchase offer dependent on certain contingencies. You can make your payout amount more or less depending on what sales actually materialize. Variable and contingent pricing terms are covered later in this chapter.

Note that *one year's figures are not sufficient.* Our examples have shown figures for only one year of business. As a buyer, you should ask to see several years, preferably five, to help provide you the opportunity to spot trends, to identify any nonrecurring expenses or income, and to determine if any single year is exceptionally good or bad.

Also, *some cash needs to be reinvested.* One final note on understanding cash flow has to do with how much cash has to be put back into the business. The cash flow shown in Tables 13–2 and 13–3 is labeled "before interest, depreciation, reinvestment, and taxes." A growing company needing large inventory purchases or plant expansion may require far more cash than is being generated from operations. You must learn whether this cash can be borrowed from outside or whether it will require your further cash investment.

Now that we have an understanding of the cash being generated, we need to look at whether that cash flow is good or bad. Simply put, will this business produce a good return on your investment? Merely calculating the percentage return is not enough. You need to know whether this is a good return in light of the risk you will take.

What Makes the Business Unique

The degree of risk and desirability is the third characteristic of a business that will affect its value. All the intangibles that make the business unique are pluses and minuses to establish the degree of risk.

No universal scale exists, and everyone's risk preference is different. For example, a buyer with a marketing background might consider a business requiring sophisticated engineering to be a high risk. An engineer might say the same thing about a restaurant.

Putting personal risk preference aside, some measures of risk do have general application (see Table 13–4). Worksheet 13 will help you with a risk assessment of the business.

Table 13–4. Risk Assessment

Factor	Low Risk	High Risk
Company history.	Long, profitable history.	New or unprofitable history.
Industry segment.	Stable or growing, highly profitable industry.	Erratic growth or decline, unstable, generally unprofitable industry.
Special skills required for success.	No special skills are required.	Highly specialized or scarce skills are required.
Location (or lease term).	The location is excellent and can continue.	The location is unsuitable and/or requires relocation.
Labor situation.	Labor is available and labor relations are good.	Labor is scarce and/or labor relations are poor.
Management situation.	The remaining management team is fully qualified and competent.	Management is not competent to run the business, or is not remaining.
Return *of* investment.	The buyer would be able to liquidate his or her investment for about what was paid.	The investment could be easily depleted or is nonliquid.
Return *on* investment.	Market, economic, and historical factors indicate that returns will continue.	There are no prospects for return without changes in the company, the market, or the economy.
Outside dependency.	Most of the requirements for success are within the company's control.	Success depends on factors such as interest rates, styles and fashions, or foreign sources that are outside the company's control.
Company reputation.	Well recognized and highly respected.	Unknown or poorly regarded.
Products or services.	High value, competitive, and responsive to market needs.	Poor quality and/or outdated for the market.
Franchises, licenses required.	No special licenses, franchises, or bonds are required.	The business requires hard-to-obtain licenses, bonds, or franchises.
Competition.	Competition is limited.	Competition is intense and/or increasing.
Technology.	The business is not particularly vulnerable to technological changes.	A change in technology could have a major negative impact.

Pricing the Business

This is a good place to stop and recap where we are. We have examined the three components that affect the value of a company:

What the business owns—the balance sheet
What the business earns—profit and cash performance
What makes the business unique—the degree of risk and desirability

The next step is to convert the value produced by these three components into price.

The technique to convert the value of the assets to a price is simple addition. Converting the value of what the business earns, the cash flow, is a bit more complicated. It uses a technique called *capitalization*, which tells how much we should pay for a stream of cash flow. Converting the value of risk and desirability to a price will unavoidably require subjective judgment.

After we understand the basics of converting value to price, we will explore the five different pricing methods (see Figure 13–2):

1. *Price based on assets*, used when assets are the main value in the company
2. *Price based on cash flow*, used when there are few assets but strong cash flow
3. *Price based on an integrated method*, where both assets and cash flow are substantial
4. *Price based on duplication cost*, where the alternative of starting a business is developed
5. *Price based on the value of future earnings*, used where the probability of such earnings is high, usually for larger companies

Pricing the Assets

The asset value on the balance sheet is the least controversial value to establish and convert to a price. Most assets can be counted, appraised, or evaluated. As a starting point, price can equal the fair market value of the assets. You are going to buy things that you will own and that you can resell.

In adjusting the balance sheet, reexamine the reserves and allowances. Be on the lookout for assets that may truly be near depletion. Many owners of long-established businesses overlook assets that have been expensed but that still have market value. Tools, dies, and spare parts are examples.

In valuing the business, pay close attention to notes, both payable and receivable. If these are borrowings between the owner and the company, they may best be removed from your transaction.

Some assets are not on the balance sheet and are not as easy to value. One unusual asset is a lease that is substantially under market rate. The value can be significant. A five-year lease on 10,000 square feet at $5 per square foot per year when the market rate is $7.50 is worth $2.50 × 10,000 square feet × 5 years, or $125,000. However, unless you plan to move the business and rent out this 10,000 square feet for the profit, you should not value the lease. The positive benefit is already reflected in the profit/cash flow, which you are going to price next.

Be mindful that a short lease is an exposure. What will the new terms be?

Other intangibles might be the company name, the customer or client list, a patent, special computer systems, or the like. Once again, the way professionals tend to value these intangibles is by assuming that they are reflected in the profit/cash flow of the business. If these intangible assets really have any value, they will have earned a premium profit return and you can reflect that value when you put a price on the profit/cash flow.

However, sometimes sellers insist that these intangibles be assigned a price. You should ask to know why any price should be attached to these intangibles if the business is not earning a premium because of them. What value is the great location or well-known name if the business isn't making any money? The concept is a tough one, but a fair one.

Pricing the Cash Flow

Putting a price on the profit/cash flow is more art than science. In theory, we are going to *capitalize the cash flow*. This means that we will divide the cash flow figure by the percentage of return on investment we think we should earn and so get the price we would pay.

If the cash flow is $100,000 and you want a 25 percent pre-tax return, divide $100,000 by 0.25 and see that you would invest $400,000 for that stream of cash flow.

The *capitalization rate* serves the same function as the rate of return. The task is to select the proper *capitalization percent (cap rate)*. That selection depends very much on the degree of risk and the prevailing interest rates.

Risk determines the capitalization rate. Assume that two businesses both have cash flows of $100,000. One is a low-risk business on which a buyer would be satisfied to earn a 20 percent return, whereas the other is a higher-risk business on which a buyer would want a 30 percent return. A buyer would be willing to pay $500,000 ($100,000 divided by 0.20) for the low-risk cash flow but only $333,333 ($100,000 divided by 0.30) for the cash flow with the higher risk.

The higher the risk, the higher is the cap rate and therefore the lower is the investment we would make. Here are some extreme examples so that you can get the idea.

- A 15-year-old newspaper delivery service has had a solid history of profit/cash flow and earns $100,000.
- A very large restaurant featuring the owner-chef's French menu has produced $150,000 in profit/cash flow in each of its three years of operation.

- A specialized design engineering company builds turntables for re-volving restaurants and earned $200,000 in cash flow in its first year.

Compare your cap rate with the market rate. Before we try to de-velop a cap rate for these companies, we should set a benchmark that will give us a practical frame of reference. We can use a top-grade bond: It has low risk, it is very liquid, it requires little or no time to manage, and at this writing, it earns 8 percent.

Any business does involve risk and does take time to manage, so a buyer must demand a higher return (cap rate) on that higher-risk invest-ment.

It may seem to you that the returns used as examples in this chapter are high, even adjusting for risk. The reason is liquidity. As a business buyer you will learn that converting the investment in a business to cash is not an easy or quick process. To compensate for this lack of liquidity, buyers demand a higher rate of return, usually reflected as a lower pur-chase price.

Lack of liquidity has another effect on price and value. You cannot com-pare private companies with public ones, even those in the same field. Attempting to use published price/earnings as a value method is a mistake. The price/earnings ratio of a public company is affected by its liquidity. The stock of a public company can be traded or sold in minutes. People will pay less if they can't readily convert their investment to cash, as is the case with a small private firm.

Investment Growth or Decline. Our frame of reference needs one other perspective, and that is the potential for increase or decrease in the value of our investment. Our top-grade bond is not going to go up or down much except to adjust for yield. The investment in a business could multi-ply manyfold or be wiped out completely.

Setting Cap Rates. Now let's set some cap rates on our examples. The newspaper delivery business has very low risk. It has been around for years, no special skills are needed, and no competition is likely. About the only risk is that the newspaper will find another firm to deliver its papers. There won't be much chance of loss or growth on our investment. Try 20 percent ($100,000 divided by 0.20 equals $500,000).

The restaurant has one big risk factor, which is the chef-owner. If he leaves when we buy the business, we will have to replace him. This is a special skill. The three-year age of the business is neither good nor bad. It does not guarantee a following, but the equipment is new enough to be sold for a good price. If you are a chef, use 30 percent; if not, use 35 percent ($150,000 divided by 0.30 equals $500,000, or $150,000 divided by 0.35 equals $429,000).

The design engineering company is a very high-risk situation. It is new, its market is very narrow and hard to influence, and the need for special skills and relationships is high. Its assets, including its round manufacturing building, have little application to anything else. A 40 percent cap rate is not unreasonable ($200,000 divided by 0.40 equals $500,000). The examples are summarized in Table 13–5.

These examples, though realistic, were contrived to make the point that degree of risk can have an impact on the cap rate sufficient to cause three businesses with widely different cash flows to be theoretically priced the same. Worksheet 13 will help you price your cash flow.

Now we have figured out how to price assets and cash flow. If a company had only one or the other, coming up with a total price would be easy.

Table 13–5. Examples of
Capitalization Rates

Newspaper Delivery Service

Risk	Low
Potential for growth or decline	Low
Capitalization rate	20%

$$\frac{\text{Cash flow} = \$100,000}{\text{Cap rate} = 0.20} \qquad \text{Price} = \$500,000$$

Restaurant

Risk	Medium
Potential for growth or decline	Medium
Capitalization rate	30%

$$\frac{\text{Cash flow} = \$150,000}{\text{Cap rate} = 0.30} \qquad \text{Price} = \$500,000$$

Specialized Engineering Company

Risk	High
Potential for growth or decline	High
Capitalization rate	40%

$$\frac{\text{Cash flow} = \$200,000}{\text{Cap rate} = 0.40} \qquad \text{Price} = \$500,000$$

Three businesses with widely varying cash flows
are theoretically priced the same when adjusted
for risk by their capitalization rates.

In fact, in a service company, such as one that provides night guards, there may be no assets to speak of and the whole price will be based on the value of the cash flow using the capitalization rate idea. Because many companies do have both assets and cash flow, we need a way to price them together.

Integrated Pricing

One method that values assets and cash flow in an integrated way is called the *excess earnings method*. It assigns a portion of the owner's cash flow to cover the cost of carrying the assets. For example, if the assets are valued at $400,000 and it costs 10 percent to borrow money, the first $40,000 of cash flow is viewed as satisfying the return on the investment in assets. Any cash flow over that is considered "excess." This excess is then capitalized using the same concept of applying a risk-determined cap rate. The capitalized figure is added to the value of the assets to get the total price. Here is a sample calculation.

Sample Calculation		
Asset value		$ 400,000
Prevailing interest rate		×10%
Cost of carrying assets		$ 40,000
Owner's cash flow	$50,000	
Less cost of carrying assets	−40,000	
Excess earnings	$10,000	
Excess earnings	$10,000	
Divided by the cap rate	.333	
Equals value of excess earnings		$ 30,000
Plus value of assets		400,000
Total value of business		$430,000

In cases in which the earnings are negative or not enough to carry the cost of the assets, the business is considered to be worth less than even the value of the assets.

Sample Calculation		
Asset value		$400,000
Interest rate		×10%
Cost of carrying assets		$ 40,000
Owner's cash flow	$ 25,000	
Less cost of carrying assets	40,000	
Excess earnings (negative)	$(15,000)	
Negative excess earnings		
Cannot be capitalized		
Value of excess earnings		$(15,000)
Plus value of assets		400,000
Total value of business		$385,000

Duplication Cost Pricing

Another concept to apply to the value and price of a business is duplication cost. The idea is to calculate what it would cost to duplicate the *present* business. The part of the calculation relating to assets and costs is fairly easy. You can price assets in similar condition and can assume some level of working capital. You can get a good idea of prices for real estate and the costs for labor, insurance utilities, and so forth.

The problem arises when trying to calculate how long it will take for you to get any start-up company up to the level of operations and profitability of your target company. Some companies may be easy to duplicate or even surpass. New businesses, poorly run or badly located businesses, and businesses requiring little know-how are examples. If a company is efficient, well established, and profitable, it could take years of operation to achieve a similar position. During these years you could suffer low earnings or even losses. And while you might have avoided a high front-end cash investment by duplicating the business, you may end up putting as much or more cash into the business.

Duplication cost relates to the concept of the "learning curve" and its impact on efficiency. The assumption is that experience has a value, and that there is a cost to obtaining it. Before coming to any conclusion about the price of a business, you should consider what it would take to duplicate it. Worksheet 13 can help.

Pricing the Value of Future Earnings

Another pricing technique is called the *net present value* (NPV) method, and involves five steps:

1. Adjust the company's statements to show true present profit.
2. Develop growth plans (plans must be supportable by evidence).
3. Project growth plans for five years.
4. Calculate profit, investments, and returns for the five years.
5. Discount the figures to the present using a discount rate that reflects the degree of risk and projected inflation. Typically this rate is 50 percent above the prime interest rate. Table 13–6 shows a sample calculation.

NPV is used when a company's future is credible. Large, well-capitalized, established businessses can sometimes offer a degree of credibility. Nonetheless, the technique has two weaknesses:

1. The projections are always speculative.
2. Picking the discount rate is subjective.

This method is the most controversial of all methods for small, closely held businesses, because of its weaknesses. Proponents argue that buyers should be willing to pay for more than just one year's earnings. They assert that paying a discounted net present value of five years' earnings is a fair

Table 13–6. Net Present Value (NPV) Calculation

Present Value of a Future $1 Discount Rate, %:

Year	12	13	14	15	16
1	0.893	0.865	0.877	0.870	0.862
2	0.797	0.783	0.769	0.756	0.743
3	0.712	0.693	0.675	0.658	0.641
4	0.636	0.613	0.592	0.572	0.552
5	0.567	0.543	0.519	0.497	0.476

Pricing Calculation:

Year	Projected Earnings	×	Discounted @ 15%	NPV
1	$100,000		0.870	$ 87,000
2	110,000		0.756	83,160
3	125,000		0.658	82,250
4	140,000		0.572	80,080
5	155,000		0.497	77,035
Total	$630,000			$409,525

price because it reflects payment for the company's momentum, its ongoing value.

Opponents of the NPV method say that present owners can make plans and projections showing any growth and profitability they choose, simply by making assumptions that support the growth. Opponents of NPV pricing do not believe in paying for earnings that are not yet earned.

Other Pricing Concepts

You should be aware of some other concepts that relate to value and price.

Potential and Projections. The first concept has to do with "potential." A business may have few assets and little cash flow, but through either the buyer's special skills, some unexploited attribute of the business, or some change in the business' environment, projected future growth is a high probability.

There are two ways to deal with potential. One is to use the concept of variable pricing presented later. You can simply agree to pay a higher price if the seller's growth projection does, in fact, occur. The opposite view of potential gives it no value or price to the seller. After all, it is you, the buyer, who will do the work, take the risk, make the (possibly substantial) investment, and manage the realization of any potential.

The latter point of view is more common, but there are plenty of cases in which some event—such as the construction of a new highway or the demise of a major competitor—just about ensures growth with little cost or effort. Either way, buyers of smaller companies should normally be reluctant to pay for potential before it is realized.

Two Special Types of Potential. Occasionally the source of potential value can be identified. For example, if a company has just made an investment in a machine that is certain to produce earnings or savings, there can be an *expected value*.

Another special kind of potential is *conditional value*. This refers to the value that will result if some future act occurs. An example is a large pending but not yet awarded contract. Conditional value can be negative: Buyers may point out that the company could lose a large customer, too.

Supply and Demand. This very basic aspect of pricing is often overlooked when pricing a business. Supply and demand is at work in this environment just as it is elsewhere. It has direct effects on businesses of the same and similar types. Two restaurants, if similar enough to both be considered by a buyer, will compete for sale, and price will be a point of competition.

Supply and demand has indirect effects, too. Right now manufacturing and distribution businesses are in high demand. Business brokers attribute the demand to the surge in corporate layoffs and cutbacks. Many of these executives equate "business" with "manufacturing" or "distribution." Premiums will be paid for these businesses as long as demand is strong. At the other extreme are video rental stores, which are in overabundant supply and which often sell at a discount.

Special Factors of Value. Another concept to consider involves special factors that make the business worth a premium. A large backlog of business or an ongoing contract are two examples. Synergy, the elimination of a competitor, obtaining some special license, or even emotional factors may make the business worth a higher price to some buyers.

Some sellers feel that they should ask for money for "the going business" or "the goodwill." What those sellers mean is that there should be some price paid for all those intangibles such as the business name and reputation, the customer list, the business systems and controls, and all the other valuable elements that have been assembled over the years.

Buyers are willing to pay for these assets and in fact are paying for them if they offer more than the value of the tangible assets. As mentioned earlier, if all these intangible assets really do have any value, they have been earning income for the business. Whether you, as the buyer, capitalized the cash flow or used a pricing method that integrates the value of assets and the value of earnings, you have indeed given value for the intangibles. If you wish, you can call this premium over tangible asset value *goodwill** or *the key* or the *going-business value.*

Buyers Pricing Tests. You should perform several calculations and tests regarding the price of the business. Some are tests used in standard financial analysis. You and your advisors have access to standard industry ratios for almost any business. The ratios include balance sheet ratios (current ratio, assets to sales, etc.) and income statement ratios (expense ratios to sales, margins, etc.). In Chapter 12, we mentioned resources to help with these analyses.

In the case of smaller companies, you should test first against other alternatives. Decide how the price, returns, and effort required in your target business measure up to other investments of your money and your time.

The second test is sometimes called the "justification of purchase test." It states that a business should be able to provide:

---

*In fact, the generally accepted accounting definition—and the IRS definition—for "goodwill" is simply the excess over asset value.

- Sufficient cash to repay the loan to the seller
- Sufficient cash to support the operations of the business
- A reasonable return on the buyer's down payment
- A fair salary for the owner's work in the business.

The tests on larger companies are more concerned with futurity of the investment. With larger companies the future outcomes are more likely and predictable.

One test involves the idea of *cost savings value*, mentioned earlier. When the buyer is another company, savings from economies of scale or reduced competition may allow the buyer to justify a higher price than otherwise.

Decisions regarding the price of larger companies are heavily weighted by projections of future earnings and values, using the NPV method of pricing.

Now that we have spent time on methods of arriving at a price, we will turn to the idea of affordability.

What the Buyer (You) Can Afford

Some sellers feel that the buyer's ability to pay for the business is not their concern. They believe that if a buyer can't afford the business, then he or she isn't a real buyer.

The Seller Affects Affordability

The fact is, the seller and the value of the business affect the affordability to a buyer in several ways. If the business has assets of value, you as the buyer can borrow money against them. If the seller will set a lower guaranteed price and allow for higher payment on some contingency basis, the effect will be to make the business more affordable. The most important step the seller can take to make the business more affordable is to extend favorable terms of sale.

Available Debt Affects Affordability

A company that has marketable assets or other collateral and is generating positive cash flow has debt availability because it has borrowing capacity. This makes the company more affordable, though the price will already have reflected both the value of the assets and the cash flow.

If the company lacks sufficient collateral to handle debt, the buyer must carry the debt personally. In this situation, most often the buyer will borrow from the seller.

Terms of Sale

Terms of sale are:

- The cash down payment
- The length of time for paying the balance
- The interest rate
- The form of payments—interest only, fully amortizing, partially amortizing with a balloon payment

No stronger statement about the impact of terms can be made than this: "You may set the price if I may set the terms." Payment terms with no cash down, no security, minimum interest, and terms that stretch for decades would make almost any price acceptable.

What you can afford to pay and what you will be willing to pay depend much more on the actual cash required than on the price. The terms of sale can range from all cash at closing to no cash down with payment over several years. All-cash terms should bring about the lowest price but will of course result in the highest cash payout at closing. In theory, any all-cash price can be converted to a price involving payment terms over time by using standard payment tables for any specified interest rate.

Terms affect not only affordability but buyers' perceptions of how financially attractive a deal is.

Terms Affect Perceived Return on Investment. People often measure the return on their investment in cash terms. Here is an example of the impact of financing on such a buyer's calculations. In each case, the price of the business is $500,000 and cash flow is $100,000.

All cash at closing

Cash price of business	$500,000
Cash return	$100,000

$$\frac{\$100,000}{\$500,000} = 20\% \text{ return on investment}$$

With 2/3 financing, 10 years, 10%

1/3 cash down payment		$166,666
Cash return	$100,000	
− Loan repayment	−44,067	
Net cash return		$ 55,933

$$\frac{\$ 55,933}{\$166,666} = 30\% \text{ return on investment}$$

Table 13-7. Monthly Payments to
Repay $100,000

Years	7.5%	10%	15%
1	8676	8792	9026
5	2004	2125	2379
10	1188	1322	1613
15	928	1075	1400
20	806	965	1316
25	739	908	1280

You need to examine both concepts to see which one suits you better.

Constructing Terms of Sale. Calculating the effect of terms on the selling price involves four variables: the cash down payment, the length of time for repayment, the interest rate, and whether the payments are fully amortizing or involve a large (balloon) payment at the end of the term.

If you work with loan tables and do a few calculations, you will develop a general feel for the effect of certain changes in these variables. Table 13–7 gives an idea of the effect of various payments. The table shows why hard bargaining for a point or two of interest or for 20-year versus 18-year terms may earn less than the effort is worth.

In practice, sellers are willing to accept a lower real price for an all-cash transaction. How much lower will depend on the seller's personal situation and perhaps on his or her confidence in the success of the business after the sale. The sellers of small businesses usually do offer to finance part of the purchase, as we will see.

A major consideration about terms from your standpoint is security. The seller wants to sell the business *and wants to get paid for it.* Structuring the transaction to provide security is vital.

Using the Value of the Business to Help Affordability

The assets and liabilities from the balance sheet can be used to help the sale. Most sales of small businesses are sales of assets, not sales of stock. The buyer pays for the assets and the seller discharges the liabilities. But if you, the buyer, agree to take on and discharge the liabilities, you pay only for the difference between the assets and liabilities, thus requiring less cash to be paid out to the seller. Of course these liabilities do have to be paid at some time, and the creditors often have to agree to the arrangement.

Another way you can use the balance sheet is to arrange, coincidental with the purchase, to borrow against the assets of the business, provided you have not pledged them as security to the seller. As a frame of reference, banks and others will usually lend on a percentage of value:

Machinery and equipment	50%
Inventory	50%
Accounts receivable	50–75%

You may be able to borrow against an order backlog or a special contract. Selling assets and then renting or leasing them back can provide a source of cash. The obvious example is real estate, but machinery, office equipment, and even telephone systems can be leased. If suppliers will provide inventory on consignment and allow you to pay for the inventory as you use it and reorder, you can reduce your cash requirement. If there is a patent that makes up a substantial part of the price, you could let the seller keep the patent and instead set up a license to use it and pay a royalty.

Borrowing against assets as part of the purchase transaction can be coupled with the outright sale of some assets. Unused real estate or an unwanted line of business might be sold to generate cash.

While these ideas on balance sheet financing are valid, they are not appropriate in every situation. The returns projected and the basic soundness of your business financing strategy should govern any actions.

Variable or Contingent Pricing

Variable pricing is a way to structure terms, not a way to set a price. Using this arrangement, the price established for the business varies in relation to some future event.

The most common variable factor is sales volume. Variable pricing tied to sales can be used when present sales are below historical patterns and the seller claims some unusual event or now-solved problem was responsible. You can agree to some added payout schedule if sales materialize at certain levels. Lower payouts for lower sales can be negotiated as well.

Price can be tied to other variable factors, such as the number of employees who remain with the company for some time (important to real estate firms), or the number of accounts that continue with the company (important to advertising agencies).

Variable pricing can be a powerful way to add to the real price but keep your front-end cash requirements down. Sometimes it is the only method that provides fairness to both parties. As you see, the terms of sale can have a substantial impact on how much money (cash) you will need, and therefore on the affordability of the business.

Summary

Much time and money can be spent on valuing and pricing businesses. Because each business is unique, all methods of pricing are somewhat subjective. Your pricing calculations, assumptions, and logic are very valuable for three reasons:

1. You can approximate the price within a reasonable range.
2. You need a rational basis to discuss value and price with the seller. You can then avoid outrageous and ill-conceived pricing.
3. You need a rational basis to discuss and argue value and price with the buyer. You can then avoid ridiculous and insulting offers.

What a business owns, what a business earns, and what makes a business unique can be combined in a rational way to arrive at a price. Even the subjective nature of risk and uniqueness can be treated with some degree of rationality.

If you thought that determining what you can afford was a simple exercise of computing your net worth, you now know it isn't. The principles, examples, and references were presented to give you a broad look at concepts of value, price, and raising money. The ultimate test of what you can afford is a test for reasonableness, which the Institute of Business Appraisers in its publication MO-9 calls the "justification of purchase test." After investing the money you have and what you borrow, the business should generate enough cash to cover its operations, service the debt you incur, provide a return on your down payment, and afford you a fair salary for your time. The answer to the test is so dependent on the specific company being considered and on the terms you negotiate that you need to take the next big step—find a business you want and try to buy it.

Case Study: The Hillcrest Corporation

This case study prices the Hillcrest Corporation using five different pricing methods:

1. Price based on assets
2. Price based on cash flow
3. Price based on the integrated method
4. Price based on duplication cost
5. Price based on net present value of future earnings

These two most common pricing tests will also be applied:

1. The alternative investment test
2. The reasonableness of purchase test

Part One: Background

The Hillcrest Corporation is a 10-year-old manufacturer of fishing rods and other tackle for saltwater fishing. The operations of the company are sound, and growth in sales and profit have been steady. The industry has been experiencing growth for many years, and prospects look good.

The owner has trained his 15 employees well. Although he is still the key manager of the company, he has provided for a good manager as his replacement. The owner has taken only a token salary, but he and his family have taken perks and made some discretionary charges to the business. Most of these can be identified.

The company's machinery and equipment are standard metal- and woodworking devices. They are nearly fully depreciated, but they have a ready market value. Competitors, particularly the Japanese, are beginning to use high-tech equipment and exotic materials.

Distribution is made through wholesalers. Competition is strong but not predatory. The business operates one shift, five or six days per week, depending on demand, which is somewhat seasonal.

The real estate, a modern, 20,000-square-foot factory with a sales office, is owned by the business owner personally. He has not been charging the business any rent. The real estate is not to be included in the sale of the business. Two luxury cars are leased by the company for the use of the owner and his wife.

Part Two: Financial Statements and Adjustments

A. Hillcrest Corporation Balance Sheet as of Dec. 31, 19____

	Per Statement	Adjusted
ASSETS		
Current assets:		
Cash	$ 50,000	$ 50,000
Accounts receivable	250,000	250,000
Notes receivable	20,000	20,000[a]
Inventories	75,000	80,000[b]
Prepaid expenses	10,000	10,000
Other		
Total current assets	$ 405,000	$ 390,000
Fixed assets:		
Furniture/machinery/equipment	1,960,000	
Less accumulated depreciation	(1,560,000)	
Total fixed assets	$ 400,000	$1,110,000[c]
TOTAL ASSETS	$ 805,000	$1,500,000
LIABILITIES		
Current liabilities:		
Accounts payable	80,000	80,000
Wages payable	32,000	32,000
Taxes payable	49,000	49,000
Interest payable	1,000	1,000
Notes/leases current portion	38,000	38,000
Other		
Total current liabilities	$ 200,000	$ 200,000
Long-term liabilities:		
Notes/leases	$ 190,000	$ 190,000
Mortgages		
TOTAL LIABILITIES	$ 390,000	$ 390,000
Owners' equity		
Capital stock	$ 1,000	$ 1,000
Retained earnings	414,000	1,109,000
Total Owner's Equity	$ 415,000	$1,110,000
TOTAL OWNER'S EQUITY & LIABILITIES	$ 805,000	$1,500,000

[a]The Note receivable is a loan to the present owner and can just be removed.
[b]Inventory was kept LIFO, and the older material has a higher than book value.
[c]This is the real market value of the highly salable standard equipment and machinery.

B. Hillcrest Corporation Income (P&L) Statement for the Period Jan. 1, 19___ to Dec. 31, 19___

	Per Statement	Adjusted
Sales:	$2,000,000	$2,000,000
Less cost of sales (45%)	900,000	900,000
Gross profit (55%)	$1,110,000	$1,100,000
Expenses:		
Owner's salary	$ 10,000	$ 45,000[a]
Owner's benefits	2,000	12,000
Employee salaries (15)	345,000	345,000
Employee benefits	84,000	84,000
Rent	0	120,000[b]
Utilities	20,000	20,000
Travel/entertainment	23,000	10,000[c]
Selling expenses	32,000	32,000
Depreciation	10,000	10,000
Insurance	12,000	7,000
Interest	10,000	10,000[d]
Auto expense	16,000	0[e]
Legal and accounting	10,000	5,000[f]
Other	12,000	0[g]
Total expenses	$ 586,000	$ 700,000
Pretax proft:	$ 514,000	$ 400,000

[a]Salary and benefits are adjusted to show a fair salary to a full-time owner.
[b]Rent is adjusted upward to show a reasonable rate of $6.00 per square foot × 20,000 square feet.
[c]Excessive travel and entertainment are adjusted down to a reasonable level.
[d]Home and other personal insurance has been charged to the business; amount is adjusted down.
[e]No cars are necessary to Hillcrest Corporation; they are eliminated.
[f]Personal legal and accounting services are charged to the business and are adjusted out.
[g]"Other" represents donations to the owner's favorite causes. They are not required and are eliminated.

C. Hillcrest Corporation Adjusted Owner's Cash Flow for the Period Jan. 1, 19___ to Dec. 31, 19___

Adjusted profit	$400,000
Interest paid on loans	10,000
Depreciation	10,000
Further adjustments to salaries	0
Other adjustments	0
Adjusted owner's cash flow	$420,000

D. Hillcrest Corporation Risk Assessment Worksheet

Risk Factor	Rated 1 to 6 (6 is high risk)
Company history	5
Industry segment	3
Special skills required	3
Location/lease terms	3
Special relationships required	3
Labor situation	4
Management situation	4
Return *of* investment	2
Return *on* investment	3
Outside dependency	3
Company reputation	3
Products or services	2
Licenses, insurance required	3
Competition	2
Technology	2
Total	45

Divided by 15 = average, which is the desirability
multiplier, or 3. Using a 1-to-6 scale, this makes
Hillcrest a company of average risk.

Part Three: Pricing Calculations

1. Price based on assets

Estimated market value of assets from adjusted balance sheet	$1,500,000
Less liabilities being assumed	0
Price based on assets	$1,500,000

2. Price based on cash flow

Owner's cash flow from adjusted financial statements	$ 420,000
Capitalization rate (cap rate) based on desired return on investment. (This is a business of average risk, and we have chosen an average rate of return.)	30%

   Price based on cash flow:

   $$\frac{\$420,000}{.30} = \qquad \$1,400,000$$

3. Price based on the integrated method

Market value of assets	$1,500,000
Prevailing borrowing rate = 12%	×.12
Cost of carrying assets	$ 180,000

Adjusted owner's cash flow	$420,000
Less: Cost of carrying assets	−180,000
= Excess earnings	$240,000
Excess earnings	240,000
Divided by CAP rate of 30%	.30

Value of excess earnings	$ 800,000
Plus: Market value of assets	+1,500,000
Price based on integrated method	$ 2,300,000

4. Price based on duplication costs

It is assumed that it will take five years to reach the present level of cash flow of Hillcrest Corporation.

The assets will be purchased at market value	$1,500,000

The losses during the five years will accumulate as follows:

Year	Cash Flow from the Business	Lost Salary from Employment	Total
1	−$600,000	−$50,000 =	$ 650,000
2	−$400,000	−50,000 =	450,000
3	+$100,000	−50,000 =	+50,000
4	+$200,000	0	+200,000
5	+$400,000	0	+400,000
Total losses			$ 450,000
Approximate duplication cost			$1,950,000

The duplication cost can only be approximate because of the uncertainty of the projected time and losses to grow the new business. Mathematical adjustments for present value are ignored.

5. Price based on net present value (NPV) of future earnings.

Hillcrest Corporation has prepared a five-year plan that, based on available industry statistics, calls for the company to:

• Enter the market for freshwater fishing equipment
• Add fishing reels to the product line
• Develop a catalog selling division

Investment would be modest, and the factory still has capacity on the second and third shifts.

Growth in adjusted profits is projected at a rate of 20% per year.

Present	Year 1	Year 2	Year 3	Year 4	Year 5	Total Actual Cash Flow
$400,000	$480,000	$576,000	$691,000	$829,000	$995,000	$3,571,000

Discount rate is 15% (50% above prime rate), so the discount factors from Table 13–7 are:

	$480,000	$576,000	$691,000	$829,000	$995,000
	×.870	×.756	×.658	×.572	×.497
NPV is	$418,000	$435,000	$455,000	$474,000	$495,000

Price based on discounted net present value is	$2,277,000

Investment Tests

6. Alternative investment test

We determine that the buyer could invest his or her money at 10% and could earn about $50,000 in a job. Hillcrest Corporation provides an adjusted owner's cash flow of $420,000, which includes a salary of $45,000. This is what the buyer could earn in his or her other investments at the various prices we have developed.

Price based on assets	$1,500,000		
Invested at 10%=		$150,000	
Plus salary from job =		50,000	
Total from the alternative			$200,000
Price based on cash flow	$1,400,000		
Invested at 10%=		$140,000	
Plus salary from job =		50,000	
Total from the alternative			$190,000
Price based on integrated method	$2,300,000		
Invested at 10%=		$230,000	
Plus salary from job =		50,000	
Total from the alternative			$280,000
Price based on NPV	$2,277,000		
Invested at 10%=		$227,700	
Salary from job =		50,000	
Total			$277,700

The tests show that at every price we have developed, Hillcrest Corporation is a better investment than the alternatives. Of course, it should be better to compensate for the risk, effort, and lack of liquidity that the alternatives do not have. At the highest price we have developed, Hillcrest Corporation provides a return of 18.4%.

$$\frac{\$420,000 \text{ cash flow}}{\$2,277,000 \text{ highest price}} = 18.4\% \text{ return}$$

7. Reasonableness of purchase test

We will assume that the highest price we developed is being paid all in cash. $2,277,000

Can the adjusted cash flow of	$420,000
1. Support itself	
(Depreciation is covered.)	—
2. Provide a salary?	
(A fair salary is already provided in the expenses.)	—
3. Pay the purchase debt?	
(There is no purchase debt.)	—
4. Cover the equivalent of the lost interest on	
the cash payment? ($2,227,000 × 10%.)	$222,700 = YES

Even at its highest price, Hillcrest Corporation passes the test for reasonableness.

Worksheet 13
Pricing the Business

13A. WHAT THE BUSINESS OWNS (PRICING THE ASSETS)

Individual asset or liability value adjustments:

Asset or Liability Name	Reason for Adjustment	Value per Statement	Amount of Adjustment	Estimated Market Value
(+or−)				
_____	_____	$ _____	$ _____	$ _____
_____	_____	_____	_____	_____
_____	_____	_____	_____	_____
_____	_____	_____	_____	_____
_____	_____	_____	_____	_____
_____	_____	_____	_____	_____
_____	_____	_____	_____	_____
_____	_____	_____	_____	_____
_____	_____	_____	_____	_____
_____	_____	_____	_____	_____
_____	_____	_____	_____	_____
_____	_____	_____	_____	_____

Adjustments Applied to Balance Sheet

Worksheet 13 *(Continued)*

BALANCE SHEET AS OF _____

Assets	Per Statement	Adjustments	Market Value
Current Assets:			
Cash	$ _____	$ _____	$ _____
Accounts receivable	_____	_____	_____
Notes receivable	_____	_____	_____
Inventory	_____	_____	_____
Prepaid expenses	_____	_____	_____
Other	_____	_____	_____
Total current assets	$ _____	$ _____	$ _____
Fixed assets:			
Furniture, fixtures, machinery, and equipment *net* of depreciation	$ _____	$ _____	$ _____
Land and buildings *net* of depreciation	$ _____	$ _____	$ _____
Other assets _____	$ _____	$ _____	$ _____
Total fixed assets	$ _____	$ _____	$ _____
Total assets	$ _____	$ _____	$ _____

LIABILITIES AND OWNER'S EQUITY

Estimated	Per Statement	Adjustments	Market Value
Current liabilities:			
Accounts payable	$ _____	$ _____	$ _____
Wages payable	_____	_____	_____
Taxes payable	_____	_____	_____
Interest payable	_____	_____	_____
Notes/leases (current portion)	_____	_____	_____
Services or products owed to customers	_____	_____	_____
Other liabilities	_____	_____	_____
Total current liabilities	$ _____	$ _____	$ _____
Long-term liabilities:			
Notes	$ _____	$ _____	$ _____
Mortgages	_____	_____	_____
Other	_____	_____	_____
Total long-term liabilities	$ _____	$ _____	$ _____
Owner's equity:			
Capital stock	$ _____	$ _____	$ _____
Retained earnings	_____	_____	_____
Total owner's equity	$ _____	$ _____	$ _____
Total liabilites and owner's equity	$ _____	$ _____	$ _____

SUMMARY OF VALUE:

Assets being purchased (market value) $ _____

Less: Liabilities being assumed (market value)   _____

Reasonable asset price $ _____

(Continued)

Worksheet 13 *(Continued)*

13B. WHAT THE BUSINESS EARNS (PRICING THE CASH FLOW)

INCOME (PROFIT AND LOSS) STATEMENT FOR THE PERIOD ____ TO ____

	Per Statement	True Required Cost	Adjustment
Sales	$ _____	$ _____	
Cost of Sales	$ _____	$ _____	
Gross Profit	$ _____	$ _____	
Expenses:			
Owner's salary	$ _____	$ _____	$ _____
Owner's benefits	_____	_____	_____
Employee salaries (number of people ____)	_____	_____	_____
Employee benefits	_____	_____	_____
Rent	_____	_____	_____
Utilities	_____	_____	_____
Travel/entertainment	_____	_____	_____
Selling expenses	_____	_____	_____
Depreciation	_____	_____	_____
Insurance	_____	_____	_____
Interest	_____	_____	_____
Automobile	_____	_____	_____
Legal and accounting	_____	_____	_____
Other _____	_____	_____	_____
Total expenses	$ _____	$ _____	$ _____
Pre-tax profit	$ _____	$ _____	$ _____

OWNER'S CASH FLOW CALCULATION

Profit shown on financial statement above	$ _____
Interest paid on loans	_____
Depreciation	_____
Salaries/wages paid to persons not required in business	_____
Change in rent due to new owner (+ or −)	_____
Expense of previous nonrecurring items (e.g., computers, etc.)	_____
Other adjustments (+ or −)	
_____	$ _____
	_____

Adjusted owner's cash flow $ _____

13C. WHAT MAKES THE BUSINESS UNIQUE (RISK ASSESSMENT)

Risk Factor	Candidate Rank (1–6, 6 is high risk)	Risk Factor	Candidate Rank (1–6, 6 is high risk)
Company history	_____	Labor situation	_____
Industry segment	_____	Management situation	_____
Special skills required	_____	Return *of* investment	_____
Location/lease terms	_____	Return *on* investment	_____
Special relationships required	_____	Outside dependency	_____
		Company reputation	_____

Worksheet 13   *(Continued)*

Risk Factor	Candidate Rank (1–6, 6 is high risk)	Risk Factor	Candidate Rank (1–6, 6 is high risk)
Products or services	_____	Competition	_____
Franchises, licenses, insurance, or bonds required	_____	Technology	_____
		Total	_____

Divide total by 15 for overall risk assessment
(also known as the desirability multiplier) ========

13D. PRICING CALCULATIONS

Market value of assets $ _____
Less: Liabilities being assumed   – _____

Price based on assets $ _____

Adjusted owner's cash flow $ _____
Divided by: Capitalization rate   _____
(The rate of return you want on this business)

Price based on capitalization of cash flow $ _____

Cost to buy assets at market value $ _____
Plus: Start-up costs:

Year	Business Losses + Lost Earnings = Total Costs		
1	$	$	$
2			
3			
4			
5			
N			

Price based on duplication $ _____

Market value of assets $ _____
Times: Prevailing commercial interest rate   × _____%
Cost of carrying assets $ _____
Owner's cash flow $ _____
Less: Cost of carrying assets   – _____
Excess earnings $ _____
Times: Risk multiplier or divided
 by the CAP rate   _____
Value of excess earnings $ _____
Plus: Market value of assets   + _____

(Continued)

Worksheet 13   *(Continued)*

Price based on integrated method $ _____

The candidate company has special value due to some unique advantage it can provide, i.e., cost savings, elimination of competition, a hard to obtain franchise or license, a valuable location, etc.

Price premium for special value $ _____

E. PRICING TESTS

ALTERNATIVE INVESTMENT TEST:
The present rate of return on a bank CD   _____%
Salary you could earn as an employee $ _____

Rate of return on candidate company:

Owner's cash flow   =

Proposed selling price   _____%

Owner's salary and cash flow $ _____

JUSTIFICATION OF PURCHASE TEST:
Owner's cash flow from B above $ _____
  (includes a salary of $ _____)
Plus:
  Cash to be gained by selling unneeded assets   _____
  Cash to be gained by trimming inventories   _____
  Cash to be gained by extending payables   _____
  Other cash to be gained   _____

TOTAL CASH TO BE GAINED $ _____
Less:
  Cash needed to repay debt $ _____
  Cash needed for additional salary   _____
  Cash needed for repairs or replacement   _____
  Cash needed to increase inventories   _____
  Cash needed to increase accounts receivable   _____
  Cash needed to compensate for the interest which
    could have been earned on your down payment   _____

TOTAL CASH NEEDED   ($ _____)

Actual cash available (or required) $ _____

FIRST-YEAR CASH EVALUATION OF PURCHASE:
Actual cash available (as above) (A) $ _____
Divided by:
  Cash down payment $ _____
  Plus: Additional cash invested or loaned ($ _____)
  Total cash put into the business (B) $ _____

Cash on cash return (year 1 only) (A) ÷ (B)   _____%

CHAPTER 14

Negotiating, Closing, and Getting Started

The final sequence of events in your business purchase involves:

- Your offer—possibly followed by a series of counter offers
- An accepted offer—usually with some contingencies
- Your due diligence examination—and the satisfaction of the contingencies
- The drawing of the formal contract
- The closing

You will negotiate each of these steps, sometimes directly with the seller, sometimes through intermediaries. Worksheet 14 at the end of the chapter can help you stay organized.

Negotiating

Negotiating is the process whereby two parties who need or want something from each other resolve to a solution. The solution can be obtained through force, through compromise, through concessions, or some combination. As an example, consider a buyer and seller who are far apart on the price of a business. If the seller has made a commitment to move out of the area in a short time and the buyer knows it, the buyer can exert economic force (take it or leave it). If the seller has no such pressure to leave, he or she might find a compromise with the buyer (split the difference). Or the buyer might agree to make a concession on the offered price if the seller will concede good terms of sale (this for that).

Effective negotiation has some natural enemies: fear, surprise, futility, and suspicion. The best defenses are facts, consistency, alternatives, and honesty. Being honest does not mean being naive, or revealing how strongly you may want the business. It does mean that you honestly want to buy the business, but you honestly can walk away. Although there is no requirement for openness and candor, deception can be detrimental to negotiations.

The discussion that follows is based on 5 "P"s: Perspective, Preparation, Posture, Persuasion, and Preservation.

Perspective

Perspective is needed to ensure that negotiations stay within the bounds of your personal values as well as within the bounds of your personal financial objectives. To gain an appreciation for the power of perspective, understand that people act in their own perceived best interest. It does not matter that something may actually not be in a person's best interest; the important thing is that the person perceives it to be. A person's perception of reality *is* that person's reality.

A good way to maintain your perspective is to remain aware that you do not have to buy *this* business. Now that you know to find businesses, you can turn up other candidates. This does not mean that you shouldn't be fully committed to working for the purchase of the right business. It does mean that you should not pursue the business at any cost.

Mismatched or unrealistic expectations shatter many of life's undertakings. Your perspective should embrace the following expectations about business buying negotiations:

- You don't have to buy the business.
- The seller may not have to sell to you.
- Negotiations will take longer than expected.
- There will be misunderstandings and things will go wrong.
- You may learn things during the negotiations that will change your position on some points.

Preparation

Preparation for negotiations involves learning as much as you can about the seller and the business. One fact has more impact on the negotiations than any other and cannot be emphasized enough: You must find out what the seller wants.

This is not as easy as it sounds. The seller may say one thing and mean another. The seller may not know. The seller may want things that appear irrational. You need to probe any demands of the seller to learn the reasons the seller feels he or she wants something in order to uncover the seller's real goals.

A typical example involves a seller who claims to want all-cash terms. If you probe for the reasons, you might hear "I want to retire and therefore I need all cash." The seller has assumed that the best way to get money for retirement is to get all cash, invest it, and live off the income. The seller might be better off with a steady income from the higher price and extended interest-bearing terms you plan to offer.

Another common reason given is "I just want to walk away from the business with no worries, therefore I want all cash." The seller assumes that by extending terms he or she will have problems getting paid, but extending terms should not have to mean any worries for the seller. You may be able to provide excellent, well-secured collateral. (Perhaps the seller has worries about the business not being as sound as it has been represented to be!)

The seller may want many things, some of which may be contradictory:

- A high price
- All cash at closing
- Solid security
- Freedom from work
- Freedom from worry
- A reputation for getting a certain (high) price for the business
- Recognition
- A feeling of "winning"
- A stream of income/an annuity
- A quick deal
- A payment method to reward "potential"
- A continuing association
- Status
- A place to go/something to do
- Another business
- To get out from under this business
- Continued employment for friends or relatives
- Relief from debt
- Inclusion or exclusion of real estate
- To please a family member
- To buy or pay for something

The list is not complete, but it illustrates how complex the issue can be.

The seller's wants are so important to the negotiations because they determine the structure of the sale that the seller will find most acceptable. Knowing what the seller truly wants can permit you to develop creative alternatives.

What the Seller Really Wanted: A Case Study

In one of my first transactions, the buyer wanted to buy not only the business, an auto body and paint shop, but the real estate too. He was willing to pay the fair market price and even a bit more. The seller, however, would sell only the business, not the land and building. The more they negotiated, the more the parties hardened their positions.

When I finally worked through why the seller wanted to keep the land and building, I realized he had no special attachment to the property: He wanted rental income. Once I confirmed that, I was able to work with a commercial real estate broker to find the seller another income-producing property. The buyer was able to purchase the business and its property, and the seller got what he really wanted.

Other preparation will have your advisors well informed and ready to support your efforts. Prepare alternative courses of action by presupposing what will happen. (If A happens, you will do one thing; but if B happens, you will do another.)

Posture

Posture has to do with your opening position, how the negotiations will be conducted (directly or through intermediaries), where any meetings will be held, and the tone and pace of the negotiations.

A clear posture helps to prevent surprises. Abrupt changes in the flow of negotiations can put the seller off balance and, while that tactic may earn you some temporary advantage, it most often results in raising the seller's defenses against any future surprises.

Parties to negotiations sometimes adopt artificial postures to gain a negotiating advantage. Sellers may try to appear uninterested in selling or may give the impression several offers are pending. This posture is intended to convey that the seller is not desperate and cannot be bargained down easily. The real effect might be to make the buyer think that he or she will end up in a bidding war, and turn the buyer off.

Buyers sometimes adopt a posture of offering an extremely low price and permit themselves to be brought up slowly as they gain other concessions. The problem with this posture is that it can insult the seller, who sees the value of the business as a reflection on his or her life's work.

Other buyers offer a very high price to encourage the seller to make generous concessions. These buyers then reduce their offer as they find "problems." This is a common tactic that almost always generates strong resentment when the seller catches on and realizes that he or she is being manipulated.

"The Trip to Tahiti"

Buyers who are highly skilled—and somewhat cold-hearted—use a trick on sellers called "the trip to Tahiti." The buyer examines the business with obvious pleasure, remarking positively on how well the business will fit the buyer's other corporate interests. At some point during the meeting the buyer will appear to make a decision that he wants this business. The buyer tells the seller that the price is clearly within bounds and will not be much of a problem . . . as long as the seller is willing to accept all cash. The seller agrees to hold the business off the market for 90 days while the buyer examines the books and has the paperwork put together. The buyer leaves the meeting with a free 90-day option, and the seller, thinking about getting his full selling price all in cash, goes on a mental trip to Tahiti.

Unfortunately, after several weeks, the buyer confides that he has someone—a partner or a boss—who has found a different company to buy. Our seller needs to become competitive; the price of the business has to come down a little. From there it's a downward slide as the seller's inventories don't check out, and receivables look too old. And that all-cash payment? Well, the policy now is to leverage acquisitions, so 10-year installments are now the preferred terms.

By now the seller has held the business off the market for some time. Word of a sale has leaked out. The dream of a high, all-cash price has been shattered, and the seller may be demoralized and full of doubt.

The toughest of these buyers keep up the pressure right through the closing, seeking concessions for legal fees, bank fees, and anything else until the seller finally says "No!"

The fact is that professional buyers buy lots of companies and become quite skilled at it, but most sellers sell only once.

Unless you are a very skilled negotiator or there are special circumstances that exist, adopt a posture that is comfortable for you to maintain. To the extent you can, be cordial, polite, and businesslike. Be firm but patient. Be open to ideas and alert for opportunities to build toward a successful resolution. Recognize any "gamesmanship" for what it is and try to move the negotiations to a higher tone. Don't be rushed and don't be pressured.

The Offer

Before moving on to persuasion and preservation, you need to put an offer on the table. The centerpiece of the negotiations from this point on is the written offer, which should contain at least these elements:

- A description of what you are offering to purchase (specific assets, stock, licenses, etc.)
- The name of the seller or sellers.
- The date of the offer and the date the offer expires
- The price
- The terms
- The interest rate, if any
- The repayment schedule, if any
- The amount of deposit, if any
- A date for closing
- Any contingencies attached to your offer

Contingencies

There are two kinds of contingencies. One kind makes the offer subject to the occurrence of some *activities*. The offer may be contingent on your obtaining financing or on the landlord's willingness to assign the lease over to you.

The second kind of contingency makes the offer subject to the existence of certain *conditions*. For example, the offer may be contingent upon a certain level of inventory or the value of certain assets. A common contingency requires that your examination of the books must show the business to be in the financial condition represented by the seller.

Contingencies are put into an offer to break a typical log jam in negotiations. On one hand, the buyer can't make an intelligent offer without facts about the business. On the other, the seller doesn't want to open up confidential details about the business to someone who may not buy it. The solution has become the contingent offer. The seller provides information to the buyer, but does not allow the buyer to review the books, talk to employees, or the like. The seller provides enough information to enable the buyer to make a decision and develop an offer. The buyer submits an offer based on the information provided by the seller, but by making the offer contingent, reserves the right to withdraw the offer, cancel any agreements, and have the deposit returned if, upon examination by the buyer, the information is not correct or certain conditions are not met. This examination is called *due diligence.*

The wording of the contingent conditions is very important. Buyers would like the contingencies to be as broad as possible, so that any decision to buy or not buy is within their control. An example of a broad contingency is "all financial data is subject to examination and approval by the buyer's accountant." The practical impact of this statement is to give the buyer complete access to the financial records with no obligation to complete the deal. The accountant just has to "disapprove" the financial data.

Sellers want the contingencies to be very narrow, so that they are clearly identifiable and easy to meet. A narrow contingency would be "this offer is subject only to the buyer's verification that sales, costs, and expenses were as shown on the financial statements given to the buyer."

Your contingencies should cover anything that is critical to your decision. Verification of financial data is almost always needed. If certain employees or customers are essential, your contingencies can include satisfactory agreements with them. The same applies to contracts with key suppliers or the franchisor, if there is one.

A very common contingency involves the future rent or purchase of the business location. If your decision to buy the business is based on your assuming the present lease or renegotiating other arrangements, you should establish such a contingency in your offer. If you are going to borrow money to buy the business, you might want to make your offer subject to your ability to obtain financing.

Word your contingencies so that you have the *right* to withdraw your offer but not the *obligation* to withdraw. Your contingencies may not be met, but you still may want to go forward.

The offer, with all its terms and contingencies, is both critical and complex enough to warrant review by your advisors.

Persuasion

Persuasion is convincing another to accept or do something. But if, as we have said, people do things only if they perceive them to be in their own best interest, you need to show how what you want is in the seller's best interest.

Just as you have the obligation to find out what the seller wants, the seller has an obligation to learn what you want. If the seller has not been alert enough to ask you, then you have to tell him or her. This does not, however, mean disclosing your strong desire or anything else that would weaken your negotiating position. An opening negotiating dialogue between you and the seller can be a factual review of your offer and the reasons for it. Get the seller to invest time in understanding your offer. This is a way to get the seller participating in a solution, and the seller's investment in a solution works to your advantage.

Learn from rejection. You should expect that almost any opening offer you might make will be rejected and you should learn all you can from the experience. Get the reasons for it. Determine the key points in the seller's arguments. Keep asking "why," so that you can understand what is behind the objections.

Do not argue your position yet, just present your offer and make sure the seller understands it. Then wring every bit of intelligence you can from the rejection. At some point, ask for a counter offer. Once you have a counter offer, you can develop more specific negotiating tactics.

Use concessions. Assess where you are far apart and where you are near agreement. Develop a list of things you can give (concessions) and a list of concessions the seller could give. Think of as many alternatives as possible to give the seller what he or she wants. Think of alternatives for the seller to give you what you want. Restructure a new offer that reflects the sum of your understanding. This time, do argue your points. Hopefully the seller and the intermediary will develop a list of concessions, but they may not, and you should not wait passively for them to do so.

Price is the most common stumbling block. Because price is the most common area of difference, we will use it as our example. The seller may view the price of the business as a reflection of his or her personal worth. It is common for owners to think of their businesses as extensions of themselves. They will say, "All those years of hard work should be worth at least this much." You may have to point out that all those years of hard work provided a fine living, a nice home, and so on. The selling price of the business is only the residual value of the seller's work, not the value of the seller's life.

Sellers sometimes base their price on cash taken from the business but never shown on the books. (An admission of tax evasion is not a particularly good testimonial to the seller's honesty.) In Chapter 13 we learned ways to deal with unreported sales and other cash. Whether the cash ever really existed or not, don't accept any pricing logic that cannot be proven.

If the seller does have a genuine logic for the price, find out what it is. Understand it and let the seller know you understand it. Then you can ask for understanding of your pricing logic.

Involve the seller in your pricing calculations. If you based your price primarily on the value of the assets, ask for the seller's help in seeing why it should be otherwise. If you used a capitalization rate on the cash flow as your pricing method, explain your method to the seller and ask to know how you can be more correct.

You may want to compare the seller's price to the cost of duplicating the business. Review with the seller what the cost would be to start a similar business. Let the seller find any flaws in your logic. You might say, "Help me understand why your price is correct when it would cost so much less to start a similar business."

Keep your argument centered. Your persuasion should always return to the central proposition that your offer is in the seller's best interest. Point out that you want to pay a fair price, and one that will allow you to afford to buy the business. Your objective to buy the business for a fair and affordable price is in the seller's best interest because it facilitates the sale.

Be ready for the worst. Unfortunately, negotiations don't always flow as logically as our example. Outbursts of temper, seller regret, ego needs, ill-conceived positions, and almost every other vagary of human nature can turn the negotiations into an emotionally charged circus. A competent intermediary can buffer these frictions and defuse problems before they get out of hand. Your strategy when confronted with an emotional situation should be to acknowledge the other person's strong feelings and begin at once to focus away from personalities and motives and toward a range of solutions.

No detailed script can be written to cover all the variations you will encounter. Use your list of concessions from both sides to persuade the seller to move toward agreement. Use your advisors as sounding boards and as sources of creative strategies and tactics.

Preservation

Preservation of your negotiations involves building upon agreements and narrowing areas of disagreement. It involves keeping the negotiations progressing through the stresses and strains that are bound to occur. It means preventing every difference from threatening the whole negotiation process and causing it to fall apart.

Poor negotiators and those who rely on power techniques often refer to a particular issue as a "deal breaker." What they mean is that the issue is important. Their overly dramatic reference is intended to put pressure on the other party. Sometimes the pressure works, but the result all too often is to put the negotiations generally on thin ice, where any issue can become a deal breaker and no foundation for progress can be built. There may be a time for the dramatic, but negotiations that progress on solid gains stand a much better chance of success.

Closing

When negotiations are successful and an agreement is reached, a process for closing the transaction is set up. A formal contract containing all the facts of the agreement needs to be drawn. The seller's attorney usually prepares the first version for review by the buyer and his or her attorney. If you have not yet done your due diligence examination, now is the time.

Due Diligence

The term *due diligence* properly infers an obligation on your part to satisfy yourself regarding the facts of the business. The seller allows you to examine records, books, facilities, and contracts and, if your offer contains such contingencies, to talk with employees, customers, suppliers, and others. Your objective is to determine if the information you relied upon in making your decision is correct.

If your offer was well written, it provides you with a way to cancel your agreement if certain information is proven not to be true. Use your advisors and the analytical techniques discussed in Chapters 12 and 13. Your due diligence may result in the withdrawal or revision of your offer if the facts prove to be different from what you were given.

Once your contingencies have been satisfied and the contract is in its final form, you can close. The closing is the formal transfer of the business or its assets to you. Unlike a real estate closing, where the routines are well known and commonly, if not always smoothly, executed, business closings are seldom routine. Each business and the terms of its sale are unique. Even your advisors may not be thoroughly familiar with the intricacies of a business sale.

The best way to ensure a smooth closing is to set up a checklist. Things may still go wrong, but you will have a blueprint to follow. Where appropriate, each item on the checklist should be assigned to someone. More than one closing has been put off because no one got a copy of the lease or someone forgot to transfer the utilities.

The Checklist

The agreement you reached with the seller spelled out the key points of the arrangement. As the formal contracts are hammered out, more and more details are covered. Some of the items in the checklist shown in Figure 14-1 may be included in the contract; others are just reminders of things that need to be done.

An important item on the checklist covers what will happen during the time between the contract signing and closing. The time between the two

- Conduct of the business until closing
- The time and place of closing
- A list of everyone who needs to attend
- A list of all the documents required
- A breakdown of the funds to be disbursed
- Absolute assurance that the funds are available in the amount and form specified.
- Your new corporate tax and employer identification numbers
- Provision for any licenses to be obtained or transferred.
- Pro-rating calculations for taxes, wages, utility bills, etc.
- Adjustments for any deposits the seller may have with the landlord, suppliers, or utilities
- Transfer of banking arrangements
- Transfer of keys and alarm codes
- Transfer of any computer codes
- The real estate lease or purchase agreement
- Customer lists
- Transfer of utilities—particularly telephone numbers
- Any separate contracts establishing seller's obligation to consult or not to compete
- Allocation of the selling price to assets, consulting, non-compete agreement, and goodwill
- Provision for broker's fees
- Clearance of outstanding liens or encumbrances
- Compliance with bulk sales laws to notify suppliers
- Assumption or discharge of any other leases or mortgages
- Definition of the warranties and guarantees the seller will provide
- Provision for security by the buyer
- Definition of the seller's obligations to help in the transition of the business and training of the buyer
- Adjustments for actual inventory and receivables value at closing
- Adjustments in the event that accounts receivable are not collected
- Disposition of any outstanding claims or litigation against or by the seller
- Provision for continuity of insurance or bonding

Figure 14-1. The closing checklist.

events can be weeks or months. You might be waiting for your financing, or the seller may be waiting for an up-to-date appraisal. Whatever the reason, make provisions for how the business is to be conducted during that time.

Typically, the seller agrees to operate the business in its customary way. You may want to spell out specific do's and don'ts, especially as they relate to *selling activities*—a big discount price sale can bring in quick money, deplete inventory, and load up customers, making your first weeks difficult. Another example involves *purchasing activities*—failing to buy needed goods and supplies can conserve the seller's cash but leave you in a bad opening position. Finally, be alert for *personnel activities*—hiring and firing at this stage can create real problems for you as you learn the new business.

Take the Pulse Quickly

You can monitor unusual gyrations in inventories and cash levels if you are alert, but some things can't be easily detected, such as deteriorating customer service or callous treatment of employees or suppliers during the seller's last days as owner. As soon as you can after the purchase, meet with employees and talk with customers and suppliers to assess their satisfaction with your new company.

Asset Sale versus Stock Sale

Another important item on the checklist requires you to decide on the method of sale. In most cases, the sale method will be a sale of assets. The assets are identified and title is passed, usually with some warranties such as the collectability of the accounts receivable and the quality of the inventory. If liabilities are to be assumed, they, like the assets, are carefully defined. The purchase clearly circumscribes all obligations regarding who assumes which liabilities.

The principle advantage of structuring the sale as an asset sale is its clarity. In an asset sale you will know what you are buying and what obligations you are assuming.

The alternative method is a stock sale, where the buyer purchases the shares of stock of a business. The big risk in purchasing the stock of a corporation is that you are also purchasing all liabilities, both known and unknown. A lawsuit over some past activity by the company could prove to be a most unwelcome and expensive surprise.*

Under some conditions, there are advantages to a stock sale. If the company has tax losses to carry forward, a favorable lease, a transferable franchise, or other important contracts, or if the assets of the business are encumbered, a stock sale may be the method to use.

If the advantages are worth using the stock sale method, you can attempt to get the seller to indemnify you for any claims that may be made after the sale. If the seller has no means to satisfy those claims, his or her indemnification isn't worth much, however. People have tried using indemnity bonds to overcome the problem.

---

*A common problem concerns past violations of new environmental standards. The cost of clean-up could be higher than the value of the business.

The importance of these actions and the changing legal and tax environment makes having competent advice essential throughout this phase.

Manage the Closing

The checklist works to ensure that after all your hard work to find and buy the business, some glitch doesn't develop. A tantrum at the closing table over some mistake or omission is the last thing you want. Unfortunately, it happens all too often as people underestimate the complexity of the transaction. Your management of the closing can be your first management task as a business owner.

The First Month of Ownership

Your objective in the early days of ownership is to take control of your new business. Immerse yourself and learn.

Make Changes Slowly

Because you can't know all the critical interdependencies in the business yet, be careful about making sweeping or dramatic changes. If you change the name of the business, you might lose old customers. You might change some supplier only to learn later that the supplier's brother is (or was) your biggest customer. If the business is on a fairly even keel, take things slowly.

Put Out Fires

Of course, if you face serious problems, you must take action. If the crisis involves relationships with other people, such as customers, employees, creditors, and so on, a new owner can often buy time by listening, acknowledging concern, and demonstrating a sincere intent to resolve the problem. Most reasonable people will give a new owner time to learn the facts and come back with a proposed solution.

No matter what the crisis, you can usually find some help. Everyone around you has a stake in your success, including the former owner. The former owner has a special interest in your success if you owe him or her money. There may be times when you have to decide alone, but that's why you wanted your own business.

Learn the Routines and the Culture

Every business has its own flow and rhythms. Even if you think you want to change it, learn the culture you bought. The small secrets contained in every-day actions may be the keys to success or barriers to progress.

Focus on People

Your first days should be full of people contact. No matter how trite it sounds, people are what business is mostly about. Human skills, knowledge, needs, and resources form the basis for production of any kind. In all your people contacts, particularly at this early stage, be searching for others' views on the key opportunities and threats to your business.

Employees. Get to know your people. Learn their skills and knowledge. Determine if they are satisfied or not, and why. Set up a communications pattern that you can sustain. You can do harm if you start a program of heavy communication and then withdraw. As important as it is to listen to your people, it is also important for you to talk to them. They will want to get to know you. You are an important person in their lives, and what you plan to do affects them very much. To the extent you can, offer reassurance that nothing harmful to them is imminent.

Customers. How successful you are at communicating with customers may very well determine how successful your business will be. Because you now control what your company does, you represent the power to satisfy your customers. Listening to their needs and comments is a top-priority activity. Find a way to build an ongoing dialogue.

Suppliers. New owners sometimes overlook these important people. To one extent or another, you do rely on them. Their success already depends on your success, so look for ways to make them part of your business team.

Bankers, Lenders, and Investors. Many new business owners fear that their banker or investor will try to interfere with the business. To try and prevent this intrusion, new owners sometimes do the worst thing possible—they try to keep these people out of the business and in the dark. Your best course of action is to find out what your lenders and investors expect from you and try to give it to them. If they know you are performing, they will usually stay out of your way. If you do get into trouble, they will want to help.

Advisors. You will need to develop a working relationship with your advisors. Your accountant is a key person. You may also find you need some specialized advice from consultants or others. Seminars and books are available on topics ranging from personnel hiring and training to advertising to negotiating with vendors. Be prepared to learn that no matter what kind of advice you need, the chances are that someone is out there ready to sell it to you.

Set Simple Controls

In the early stages of your ownership you need to decide which few critical factors could cause major damage or possible failure for your business. Once you identify them, you can establish controls. Controls may be needed on cash, quality, expenses, purchasing, or some area of employee performance, for example. In the beginning, pick only the most important factors, and try to keep the controls easy to administer.

Learn How to Measure Results

You may be surprised at how results are really measured in smaller companies. Although financial results are the final measure, they arrive late and incomplete. Reports are available only long after they can do much good.

The true indicators of results may be the number of phone calls per day or the labor hours per unit or the number of days backlog in the order book. Every business has measures of productivity and performance that will predict results. Find out what they are in your new business and begin tracking your progress.

Define Key Opportunities and Threats

Whether you actively develop a formal business plan or not will depend on your philosophy about planning and the requirements of your lenders and investors. Regardless of what you think of business plans, you should at least define the key opportunities and threats your business faces. You were urged to review this subject in your discussions with employees, customers, and others. If your business is part of an association, get its views on your environment. Ask for ideas from your Chamber of Commerce and neighboring businesses.

Missing opportunities and threats early can be compared to getting off course early in a trip; the longer you wait to make corrections, the more work it takes.

Worksheet 14
Negotiating Data Sheet

14A. PEOPLE

		Telephone	
Advisor	Name/Address	Business	Home
Seller			
Seller's attorney			
Seller's accountant			
Your attorney			
Your accountant			
Broker			
Other			
Other			
Other			

14B. WHAT THE SELLER WANTS MOST

1.
2.
3.

14C. OPENING POSITIONS

Item	Seller	Buyer
Price		
Cash down payment		
Terms		
Years		
Interest rate		
Other		
Other		

14D. POSSIBLE CONCESSIONS

Seller Could Concede	Buyer Could Concede
1.	1.
2.	2.
3.	3.

CHAPTER 15

Franchises: An Introduction to Turnkey Entrepreneurship

Franchises offer some special appeals, particularly to the midcareer, first-time business owner. Most good franchises come with tested systems to help manage the business. From the sign over the front door to the payroll accounting system, the franchisee often has the franchisor's experience and support available. Many established franchisors have field consultants who visit the locations on a regular basis, and who respond when called to help with problems.

A common expression used to describe owning a franchise is "be in business for yourself but not by yourself." Owning some franchises can make you instantly a part of a large organization with sophisticated advertising and strong market recognition. For many people at midcareer, this makes the transition from employee to owner less frightening.

The franchise industry enjoys a better reputation than in years past, and is growing rapidly. The super successes in the field, such as McDonald's, coupled with tight government regulation and policing by the industry itself, have raised the image of franchises. While there are still bad franchises and dishonorable franchisors, there is generally a more positive view toward franchise ownership.

Franchises are now available in a wide variety and price range. One recent collection of franchise offerings included a $99 franchise for personalized books, a $3,000 franchise to provide business education seminars, and a $1 million top-name restaurant franchise. In between were franchises for instant printing ($35,000), hair styling ($75,000), automotive repair ($100,000), and even a minor league sports franchise ($250,000). One franchise, Haunted Hayrides, offers a business opportunity for those who might want to work at it only in the month of October!

This variety means that people have more chance to find opportunities that match their desires and their financial capabilities, making franchises attractive and affordable to more people who are seeking to become entrepreneurs.

Buying a franchise for a new location directly from the franchisor is a fairly straightforward proposition. Federal and state laws require the franchisor to disclose the material facts about the franchise in the offer to sell. There is relatively little negotiating. The transaction of buying a franchise directly from the franchisor varies considerably from buying an established, nonfranchise business, where, as you have learned, financial data may be vague and the price is determined only after lengthy negotiations.

Much of what we covered in Chapters 7 through 14 applies to this route to ownership. However, whether you buy an existing franchised location from a previous franchisee or a new location directly from the franchisor, there are some special procedures to follow.

What Is a Franchise?

Franchises have become a "first business" for millions of people, but surprisingly, many business seekers don't have a clear idea of what a franchise really is. A franchise is a license. In most cases, it is a license to use a franchisor's name and to offer its products or services for sale in exchange for certain fees. The terms of the license are spelled out in the franchise agreement.

The Franchise Agreement

The franchise agreement covers in detail the obligations that you and the franchisor have to each other. It will include such items as the following:

The price of the franchise. The agreement includes the terms of any financing and the ongoing royalty schedule.

A list of exactly what you are getting for your money. In addition to the right to use the franchisor's name and to sell the products or services, you may be getting training, certain equipment, a starting inventory, special promotions, or a number of other assets.

The procedures you must follow in operating the franchise. Some franchises have very detailed manuals that cover all aspects of operations, from what color uniforms are required to how to clean the floors. Some franchises permit a degree of flexibility; others require strict adherence to procedures. All require some form of reporting and controls.

The duration of the agreement and the procedures governing sale, renewal, and transfer. Also covered are the conditions under which either side may cancel the agreement.

A definition of the territory. Your territory may be narrow or broad, exclusive or unprotected, or some combination that might even change over time.

A definition of the responsibilities for operations. The agreement covers the responsibility for pricing, purchasing, advertising, paying invoices, hiring, training, insurance coverage, maintenance, security, and similar items. Some franchisors require the franchisee to operate the franchise personally. If the franchisor provides consulting or troubleshooting support, it should be covered in the agreement.

A description of any obligations you will have to purchase materials, services, or supplies from the franchisor. If there are such obligations to be a captive purchaser, the conditions under which you can purchase on the open market will be spelled out.

The plan for the facility. Some franchisors provide the complete facility, others give detailed specifications, and others offer little or no guidance. Some franchisors own the facility and lease it to the franchisee. In other cases, the facility is rented from a landlord—sometimes from the franchisee.

The franchise agreement is an imposing document, which you must review with your advisors.

The Pluses of a Franchise

The most obvious benefit provided by a proven franchise is its reduced risk. A good franchise has an established, tested product or service. Equally important can be the methods and systems, which have been refined to a smooth set of procedures and which have been proven successful. You are able to benefit from the franchisor's learning curve, and that means you most likely face less risk.

A strong franchisor is almost certainly able to secure a better location than an individual. The franchisor has more technical expertise in site selection. Franchisors know how to assess traffic count and flow. Strong franchisors have more financial clout to negotiate and sign up good locations.

If the franchisor is a heavy advertiser and promoter, the recognition factor can be a big plus for the franchisee. The economy of scale available to the franchisor can permit advertising on television and other media that are too expensive for the independent operator. Economies of scale may extend to purchasing of materials and supplies, giving you lower prices than you could obtain on your own.

Training, consulting, and any other help the franchisor provides can be very meaningful. The independent operator has limited and often expensive resources for help. If you came from a large organization, you may appreciate the availability of the franchisor's field staff.

If you are buying a franchise direct from the franchisor, and not in a resale, you will have no complicated analyses of past operations to conduct. You will, in effect, have a clean slate.

The Minuses of a Franchise

Owning a franchise is "being in business for yourself but not by yourself." The restrictions and controls imposed by the franchisor are the greatest drawbacks to a franchised business. If you want complete freedom of operations, it may not be found in a franchise. You may be required to follow detailed regulations and procedures.

The initial license fee and the ongoing royalties can seem onerous, particularly if franchisor support is weak. Royalty fees can easily exceed what the operator is earning. Most disputes between franchisors and franchisees center on this issue.

Your options for the eventual disposition of the franchise need to be understood. Any restriction on your ability to resell or bequeath your franchised business can be a significant minus. The ownership of the franchise license is not permanent. This could pose a serious problem later on. You may be required to meet some conditions for renewal. You may not be able to resell your franchise to anyone you wish. In some cases you can sell back only to the franchisor. Even after years of building the operation, you may not be able to pass the business on to your heirs.

The franchisor's management and financial strength may become weak or may fail. You could be adversely affected by events outside your control.

You may be prohibited from expanding or relocating your business because of the franchisor's licensing of others.

If the franchisor requires you to purchase its products and supplies and does not permit you to buy on the open market, you may pay noncompetitive prices.

If the Franchise Is a Resale

You don't always have to buy a new franchise directly from the franchisor. Many franchise businesses are offered for resale by their operators. Buying a franchise in a resale is like buying any other business but with some additional steps. In effect you are buying the business the operator has built plus the franchise license of the franchisor.

In almost all cases you will need to obtain the approval of the franchisor. Expect to be asked to submit your personal financial statement and your plan for the business. Provision will have to be made for your training. You will have to familiarize yourself with and accept all the terms and conditions of the franchise agreement and the requirements it places on your operating procedures. You may have to be interviewed as a part of the franchisor's acceptance procedure. Your business experience can be a plus for you.

While these may seem to be added burdens, you have access to one very beneficial step that is possible only when buying a franchise: You have the ability to talk to the owners of similar businesses. Talking with other franchisees can give you information and insights unavailable to you with other businesses. Be alert to the fact that the franchisee of the unit you are considering wants to sell and might paint an overly rosy picture. Go find other owners to talk to. You can get the first-hand experiences of people who own, manage, and work a business very similar to the one you are considering.

The balance of your investigation, analysis, negotiations, and closing will be very similar to the process outlined for buying a business.

If the Franchise Is a New Location

There are several major differences between buying an ongoing business and a new franchise location.

Deciding What You Want

In deciding what you want, there are some new choices to make if you are considering franchises. We have mentioned buying an existing versus a new franchise, but among new franchises you may find a bewildering array of choices. If you are considering a fast-food business, there are franchises selling pizza, hamburgers, and all kinds of sandwiches. Even if you have narrowed your choice, say to quick printing, there are several franchises from which to choose.

Determining What You Can Afford and Pricing the Business

Determining what you can afford requires a new approach because you do not have historical financial data to analyze and you cannot follow the classic methodology for pricing the business (Chapter 13). The complication results from the need to deal with projections of future financial performance. No reputable franchisor will guarantee what your results will be. You will be forced to make judgments and take risks on your own evaluation of the franchise and the location.

Of course, you do have the unique source of help which was mentioned earlier—owners of other franchise locations. You can ask other owners how close the franchisor's projections matched their experience. You can learn about the problems and any surprises these owners encountered. You can also ask about any flexibility the franchisor might have with regard to price and terms.

Finding the Business

Finding the business is actually a little easier with a franchise. If you know which one you want, you can contact the franchisor directly. If you don't know, you have all the sources presented in Chapter 9, plus some new ones:

Franchise Opportunities Handbook
Superintendent of Documents
U.S. Government Printing Office
Washington, DC 20402

Membership Directory (and other publications)
International Franchise Association
Suite 1005
1025 Connecticut Ave., NW
Washington, DC 20036

Directory of Franchising Organizations
Pilot Books
347 Fifth Avenue
New York, NY 10016

In addition, almost any big newsstand has several business opportunity or franchise opportunity magazines for sale. These magazines offer hundreds of listings.

Analyzing the Business

Analyzing the business is the step that will be the most different when the business is a franchise. The whole process of learning about the seller and finding out what he or she wants is not relevant to a directly purchased franchise. Neither are all the balance sheet and income statement adjustments.

The Disclosure Document. Franchisors are required to publish a disclosure document that gives you more information than you can ever hope to get from a regular business owner, as Figure 15–1 shows.

Other Franchisees. The last item in the disclosure document can help you locate other franchisees. You can get valuable insights into the franchisor's behavior and performance by talking with people who have had first-hand experience. You can find out if promises were kept and how the quality of the goods, services, training, and other support compared to what was expected.

If you can locate the former owners of failed locations, you may be able to get some very useful, although possibly tainted, insights into the downside risks of the franchise.

The Franchisor. Of course, the franchisor itself is the prime source of information. You may be subjected to a high-pressure sales approach or you may have to initiate the contact, but either way, there is plenty of information available.

The franchisor will want information about you, too. References, a summary of your experience, and your financial statement are a minimum. You may also be asked to prepare a business plan to demonstrate your ability to manage the franchise.

A description of the franchise
The franchisor's ownership and financial condition
Background data on key people
The price, royalties, territory, and other terms of the franchise license
   (including any financing that may be available)
The operational duties of the franchisee
Any other obligations of the franchisor, such as training, advertising,
   and promotion
The procedures for sale, repurchase, default, termination, renewal,
   and transfer of the franchise
The procedure to establish the physical location
Any litigation in which the franchisor is or has been involved
Any restrictions on purchases or sales by the franchisee
Information about past, present, and projected franchisee locations,
   including, where appropriate, the names of the franchisees

---

Figure 15–1. Contents of the disclosure document.

Judgment. Your real job when buying a franchise is to exercise good judgment about all the information you will have.

- Is the franchise a good value? What are you getting that you couldn't provide for yourself or obtain by buying a nonfranchise business for the same price?
- Is the franchisor reputable and financially stable? Are the people competent and trustworthy?
- Do you have confidence that the financial projections you have developed are realistic and achievable? The key element in the projections is market potential.
- Does this franchise satisfy your basic criteria, and does it meet the risk preferences you established in earlier chapters?

Franchising is a dynamic field. More and more kinds of businesses are available as franchises. Don't consider your search for a business complete unless you have investigated franchise opportunities.

The following case study capsules a typical buying process for a franchise.

A Franchise Case Study

Mr. Ken Jackson, 48 years old, was born in Illinois, one of four boys. Ken began work after high school in a nearby manufacturing plant. After a two-year break for a stint in the Army between 1966 and 1968, Ken returned to his former employer. He enrolled in a correspondence course in accounting and was soon moved from the plant floor into the office as assistant office manager. Two years later, in 1971, Ken was transferred and promoted to office manager and then to plant accountant. Another promotion brought him to the position of division controller in the company's Jacksonville, Illinois, facility.

It was in Jacksonville in 1978 that Ken began to take stock of his personal situation. He determined that his career with his company was probably not going much further. He had come to enjoy accounting thoroughly and to dislike the cold weather just as thoroughly. He set a personal target: He would be out of the cold weather and into something new in a year and a half.

In September 1978, only a few months into his timeline, he saw a three-line advertisement in the local paper. The ad said "Tired of working for someone else? Call us to learn about a business of your own." Ken and his wife, Barbara, a computer operator working in a CPA firm, contacted Comprehensive Business Services and received from them a substantial bundle of information and an equally substantial application package. Put off by the paperwork being asked for, they let the application package sit until December, when they did make the time to complete and submit it.

The Comprehensive Package

Comprehensive Business Services offers a license to use and market their accounting systems. The concept, aimed at smaller businesses, has franchisees provide accounting and other services such as tax return preparation, loan application development, payroll, and so on, using Comprehensive's system of forms and computer programs.

In addition to accounting processing systems, Comprehensive provides a practice management system to help franchisees manage their own businesses. The practice management support includes periodic practice evaluations.

Finally, Comprehensive provides its franchisees with marketing and sales support. In addition to national advertising, Comprehensive supplies printed materials and assists franchisees in developing marketing programs targeted at prospective clients. The programs are tried and proven to work.

Comprehensive has built its package around a key premise: to be on your own you need more than just your technical or professional skills, you need business management skills and you need to be able to get clients and customers.

The Jacksons were invited to Comprehensive's (then) headquarters in Aurora, Illinois, in March 1979. They felt they were being interviewed and didn't receive any hard sell on buying Comprehensive's franchise. In fact, after returning home, Comprehensive didn't follow up at all, so the Jacksons called them. In their second meeting they were asked by Comprehensive to draw up some projections of how much business they might bill. Comprehensive supplied them with background data, forms and instructions, and a list of other franchisees to call so that Ken and Barbara could hear first-hand about the business and how it operated.

They called several franchisees on the list. To quote Ken, "We heard some positives and some negatives, but we pretty much heard what we wanted to hear. We located a man-and-wife franchisee in St. Louis and in March went to visit. After meeting with them for a few hours, Barbara and I agreed, if they could do it, we could do it!"

The Jacksons went back to Comprehensive's headquarters and met with several key decision makers, including Comprehensive's owner. In what was either a clever negative sell, or more likely honest candor, the Jacksons were told that they lacked the background and their projections were viewed as far too optimistic. Comprehensive's owner said the projections were high, but it seemed likely that the Jacksons might hit 60 percent and so contracts were drawn and signed.

During this time Ken and Barbara also worked on selecting a location. Ken wrote 18 different Chambers of Commerce in the South and West requesting information about their business—and weather—climate. Comprehensive suggested Houston because of its economic growth. In March they flew to Houston and fell in love with the city.

Ken gave his firm notice that he would leave in August. His first task with Comprehensive was a four-week training program. The first two weeks Ken learned the actual operations of the automated accounting and report-generating business and the office operations. The second two weeks Ken spent learning how to market and sell.

In August he and Barbara moved to Houston. After spending a week in another franchisee's office as an introduction, they opened their business on September 17, 1979.

The Jacksons had purchased Comprehensive's systems for producing financial statements and their marketing systems and support. While they received no furniture, fixtures, or equipment, they did receive supplies enough for 20 clients. Their $42,000 investment also granted them exclusive rights in five of Houston's zip codes. Ken had paid $12,000 in down payment, money gained from the sale of their home in Illinois, and Comprehensive financed the balance. (As it turned out, the Jacksons were successful enough to refinance the Comprehensive loan, and save some money.)

When Ken is asked what surprised him most about his new life beyond the corporation, he quickly answers that it was his discovery that he had a talent for selling. In fact, he scrapped his original plan to run the inside operations and hire an outside salesperson, and reversed the plan. He hired an inside person and kept selling on his own.

The transition to ownership for Ken was easier than for some others because his previous jobs had placed him at a distance from his bosses and had granted him a good deal of autonomy.

In trying to balance the good and bad of his transition to ownership, Ken is hard-pressed to find much bad. While he and Barbara have had some ups and downs, the good stands out most clearly to Ken. His earnings have far exceeded what he earned as an employee. His standard of living mirrors his earnings and, coupled with the warm weather of Houston, grants him a lifestyle far superior to his previous life working for someone else in Illinois. In a philosophical reflection, Ken says, "One of the really good things about being on my own is something I hardly ever take advantage of. . . . I have the flexibility to come and go as I please. Even though I don't do it, I love the feeling that I have the option to take off if I want to."

Ken and Barbara now find themselves facing some competition from accounting software packages, but they still bill over a million dollars a year by emphasizing service and consulting such as tax advice. They service about 350 accounts and employ 11 people.

Ken's advice to others who are considering a career beyond the corporation reflect his own positive experience with his franchisor, Comprehensive Business Services. He knows that not all franchisors are as supportive. He urges people to investigate thoroughly any franchisors they are considering. He found his discussions and visits with other franchisees to be of unquestionable value.

In summing up his career decisions and choices, Ken is clear about one thing: His background and experiences as they were back in 1978 would not, by themselves, have enabled him to succeed on his own. Instead, he and Barbara now find themselves solidly established as a self-reliant, personal economic enterprise. They have earned the ability to decide their own future. They can keep up their successful pattern and continue to grow, they can ease up a little and hold their business steady, or they can cash out and sell their business and use the proceeds for an even newer life.

They have worked hard and purposefully and have created their own life options.

CHAPTER 16

Starting a Business

Starting a business may sometimes represent a better route to ownership than buying one. A start-up can be cheaper, faster, and less complicated. A business you start can result in a business that matches your criteria exactly.

Some businesses are easy to start. Some businesses, particularly service businesses, are easy to start. Consulting practices, real estate sales companies, repair services, small restaurants, and professional service practices (accounting, legal, financial, medical service) can all be started without great difficulty. They may take time to grow and you still may come out ahead by buying, but starting some businesses is easy.

Some businesses should be started. If you have a unique idea or some special personal advantage, you should examine the alternative of starting a business. Unique ideas spark new businesses. If your idea for your own business is unique, then starting a business is the route to follow.

A special personal advantage might result from a patent, a location, or a ready-made client/customer base. You may possess a one-of-a-kind source of supply or some special relationships—the often referred to "connections"—that will ostensibly ensure success.

Sometimes it's the only way. The business you want may not be available or affordable to buy. In the case of a unique idea—a new product or service, say—you may have no alternative because there are no such companies to be bought. More often, there are companies that closely match your criteria, but they either exceed your financial capability or are just not for sale, and starting your own is the only alternative.

But the risk is higher. "____ out of every ____ new businesses fails within the first five years." This often-quoted statistic shouldn't surprise you.* A business that has survived five years has proven that its products, prices, location, and methods of operation are at least acceptable to its market. These key components all remain unproved in the start-up business.

You may plan to have your first positive cash flow in 12 months, and it may take 24. Perhaps a slow start means you need to have more cash to keep going for much longer than you anticipated. You may find that some part of your business is more difficult to maintain than you thought. Perhaps developing new customers takes more selling skills than you possess.

The two big dangers are undercapitalization and lack of required skills. These are the two major reasons for new business failure. Both result from the high uncertainty in business start-ups. A profitable, cash-generating, existing business or a well-conceived franchise may cost a premium to buy, but it may have earned it. The danger from undercapitalization can be minimized by careful planning, as we will discuss later.

The danger from lack of required skills can be minimized by having or gaining experience in the business you are considering. Several times in this book we state that two actions mean more to your success than any others. Getting experience in the kind of business you are considering is one of them. (Having real customers is the other, and we cover that later in this chapter.)

Gaining valid experience requires that your skills be acquired not only in the type of business you are considering, but in the size and, if feasible, in the market location you are considering.

The Classic Start-up Process

The classic process of starting a business involves three things: an *idea*, a *plan*, and the *resources* to carry out the plan.

---

*However, you should be critical of all statistics tossed around about small businesses. After all, no one knows exactly how many small businesses start every day in kitchens and garages, and no special agency is notified when someone just stops doing business.

The Idea

The idea for the new business need not be a new idea, but it does have to be a marketable idea. Challenge any new business idea by posing these questions:

- Does the idea address a real need or want? Is there, or could there be, a demand?
- Will the demand be big enough to support a business? Is the field open, or crowded with competition?
- Can the idea actually be transformed into a business? Is the technology available?
- Will the cost result in a product or service that can be priced so that the market can or will pay for it?
- Do you have the capital it will take to start and, more important, sustain the new business?
- Do you have the knowledge and skills required? Has anyone else tried this idea? What was the outcome and why?

Answering these questions will take much thought, a lot of research and, very often, some intuition.

Research versus Intuition. Research is a sometimes maligned activity in new business development. Research may occasionally kill a good idea, but it has killed far more bad ones. Intuition, or gut feel, has launched many businesses, but not all remain afloat.

Using both research and intuition makes obvious good sense. Even if you have overwhelming gut feel for your idea, your banker or venture capital firm or, for that matter, your relatives, if they are lending or investing, will want answers to the questions above.

It also does not matter if no one else asks the questions. You should ask them and do the research to answer them. Don't neglect important information that can be available to you. You can always reject the answers in favor of your intuition.

In the end, you will have to use intuition to make a judgment on the idea, anyway. Research and analysis can spot extremes and raise warnings, but they will provide only estimates and probabilities. You will decide.

The Plan

Any plan developed for a new business will create a paradox. Such a plan will, by necessity, offer a program centered on projections and conjecture. No historic pattern or experience base exists as a guide, yet investors and lenders expect the new business plan to be exceedingly detailed. Figure 16–1 offers a basic plan outline.

| A general concept statement |
| The product or service |
| The market |
| The people and organization |
| The schedule of events |
| The financial budget |

Figure 16–1. Business plan outline.

General Concept Statement. Your business idea may not be obvious to anyone else, so if you expect others to be financial or human resources for you, you need to provide them with a description. Write the concept statement so that you describe the idea and summarize its potential risks and rewards.

Make the concept statement as alluring as you can, but follow these two rules:

1. Never misstate a fact. One uncovered flaw can cast suspicion over you and your whole plan.
2. Keep it short. If you can't describe your business concept in a couple of paragraphs, readers may view it as too complex or abstract.

The Product or Service. Explain your product or service. Show costs for varying levels of production. Try to show the name and the packaging if possible. Explain any uniqueness or competitive advantage. Describe the protection you have for your product or service. Define the barriers others would face entering the field.

The Market. Define the market in several ways.

- Size
- Composition/segments
- Growth and trends, including pricing
- Location
- Demographics
- Competition
- Technological factors

Describe how the buying decision for your product or service is made, and who makes it. Present your pricing rationale. Describe the competitive environment. Explain any special features about the market, such as distribution methods, technology, cyclicality, government impact, and so on.

Most important to the readers of your plan (and to the success of the plan) is the validity of your market assumptions. How did you develop the marketing section? Where did you get the information? How did you test the market assumptions?

Professional market research can be expensive, but asking friends and family, sometimes called "mother-in-law" research, can be deadly. You can do several things to check and test your market which will not cost a lot. For a do-it-yourself approach, consult Alan R. Andreason's *Cheap but Good Marketing Research* (Business One Irwin Press, Homewood, IL, 1993).

- Comb industry trade associations, books, and magazines for market data and trends.
- Go to trade shows and other places where customers or other suppliers meet, and talk about needs, prices, competition, and more.
- If your business involves a product, make some prototypes and have potential customers test them. Find out the good and bad features and learn what price they would pay. Find out how many they would buy.
- Conduct interview surveys in shopping centers if your kind of customers can be found there. Have your family help.
- Develop, perhaps with some professional help, a mail survey. You can get mailing lists of potential customers of almost any kind. Look in a large Yellow Pages for mailing list brokers or visit a library that has lists on disks. If you haven't been in a library lately, you're missing out on a truly valuable resource. All but the smallest are mini research centers.

The Organization. The first organizational issue is the legal form of organization. Chapter 8 included descriptions of the various organizational forms and the considerations for selecting one form over another. Your attorney and accountant should give you guidance on this choice.

The second organizational issue relates to how you have defined the work to be done and the structure you plan to put around that work, and the people you plan to put in that structure.

Your years of experience can be a big plus to build credibility with investors. Any investor or lender will consider it vital to know how you and your associates are qualified to succeed. If you have followed our earlier advice, you either already had or have found a way to get some valid experience. Prepare resumes and provide references for you and your key people. If you don't have your people in place, describe how and when you will get them.

The Schedule of Events. Prepare a detailed schedule of all the events that are involved in bringing your new business on stream. The schedule should show *what* the event is, *when* it occurs, including, if appropriate, when it begins and ends, and *who* is responsible for each event. No list could be complete, but Figure 16–2 shows the kinds of events you should schedule.

The Budget. You can use several of the worksheets in this book to help set up your new business budget:

- Worksheet 6A, "How Much Money You Need" (your personal budget), Chapter 9
- Worksheet 7, "Sources of Money" (a personal balance sheet and a list of sources of money), Chapter 10
- Worksheet 10, "Income Statement" (a format for budgeting income and expenses), Chapter 13
- Worksheet 11, "Balance Sheet" (a format to project your assets and liabilities), Chapter 13
- Worksheet 12, "Sources and Applications of Funds" (a format to show the flow of funds in and out of the business), Chapter 13
- Worksheet 15, "Business Start-Up Budget" (a more detailed, *monthly* breakdown of income, costs, expenses, and cash flow), at the end of this chapter

Cash flow is especially important for a new business. Not only do you have to deal with the uncertainty of a start-up business budget, you have, in all likelihood, had to put your personal and household finances on a matching budget. Make certain you integrate these two budgets to get a complete picture of your cash situation.

Finally, because start-ups have so much uncertainty, prepare a contingency budget. The contingency budget should reflect a "worse-case" situation where cash flow would be at its reasonably poorest level. Integrating

---

- Completing the design of the product or service and its packaging
- Selecting suppliers
- Hiring employees
- Choosing a location
- Developing brochures
- Creating advertising and promotion programs
- Obtaining licenses and permits
- Setting up special announcement meetings
- Scheduling customer contacts
- Setting up shop—furniture, telephones, tools, computers, supplies, etc.
- Selecting distributors
- Establishing controls and measurement check points

Figure 16–2. Schedule of start-up events.

this worst-case contingency budget with your personal budget will point out potential problems and give you the opportunity to make judgments about your plan.

The Resources

The resources to help you carry out your start-up plan include financial resources, physical resources, and human resources for help, information, and advice. These resources are not always easy to find or convenient to use.

Sometimes entrepreneurs, in an attempt to match resources to their plans, have to modify their plans. The start-up may have to move more slowly than originally envisioned, or some opportunities may have to be put off for later exploitation. People starting businesses need to be downright ingenious in recognizing and utilizing everything that can help in the extraordinarily difficult task of creating an enterprise.

Financial Resources. Lack of financial resources, often through poor planning and forecasting, remains one of the two major causes for new business failure. In Chapter 10, we presented an array of financing alternatives. Here is a review summary:

What You Have

A second job	Investments
Assignable assets	Overtime, freelancing, and
A working spouse	moonlighting
Cash and near cash	Partnership interests
Deferred compensation	Personal property
Equity in your home	Retirement accounts
Income from trust and annuities	What you save
Insurance policies	

Once you have added up all the money you already (could) have, it is time to see where you can borrow more.

Where You Can Borrow Personally

Against your credit cards	Your bank or credit union
Against your insurance policies	Your margin or borrowing
Friends and family	account

Although there are relatively few sources for personal borrowing, there are many sources of money for business borrowing.

Where You Can Borrow Through the Business	
Asset lenders and factors	Partners
Banks	Small Business
Bartering	Administration
Customers	Suppliers
Insurance companies, foundations	Venture capitalists and
Many states and some	investment bankers
cities	Venture groups
Other federal agencies	Your landlord

These same business borrowing sources are relevant for start-ups with one major exception: There is no seller financing. The most important source of money for buying a business is not available to the start-up.

Physical Resources. An objective of most start-up businesses is to keep costs low. Physical resources such as your plant or office, machinery, office equipment, and raw materials can represent a large part of start-up costs and need special attention. Here are some ideas:

Lease or rent rather than buy. Of course, the lease-versus-buy decision has to make basic financial sense, but you should be looking for ways to avoid large purchases by renting what you need.

Keep the scale small and avoid extravagances. Investigate used equipment and furniture if you can use it. If you can get by with a small amount of space, find out if there are any "incubator"-type facilities in your area. These are typically facilities sponsored by a development agency or academic institution to aid start-up ventures by providing very small-scale facilities and, often, shared support systems.

Borrow or share where you can. The easiest opportunity for sharing is office space, as discussed in Chapter 8, but many others may exist if you have the courage of your convictions to ask for help. People tend to admire the entrepreneur starting a business; they are often willing to help.

Human Resources. The help you get from other people can make the difference between success and failure. Before you discount this resource, look at all the people who might help you if you ask:

- Employees
- Friends

- Family
- Suppliers—present and potential
- Business associates
- Government agencies such as the SBA and its Service Corp of Retired Executives (SCORE)
- Educational and other professionals
- Customers
- Association members

Information and advice are available almost to the point of excess. In Chapter 12 we listed 31 sources of information, most of which are applicable to the start-up.

Your start-up may not require the intense advice and support of the negotiations and the purchase of a business, but there are a host of details—setting up the books, getting tax identification numbers, obtaining licenses and permits—that will require a paid advisor's help.

The Elementary Start-up Process

The process of starting a business involves a marketable idea, a workable plan, and ingenious use of resources. If you ask small business owners what it really takes to start a successful business, most will tell you that one thing and one thing only outweighs everything else: *having customers.* If you have people who want to buy what you're planning to sell, you can be pretty sure you have the three elements of the classic start-up process.

- If you have people who want to buy what you are selling, you know that you have *a marketable idea.*
- If you have people who want to buy what you are selling, you can confidently develop *a plan.*
- And if you have people who want what you are selling you can almost certainly get *the resources you need.*

The Trap of the Illusionary Customer

More than one entrepreneur has fallen into a trap made up of one part optimism, one part well-meaning friends, and one part gullibility. The trap is set when the entrepreneur asks potential customers, friends, or associates, if they will buy the product or service being planned. The response is predictably a resounding "yes!" because it's in everyone's interest to be encouraging. Friends want to seem supportive and potential customers always want another source of supply to make sourcing (and prices) more competitive.

The trap is sprung when, after the entrepreneur expends the time and resources to get the business started, these "customers" explain that they didn't really mean they would buy now, or buy at that price, or buy that much, or in fact that they would ever buy.

You can avoid the illusionary customer trap by taking one precaution: Get it in writing. Get a signed purchase order. If you can't get that, get a signed binding letter of intent. If you can't get that, get a signed nonbinding letter of intent. If you can't get even a nonbinding signature, the trap is about to be sprung on you and your new business.

Get It in Writing

Richard H. has been a successful executive recruiter for both a head-hunting firm and a major corporation. He was well known and skilled, and sure that he could start his own executive recruiting company.

To test his theory he called several of his friends and asked them what he might expect in the way of business if he went on his own. To his pleasant surprise, his contacts told him about close to a dozen searches he could expect. At an average of $75,000 for each position, his 30 percent fees would total $270,000. And that was just from a few friends!

Richard cut the estimate from his friends in half, and began to budget on the reduced $135,000 estimate, certain that he was being superconservative. Just before he committed to a substantial lease, the concerned landlord suggested that Richard try and get some form of commitment from his friends. He tried. He didn't ask for a contract, just a letter of intent; in fact, he told his friends he would be happy with nonbinding letters of intent.

The answers bore a disappointing similarity.

"I expect to hire, but I can't say for sure and I certainly can't say when."

"We have to keep an eye on the market before we can commit."

"It's just about certain, but there is always a chance of promoting from within."

And so on.

Richard decided to lease small, shared office space. Though he is successful today, his first year—1989—produced only $48,000 in revenue.

Your greatest risk of failure is that no one will buy what you plan to sell. You can gain no greater insurance of success than to have real* customers waiting to buy what you plan to offer for sale. By getting it in writing you have identified who and where your customers are, what they want, how much they want, and when they want it. If you have the rest of the elements needed to run your business, you probability of success is very high.

The Most Important Element in Starting a Business

Your time is the single most important element in the business start-up. This book makes the point that nothing happens in your own business unless you make it happen. Your time is even more important to the start-up process. There are no employees around to give help, no long-standing bankers, vendors, and suppliers to provide support, and no established customers to offer encouragement. You have to create and build the enthusiasm that will attract others to your idea and to your business. In the beginning, only you will own your vision, and only you will own a stake in its success.

Summary

Starting a business may be the right route to ownership for you. Some businesses are easy to start, some should be started, and sometimes starting a business is the only way to get going, even though it's more risky.

A special kind of start-up, consulting, is discussed in the next chapter.

---

*Of course, real customers need to be able to pay their bills, too. Don't overlook credit-worthiness.

Worksheet 15
Business Start-Up Budget

15A. MONTHLY PROFIT AND LOSS STATEMENT

	Month 1	Month 2	Month 3	Month 4	Month 5	Month 6	Month 7	Month 8	Month 9	Month 10	Month 11	Month 12	Total
Sales													
Cost of sales													
Gross profit													
Expenses													
Owner's salary													
Owner's benefits and taxes													
No. of people													
Employee salaries													
Employee benefits and taxes													
Rent													
Utilities													
Travel/ entertainment													
Selling expenses													
Depreciation													
Insurance													

(Continued)

265

Worksheet 15 *(Continued)*

	Month 1	Month 2	Month 3	Month 4	Month 5	Month 6	Month 7	Month 8	Month 9	Month 10	Month 11	Month 12	Total
Supplies													
Interest													
Automobile													
Dues, licenses, subscriptions													
Legal and accounting													
Other													
Other													
Other													
Total Expenses													
Pretax profit													

15B. CASH FLOW PROJECTIONS

	Month 1	Month 2	Month 3	Month 4	Month 5	Month 6	Month 7	Month 8	Month 9	Month 10	Month 11	Month 12	Total
Cash on hand													
Cash in bank													
Near cash investments													
Cash balance beginning													

266

Worksheet 15 *(Continued)*

	Month 1	Month 2	Month 3	Month 4	Month 5	Month 6	Month 7	Month 8	Month 9	Month 10	Month 11	Month 12	Total
Cash added													
Cash sales													
Collections from accounts receivable													
Interest investment income													
Loans to the business													
Other													
Total cash added													
Total Cash Available													
Cash Expenses													
Purchases of materials and equipment													
Salaries and benefits													
Rent													
Utilities													

(Continued)

Worksheet 15 *(Continued)*

	Month 1	Month 2	Month 3	Month 4	Month 5	Month 6	Month 7	Month 8	Month 9	Month 10	Month 11	Month 12	Total
Travel/ entertainment													
Selling expenses													
Insurance													
Suppliers													
Interest													
Automobile													
Dues, licenses, subscriptions													
Legal and accounting													
Other													
Other													
Other													
Repayment of loan principal													
Taxes													
Total Cash Paid Out													
Cash Balance Ending													

Worksheet 15 *(Continued)*

	Month 1	Month 2	Month 3	Month 4	Month 5	Month 6	Month 7	Month 8	Month 9	Month 10	Month 11	Month 12	Total
Cash Flow (Deficit) Month													
Cash Flow (Deficit) Cumulative													

CHAPTER 17

Forming a Consulting Practice

Understanding Consulting

Functions of Consultants

The word *consultant* brings different pictures to different peoples' minds, because so many kinds of functions lend themselves to consulting work. Consulting can encompass many functions, as shown in Figure 17–1. These consulting functions arise out of needs that have sparked the entrepreneurial consulting profession to respond with services—and products—to fill those needs. Some consulting practices are structured to offer only advice. Others, such as many of the computer consultants, offer products and systems as well. It is not important that everyone have the same definition of consulting, but you should think about what you mean when you think about being a consultant. Generally, a consultant is from outside the organization, has special expertise, and the relationship with the client is proscribed by either task or time.

Models of Consulting Practices

You can set up your consulting practice in several ways. Figure 17–2 shows five dimensions of consulting each of which has its extremes.

Degree of effort relates to how much time you plan to put into your consulting practice. The extremes here are fairly obvious: part time to full

```
Executing special tasks
Giving opinions and advice
Problem identification and assessment
Problem solving
Product development
Program development
Training
```

Figure 17–1. Consulting functions.

time. Part-time effort can be a way to try out your consulting concept and keep your risk of failure low. If successful, it can provide a supplement to your regular income. Some consultants, however, find it difficult to meet clients' demands on a part-time basis. An assignment may require a concentrated, continual—though short—time commitment. Should you want or need consulting to provide your total income, you will work at it full time.

Another dimension focuses on whether you will do your consulting *alone or in association with others.* Consulting firms range from solo practices to huge groups such as McKinsey & Company. Big companies can provide resources and clients, but even as an independent contractor you may be subject to all the vagaries of employment that got you to read this book in the first place. The solo practice carries both the risks and the rewards of independence.

Between these two extremes lies the small partnership, a structure of association many consultants find desirable. In a consulting partnership, work might be divided between *business development activities* such as marketing, selling, and getting new clients, and *assignment activities* of actually doing the consulting.

The next dimension relates to the consultant's *market and client strategy.* The issue here is selecting the market the consultant plans to serve. The extremes range from serving anyone who will buy to serving just one client. The one-client consultant is freed from having to market and sell,

1. *Degree of effort:*	Part time	Full time
2. *Association:*	Solo practice	Group
3. *Market strategy:*	Any/all	One client
4. *Breadth of offering:*	Advice only	Products, newsletters, etc.
5. *Fee basis:*	Per diem	Retainer

Figure 17–2. Models of consulting practices.

but faces real risks. Any adverse change at the client company can mean the end of the dependent consultant's practice.

Serving anyone who can pay is not an uncommon start-up strategy, because any income is better than no income to the start-up consultant. Unfortunately, this strategy can lead the practice into low-value assignments that provide little return on time and no opportunity to build on success and gain new assignments. New consultants can find themselves trapped.

The middle-range market strategy calls for segmenting a market according to some criteria, typically based on the consultant's ability to serve it and the segment's projected profitability.

Another dimension of consulting is the *breadth of offering* the consultant will extend. The extremes here range from offering only assessment and advice to offering products, services, project execution, newsletters, seminars and more.

Your market may dictate what it needs. A real estate consultant engaged to relocate a factory may provide that single service and may provide it only once to that client. The consultant who trains employees how to use personal computers may offer a minicatalog of services, software, and accessories. Your preferences and abilities may determine what you offer, and your offerings may change with experience and with market demand.

The final dimension of consulting practices has to do with *how fees are set.* The extremes here run from a per-hour or per-diem basis to the retainer basis. The per-hour or per-diem basis has been the most common fee arrangement. After reviewing the assignment, the consultant estimates the length of time the job will take and tells the client what per-hour or per-day rate will be charged. Some negotiation may take place. A common variation is the per-project fee, where the consultant agrees to do a whole job for a fixed price.

Retainer fee arrangements may be for a period of time to be worked (say, three days each month), or for specific tasks to be done (say, handling all export orders each month). Being "retained" in these arrangements means that the consultant reserves the time and does not book other work for that time. The consultant receives the retainer whether or not the client uses the consultant. However, work done beyond the time agreed or for other tasks may be charged.

A special variation that is growing in popularity uses a commissionlike basis, where the fee, or a portion of it, varies with some measure of your success. The variable measure might relate to how much money you saved the client, how many people you trained, how many orders were received, or some similar measure of your success.

Consulting, then, is not a single thing. Your exploration of a business of your own may uncover rich opportunities in consulting.

Pluses
Freedom	Earning potential
A way to another job	Inexpensive to start
Flexibility	Uses knowledge, skills, contacts

Minuses
Lonely	Lack of peer stimulation
Flow of business is erratic	May involve excessive travel
Requires special skills such as selling	
May provide income, but won't build wealth	

Figure 17–3. Pluses and minuses of consulting.

Pluses and Minuses of Consulting

Offering your knowledge and skills for sale as a consultant is very different from steady corporate employment. Let's consider the pluses and minuses of consulting as shown in Figure 17–3.

Kinds of Skills and Knowledge Involved

At midcareer you have ample expertise and may feel you could become a consultant by selling what you know. If consulting were just plying your expertise in exchange for money, it would be a relatively simple task. In fact, consulting requires not only the professional or technical skills you plan to offer to clients, but other kinds of skills as well. The four kinds of skills and knowledge required in consulting are:

1. Technical or professional skills
2. Business skills
3. Interpersonal skills
4. Consulting skills

Technical or professional skills are the ones you plan to market. They can be viewed as being of three types, though in practice they will often be integrated:

- Specialized skills such as writing or selling
- Specialized knowledge such as appraising or regulatory law
- Specialized industry or segment skills and knowledge such as hotel or hospital operations

Now let's consider the *business skills* required. Your consulting practice will be a business and, as such, you will be required to manage it. Figure 17–4 lists several needed business skills.

Bookkeeping	Promotion
Goal setting	Research
Marketing	Selling
Negotiating	Strategic and tactical planning
Pricing and fee setting	

Figure 17–4. Business skills.

Consulting also requires a solid base of *interpersonal skills*. Consultants have no authority to direct change, yet they are expected to be agents for change. Added to that, consulting often takes place in emotionally charged, troubled organizations. Figure 17–5 lists some of the interpersonal skills required of a consultant.

Because consulting is an activity of its own, it has its own requirements for *knowledge and skills about the consulting profession*. A few are listed in Figure 17–6.

The Consultant as Change Agent. One of the most valuable models of consulting views the consultant as a change agent. You should become familiar with this model. This theory of change says the uncoerced change occurs only when the following conditions exist:

- A perceived need to change
- A readiness to change
- A willingness to change
- An ability to change
- An expectation that change is possible and positive

Test this model on any change you can think of, from quitting smoking to developing a new business strategy. When this model is related directly to consulting, two more elements are added:

- A "contract" to effect change
- A point of entry to the organization

Using Worksheet 16 at the end of the chapter, you can conduct a personal assessment to get an idea of how your knowledge and skills match up to those that have been suggested as requirements for consulting.

Communications	Listening
Conflict resolution	Meeting skills
Diplomacy	Overcoming fears
Gaining trust	Persuasiveness
Group dynamics	Setting realistic expectations

Figure 17–5. Interpersonal skills.

Contracting	Reporting, presentations
Developing recommendations	Supporting the sponsor
Diagnosis	Working with the
Proposal writing	organization

Figure 17-6. Consulting skills.

Positioning Your Consulting Services

As a consultant you will position your consulting services by defining your offering so that it matches the target market while at the same time differentiates itself from its competitors. The objective is to create a defensible "position" in the market. To create a position you will need to know your competitors and their services, and you must fully understand your market needs.

Defining Your Consulting Services

The consulting services you will eventually offer will be based on how you bring together three elements:

1. The market's needs
2. Your marketable knowledge and skills
3. Applications of your knowledge and skills to those needs for which the market will pay

The market's needs are typically determined through market research, which we will discuss in the next section. However, the market's needs are not as straightforward to ascertain as the name might imply. The problem stems from the fact that the people you will deal with in companies also have their own personal needs and those personal needs may or may not be the same as the company's needs. The company may need your consulting service but the purchasing agent may need to buy from another consultant to satisfy old loyalties.

More complications arise when different people in the same company have different needs. The purchasing agent wants the lowest-cost consulting service, but the manufacturing boss wants the consulting service with the broadest range of skills and experience. Present needs may not be the same as future needs, adding another complication.

And we need to accept that the customer's perceived needs, right or wrong, are the customer's present needs. If you are selling what the company truly needs to someone who perceives those needs differently, you won't sell much until you change those perceptions.

Finally, some people don't know what they need. They may know their problem but not the solution. Some people will lie, perhaps because they are embarrassed or perhaps because they don't want to deal with you. Most will change. Needs can change rapidly, and you could be responding to a need that no longer exists.

Finding a need and filling it, then, is no simple matter. Need identification is an important research and selling skill and is discussed more fully later in this chapter. Even though it will give you only a preliminary indication at this point, you should use Worksheet 17 at the end of the chapter to organize your data.

Researching Your Market

The result of your work so far has given you a first cut at what services you will offer. Now you need to verify your conclusions in the marketplace. If the services you plan to offer are in some way already being offered, you can draw some positive conclusions about market acceptance. If your offering is new, you need to do some market research. Design your research by first setting your research objectives and then deciding what you need to know and whom you can ask.

Your objectives:
- Determine if the idea has real potential
- Determine what services to offer
- Determine the market size
- Assess the revenue potential
- Assess your ability to reach the buyers

Your questions:
- Is this what's needed?
- Is this what's wanted?
- How much will people buy?
- How much will they pay?
- How do they buy?

Your sources:
- Potential clients
- Other consultants
- Industry experts/contacts
- Academicians
- Trade Associations

A word of caution is necessary here about asking your friends what they think. In their eagerness to offer encouragement, your friends may applaud your idea regardless of its merit. Furthermore, your friends may not be qualified to offer valid opinions.

One general rule in asking for help or information is to convince the source that answering your questions is in his or her best interest because you will then be a more responsive vendor. Another general rule is to try and quantify the answers where appropriate.

If you are worried that asking potential clients will reveal a lack of knowledge on your part and possibly hurt your chances of getting business later, you can disguise your identity or hire someone else to do the research. The research, however, is essential, so you must use one method or another:

- Ask personally
- Have someone else ask
- Guess at what's needed
- Use trial and error
- Copy an already successful practice
- Use existing research

Before thinking about the actual questions to ask, let's acknowledge that making cold phone calls and asking strangers for something can scare most of us. (We'll return to this subject in the section devoted to marketing and selling.) Experts in telemarketing strongly advocate *a comfortable script* and *lots of practice* as the two keys to effective use of the telephone as a selling or research tool. Here is a sample script for a telephone solicitation for information.

My name is _____. I'm doing some research on the need for _____ consulting services.

- Can you please connect me with the person responsible for that activity in your company?

or

- Are you the person responsible for that activity?

Or, once you have the right person:

- May I take 10 minutes to ask you some questions so that I/we can develop services that will best meet your needs?

What to ask:

- Do you have a problem or opportunity such as _____?
- What are your problems or opportunities in _____?
- Do you use consultants?
  How often?
  Who decides?
  What do you typically pay?
- If I could _____, would your company be interested?
- How would a consultant approach your company?
- If your company doesn't have such a need, do you know someone who does?

Developing Your Plan

This next subject will be familiar to you, as most midcareer readers will have at one time or another had to develop some kind of business plan. Here are some standard elements as they might apply to a consulting practice:

The concept or mission
A definition of the market
- Size
- Needs
- Competition
- Trends
- Behavior

A description of services and prices
A description of structure or organization
A schedule of events, with special emphasis on the sales plan
Financial projections

Table 17–1 is an outline of a business plan for a consulting practice.

Marketing and Selling Your Services

Define, Segment, and Prioritize the Market

No matter which of your skills you plan to exploit, or what functional area or industry you plan to pursue, you need to define clearly the market you plan to serve. Beyond defining the market, you need to decide which part of it you will address first.

The burning need for revenue can cause new consultants to chase after any opportunity that pops up. Time, effort, and money can be wasted, and you can become spread too thin by trying to grab too many things. You need to have some criteria against which you can compare various opportunities. Worksheet 18 at the end of the chapter provides one model for evaluating market opportunities. Feel free to add your own criteria.

Once you complete your evaluation and go to work on your priority segments, remember to repeat the prioritization periodically to cut your low-end business and focus on your top prospects.

Prepare Promotional Materials

Like any business, your consulting practice will need to be promoted and, probably, advertised. Figure 17–7 lists some common promotional materials.

Table 17-1.   Consulting Practice Business Plan Outline

I. The idea

Write a general concept statement about your consulting idea. Your consulting practice needs to be defined in terms of its purpose. Why does it exist? What real need is it going to fill? What, if anything, makes it special?

Is this idea the basis of a real business? Can the idea be transformed into a practice? Is it deliverable? Can it be done cost effectively? Will it be affordable?

Can you do it? Do you have sufficient personal and financial resources? Has anyone else tried the idea? What happened?

II. The plan

A. The market

Everything starts with the market. Define your market. What are the needs? How large is it? Where is it? What are the segments? What is the growth of the market? To whom do you plan to sell? If you have any specific clients in mind, name them.

How do clients buy? Why? How much do they buy? How do you know?

Is the market demand large enough to build a practice? What's the competitive situation?

B. Your services.

Only after you know the market and its needs can you define your service and product offerings. How will you produce them? What will it cost you? What uniqueness can you incorporate?

How do you plan to price your services and products?

C. Your organization

You do need to spend some time on your organizational structure, even though it may be small. What is your legal form (see Chapter 2)? How will typing, phones, billing, proposals, etc., be handled? Will you have partners, associates, and/or employees? Do you have stationery and business cards?

D. The schedule of events

Prepare a calendar that will spell out every key step. The schedule should show *who* is responsible and *when* each step will occur.

• Complete market assessment.
• Complete design of services and products.
• Select/hire associates and employees.
• Set a location—phones, typewriter, computer, furniture, supplies, stationery, bank accounts, etc.
• Develop promotional materials.
• Develop advertising and marketing programs.
• Build a network.
• Obtain licenses and permits.
• Complete any research.
• Schedule initial client contacts.
• Procure needed resources—financial, physical, information/advice.
• Set controls and check points.

E. The budget

The budget for any start-up has two special considerations: cash flow and early warning signals. The two budget formats on pages 265–269 are intended to address both.

The driver behind your budget will be your revenue forecast. Do budgets at high and low estimates of revenue. (If appropriate, you may need to integrate your business budget with your personal budget.)

F. Review and revision

Prepare some alternative courses of action should you find yourself ahead of, or behind, your plan.

Advertisements	Newsletters
Audiotapes	Photographs
Brochures	Samples
Business cards	Solicitation letters
Case histories	Statement of qualifications
Computer disks	Stationery
Give-away items	Survey results
Information	Testimonials
Letters of reference	Videotapes

Figure 17–7. Promotional materials.

Your Brochure. The cornerstone of most promotional activity for your practice is your brochure. The brochure serves several functions:

- Introduces you and your services
- Explains the features
- Explains the benefits
- Explains your qualifications
- (Sometimes) asks for some action by the client
- (Sometimes) describes fee schedule
- (Sometimes) contains references

Some brochures used by consultants are elaborate, some are simple. Some are self-mailers, some require envelopes. Some have a fixed format and others allow for inserts to customize the package. You do not have to design your own brochure. Advertising agencies, design consultants, and others are available to help you.

Your job is to develop the key copy points of your story. Start by picturing your client in a situation that calls for your services. The client is facing either a problem that needs to be solved or an opportunity that needs to be grasped. No matter what your consulting service, you can only do two things of value to a client—add to revenue or reduce costs. Now imagine your prospective client reading your brochure. The client does not need a lecture on why industry today is facing such-and-such a problem or how neatly your solutions fit a model. The questions your client wants answered are

- Who are you?
- What do you do?
- How do you do it?
- What do *I* get?
- Why should I choose *you?*
- What do you want me to do? (optional)
- How much money or time will this take? (optional)

Use Worksheet 19 at the end of the chapter to help you develop your brochure. The worksheet is divided into three sections:

1. *Preparation.* This first section forces you to spell out exactly who you are trying to reach and why.
2. *Copy points.* The second section asks for key copy points, usually short phrases, about you and your services. Remember to answer the clients' questions. The key question is "What do *I* get?
3. *Production considerations.* The third section addresses some of the specific considerations that will affect the cost and appearance of your brochure.

Test and Use a Mix of Marketing Elements

Once you have defined your market and have developed your marketing tools, you are ready to reach out to your market. *Marketing* can be defined as all those activities that connect the means of the seller with the needs of the buyer. Marketing texts list a variety of promotional, communications, and selling activities that can be used in varying degrees and combinations. Figure 17–8 is a partial list. All of these elements can be treated as trade-offs; you can spend more on advertising, or you can lower your price and advertise less. The concept is called the *marketing mix*, because you select the mix and emphasis of the marketing elements best suited to you and your market.

We will examine seven marketing elements that are most often appropriate for a beginning consulting practice, to see what each can do:

1. Personal selling
2. Advertising
3. Direct mail
4. Telemarketing
5. Networking
6. Price
7. Presentation and proposals

Advertising	Price
Delivery	Product or service design
Direct response	Promotion
Distribution	Quality
Networking	Selection
Packaging	Service
Personal selling	

Figure 17–8. Marketing mix elements.

Personal Selling. A well-known model of selling that describes the sales process is based on the theory of change presented earlier. After all, selling is a change event: Someone does something differently. This theory of change says that uncoerced change occurs *only* when the following conditions exist:

- A perceived need to change
- A readiness to change
- A willingness to change
- An ability to change
- An expectation that change is possible and positive

The selling model recognizes these elements of change in an order of its own:

- Permission to proceed
- Need identification
- Agreement on needs
- Present features and benefits
- Tentative close
- Overcome objections
- Restate'
- Close

We will look at each of these elements.

Getting *permission to proceed* does two things: It ensures that you will be heard, and it should ensure that you are talking to the right person.

As obvious as it sounds, the biggest mistake in selling comes from not *understanding what is needed.* A good salesperson knows that the customer is always right because the customer's perception of need *is* the customer's reality. If the customer's perception is faulty, the good salesperson works as an agent to change it. Before any selling can begin, there must be an agreement on need.

Once you are in front of the right person and the needs have been agreed upon, you can begin presenting the *features and benefits* of your offering. Features are what you have or can do; benefits are what they mean to the buyer.

The differences between features and benefits is extremely important. It is easier, more common, and very tempting to talk about the features of your product or service. You know them and you know how hard you worked to develop them into your offering. The fact is that customers and clients don't buy your features; they buy the benefits they perceive your product or service gives them. Before you shrug off the difference as semantic, be aware that converting a feature to a benefit is not as easy as it might seem. For example, most consultants devote a majority of their selling activity touting their service's special process of *fact finding*, *analysis*, and *recommendation*, but those features are not what the client needs. They may be important to know to build credibility, but they are of no direct benefit.

Features:	*Benefits:*
All-steel construction	Will last longer and save money
20 years of experience	Will perform better for you
50 percent stronger	Will be trouble free
On-time delivery	Will serve you faster
The largest	Will have the means to perform

Benefits are what people buy. Features are what the salesperson offers as the "what, how, and why" you can fill the needs.

After presenting the features and benefits of your offering, *ask for the business.* ("May I begin on Monday?") If you are refused, find out exactly what the objections are.

The next step is to *overcome the objections.* The methods depend on the objection, but one rule is irrefutable: Listen to and understand the objection very carefully. Probe for the real reason. Restate the objection as merely something to be resolved. Here is an example dealing with price.

Objection:	"I'm afraid your price is too high."
Restate/clarify objection:	"I understand that price is an important consideration. Why do you feel the price is too high?"

Check to see if you are being compared to a competitor. Find out the basis for the price objection. It may be simply an attempt to pressure you for a reduction, or it may be that the client has not really understood the value of your offering.

Once you have responded to objections, *reposition your selling proposal*, based on the response to your questions and focusing on the value of your services. Negotiate your value, not price. Clients may have many reasons to use your services. Figure 17–9 is a partial list. The list contains subtleties, but you can do only two things of real value for your customer: add to revenue or reduce costs.

Finally, you must *ask for the business.*

The model for selling shows the need for both knowledge and skill. In order to sell well you need knowledge about your service, the customer, the market, competition, the needs, and more. You obtain knowledge through study and experience. The skills in selling include listening, think-

To avoid criticism	To gain control over his/her life
To avoid trouble	To gain recognition
To be different	To increase well-being
To be in style	To obey the law
To be popular	To please someone important
To be safe and secure	To profit from opportunities
To conserve possessions	To protect a reputation
To copy others	To save effort
To end confrontation or sales pressure	To save time
	To solve a problem
To feel good	To win praise

Figure 17–9. Reasons to use a consultant.

ing on your feet, speaking, persuading, building trust, and so on. You obtain skills through practice and feedback. Unless you are already a skilled salesperson, reading books on selling and attending sales training programs should be part of your personal preparation for consulting.

Advertising. Advertising is usually thought of as a broad-reaching marketing tool. It works well when you can reach your audience cost effectively. Advertising can be in print, on TV or radio, on billboards, in flyers, and more. For practical reasons we will focus on print advertising as the most likely medium for a consulting practice. To decide whether advertising can be cost effective for you, ask yourself these questions:

- Who are you trying to reach? If you can define your target audience sharply enough, advertising may be able to reach it.
- Where are you going to find them? Now that you know who they are, where are they? Are they in large companies? Small companies? At home? On the West Coast? At conferences? In machine shops?
- How are you going to reach them? What medium—magazine, newspaper, newsletter—does your target audience read? How do you know?
- What is your message? What do you want to say? What does the market need to know? What is the best way to say it? This is the creative, ad agency part of advertising.
- How will you measure the results of advertising? (This is an age-old problem, but you do need to try.)
- What would the advertising cost? What do you estimate it would gain?

If you can give well-defined answers to these questions, and if you can find a way to pinpoint those who would buy your services, you might want to use advertising as one of your marketing elements.

The major drawback of advertising for consultants is that you may be paying to reach hundreds of thousands of people when only a handful can use and buy your services. Two indicators suggest that advertising might be effective:

1. Your offering appeals to a broad market and can be reached through broad media coverage.
2. Your offering appeals to a narrow market and there is a good medium (magazine, newspaper, newsletter) that focuses on your market.

Direct Mail. Direct mail, direct marketing, or direct response marketing has become a marketing darling with the advent of easy-to-develop mailing lists and sophisticated word processing and desktop publishing systems. The questions to ask about using direct mail are similar to those for advertising.

- Whom are you trying to reach? You should be able to be more specific now and think about people *by name* or *by title*.
- Where are you going to find them? This now has to be specific enough to reach them by mail.
- How are you going to reach them? What mailing lists can you buy or compile?
- What is it you want to say? What is your offer or message? What do you want to happen?
- How much will it cost to reach your market?

Direct mail, when coupled with a response mechanism, becomes direct response marketing and can be done in ways so that results are measurable. Direct response marketing typically invokes an offer-and-response mechanism such as a return card or a special telephone number. Responses are tracked as a first measure of success. (True success will depend on more than just the number of responses. You will need to see how many responses you convert to real sales.)

List technology makes direct marketing appealing, but it can be very costly. Design, printing, list development, labeling, and postage can add up to per-piece costs of a dollar or more in short runs.

There are shared mailing decks—those bunches of cards that come together—and for some consulting practices they might be effective. The key is to know who receives the deck and to assess whether they will respond to your offer and whether they will actually buy.

Testing is a must. In fact, testing direct marketing programs is a discipline in itself. Skilled direct marketers can test all the elements of a program to see whether the list was a good one, which variations of the offer were best received, which variation of the mail piece worked best, and more.

Telemarketing. Telemarketing is another form of direct marketing that is much used by consultants. Most often it is used in conjunction with direct mail and the other marketing elements. The prospects for telemarketing are the same people as for direct mail, and they will be in the same places.

Now, of course, you need to be able to get to people by phone. You need to be part detective and all persuasive to get through secretaries, identify the decision maker, and get a willing ear. In most cases, the objective of telemarketing in consulting is simply to get an appointment, not to sell your services.

The key to effective telemarketing is a good script, well rehearsed, and with ample flexibility. The more rehearsed the script is, the less "canned" it will seem.

It is relatively easy to track measurement and cost in telemarketing because there is nearly instant data.

Networking.* Networking is the development of a series of linking personal contacts. The name comes from the interconnections, which are similar to a rail network or a broadcast network. Many consultants believe that networking is the key to marketing a practice. Consulting is a personal service and, say consultants, personal marketing is the most effective.

When using networking as a marketing tool, you want to reach more than just those who can buy; you want to reach those who can lead you to those who can buy, and those who influence them. The question thus becomes not only where they are, but where they congregate. Meetings, conventions, mixed groups, associations, clubs, and other gatherings may be appropriate places to find people with whom you can network.

Meeting people and getting them to help you reach potential clients requires four key elements:

1. Tell people who you are and what you want.
2. Convince people that you offer worthwhile services.
3. Make it easy for people to help you.
4. Make networking a habit whenever you are with people.

You can use your promotional material, but most networking is done with a business card and a simple sentence, "Who do you know who could benefit from my services?"

Price. Often, price is not thought of as part of the marketing mix, but price is a marketing element. If your market is sensitive to price, it will re-

---

*This is a conventional, though still useful, view of networking. A fresh approach to networking will be discussed in the next section on practice building.

sult in an elastic relationship where lower price equals more volume. If the market is inelastic—that is, price has little impact—you may be able to charge more and use the added funds for advertising, mail, and other marketing.

As with all marketing mix elements, price should be tested for its net impact on profit contribution.

Presentation and Proposal Skills. Consulting requires a special set of skills. Because consulting is a personal service business, you will personally make presentations and proposals. Whether oral or written, proposals and presentations usually serve two purposes: to get business and to report findings or recommendations.

The rules regarding presentations and proposals are the general rules of communication: know your audience, know your purpose, match your message.

The single best advice on presentations is to prepare and practice. Prepare any visual aids. Double-check the settings for electrical outlets, microphones, flip charts, markers, and anything else you need. If you are not a natural presenter, take a course in speaking or hire a coach. Practice your presentation until you are relaxed and comfortable.

Learning how to prepare proposals can best be done by examining good ones. Review proposals you liked and determine why you thought them effective. Ask others who receive proposals what they look for. One good general rule to follow helps make the proposal easier to read. Separate data and reference material from the flow of your text and put them in the back of your proposal as appendixes. Today's computer graphics and data tabulation facilities provide a wide range of proposal capabilities. An outline of a typical proposal is shown in Figure 17–10.

The consultant faces a special problem when preparing proposals or doing presentations, which gives rise to a special rule: *Don't give away your services!* Clients may or may not intend to get your ideas for free, but if your presentation or proposal contains all the information a client needs

---

Introduce yourself.
Demonstrate your understanding of the needs.
Offer your analysis.
Briefly describe your approach.
Propose your assignment:
  • Deliverables—what the client will get
  • Time
  • Resources required
Discuss fees (subject to your judgment).

Figure 17–10. Proposal outline.

- Rephrase your work experiences to show problem-solving accomplishments.
- Start by assisting other consultants.
- Start part time.
- Start with your current employer.
- Take small, even volunteer assignments

Figure 17-11. Ways to get a first consulting job.

to do the job itself, there is the temptation and a risk that this will happen.

Presentations and proposals represent an important part of a consultant's business. Help is available from dozens of books and from people who teach people how to speak and make presentations.

The new consultant faces an obvious "Catch 22": If it takes experience and credentials to get an assignment, how do you ever get the first assignment? Figure 17–11 offers some tips.

Building Your Practice

The Need to Build and Promote

A consulting practice differs from some other kinds of businesses because of the way business is generated:

- Clients' needs are constantly changing.
- Little repeat business.
- There is no way to forecast future business.
- Volume has many peaks and valleys.
- It is hard to influence demand.
- Concepts of market and market share do not apply.

The needs of past clients are constantly changing. Sometimes when a consultant solves a problem, he or she has effectively erased any chance of further employment with that client. At the same time, contacts are constantly changing. More than with product sales, consulting is bought on the basis of personal contacts and relationships. Because people change jobs and companies, even a long successful consulting practice can find itself with no business when it loses its contact at its largest client. The implication is that you need to be continually generating new business and build on every opportunity.

Developing and building a consulting practice has been called a numbers game. If it takes five presentations to get one contract and 20 contacts to get one presentation, then it takes 100 contacts for each contract. Imagine a funnel that constantly needs refilling.

An often-used illustration suggests that growing most businesses can be likened to farming, whereas building consulting practices compares more to fishing. In farming you plant seeds, tend them and wait through a cycle, and they grow, the way most businesses do. In farming you can store extra harvest for bad times ahead. With fishing, like consulting, there is no planting and waiting: You have to work at it all the time. There is no natural growth cycle, and fish don't keep well. In farming, if the soil grows weak you can fertilize and stay at it; in fishing, if there aren't any fish you have to move to another place.

Methods to Build and Promote

There are a number of well-accepted ways to build and promote a solo consulting practice. The computer allows the consultant to engage in *database marketing*. Database marketing has two components:

1. A database (file) of present and potential customers, and of course your network
2. A planned program of communication

The program of communication can be periodic solicitation, announcements about you and your business, or just information that may be useful to your clients. The ideal communications program is two-way, in which your clients tell you about their activities and their needs.

Present clients are still your best bet. Even though a flow of new business is essential, always promote first to your present clients. They know you and presumably like you. You have two objectives when you promote to your present clients:

1. To get more business from them
2. To get your present clients to bring you new clients

Your practice may allow you to offer discounts, allowances, free goods, or other incentives in your promotions. There are other forms of promotion that are especially well suited to consulting practices. These include publishing newsletters, joining speaker's bureaus, writing articles and books, presenting seminars, joining high-visibility organizations, engaging in public relations, and conducting surveys. All of these have merit at times.

Networking

The key to building a consulting practice is building relationships. Years ago most business was done at either the buyer's location or the seller's location. A few people made use of the golf course and "the club." If a seller made a network connection someplace else, it was considered just luck. Today networking is an accepted sales and business development strategy. It is planned and organized. Base your networking plan around these four keys elements:

1. People who can buy or recommend your services
2. A way to meet them
3. A way for you to let them know what you do and what you want
4. A way to build on and show appreciation for each contact

Network—But with Care. While networking is accepted as the most effective of the practice-building methods, today this channel is crowded with job seekers and others who are searching for opportunities. "Net-not-working" is a new phrase popping up in marketing circles as broadcast networking becomes overdone. Many people learned the old rules of networking:

1. Always view everybody as a potential network member.
2. Always be ready to network.
3. Keep records of everyone you meet.
4. Put a tickler on your records and stay in touch with everyone.

Today people recognize that without a more strategic approach, your efforts may lead to shallow and overloaded networks that do little to help your practice. If they are not properly maintained, networks end up as little more than piles of business cards with notes scribbled on the back.

Experts advocate strategic networking, targeting the best probable sources of assignments, as a more effective way to network than the cold-call "information" contact to strangers.* Networks now need to be managed by new rules:

1. View your network as a long-term commitment.
2. Carefully pick network members who can help you and whom you can help.
3. Build quality relationships, not quantity contacts.
4. Produce results for your network members and let them know how to produce results for you.

Start your network through friends, family, and others who know you and who will actively help. The surprise is how long and productive that list can be.

---

*The cold call can work when the consultant has a special story to tell the prospect.

Networking "Tips" Groups. To get an idea of how one kind of networking operates, consider this "tips" group. The group meets at a hotel every Thursday morning from 8 to 9 a.m. Coffee and rolls are provided. It costs $180 a year to belong.

This is a general "tips" group with members from all kinds of businesses. It has 30 members, none who are competitors. The roster is shown below.

Tips Group Members

Accountant	Insurance sales agent
Advertising agent	Janitorial supplier
Advertising specialist	Magazine space salesperson
Architect	Marketing consultant
Attorney	Moving company owner
Banker	Office supplies store owner
Building contractor	Personal image consultant
Burglar/fire alarm consultant	Photographer
Business broker	Radio station owner
Commercial real estate broker	Residential real estate broker
Engineering consultant	Telephone systems and
Florist	services consultant
Freelance writer	Travel agent
Health-care consultant	Waste removal specialist
Hotel owner	

These people can be expected to bring two kinds of information—tips—to meetings:

1. General leads for the group
2. Specific leads for the members

Members also try to patronize each other, and that can be good business.

Members are expected to reward each other symbolically with a dollar when a lead turns into business. (Some members offer much higher finders' fees for new business.) This group averages 25 leads and $10 for 10 pieces of business each week.

The group also provides emotional support for its members.

If you can't find an appropriate sales network group, you can start one. You may have to start with close contacts such as family, friends, alumni, and fellow club members, but just keep asking the "Who do you know who could be interested . . ." question. Worksheet 20 at the end of the chapter can help you form a "tips" sales network group.

Create your own self-promotion network. You can even form a special self-promotion network group. Think of three people who have similar but not conflicting objectives to promote themselves personally. Meet with them and explore the idea of associating for the purpose of supporting and helping each other. If it is practical, each of you could invite two or three others until you have the size group you feel will be most effective, but smaller is better.

Help in the beginning might include giving each other ideas and developing self-promotion programs. More specific cooperation could take the form of help with introductions, support for club membership or public office, and direct assistance in calling each other to the attention of the public or the specific target of your self-promotion.

Throwing a party in your own honor is easier if someone else makes all the arrangements. An added value of a personal self-promotion network is that individual members can better avoid the risk of appearing too pushy, crass, or ill mannered by openly promoting themselves. As each others' "press agents," network members can make far more direct and favorable comments about each other than they could make about themselves.

Your self promotion network can become the equivalent of a trade association for your personal enterprise. You will have your own PR firm.

Afterword: Consulting One-Liners

As a last word, and with recognition to the late Howard Shenson, the "dean of consulting," here is a list of promotional one-liners for every consultant.

Always use written contracts of some type.
Answer *all* letters and phone calls.
As a credibility builder, say what you *don't* do.
Ask for referrals and show appreciation for them.
Avoid general advertising of services—advertise a "product."
Avoid mass mailings—test first.
Avoid appearing desperate for business.
Be assertive when describing your qualifications.
Be prepared to provide references.
Charge expenses flat per diem, not reimbursable (except travel).
Check out speaking locations in advance.
Communicate your success to clients—past, present, potential.
Communicate your successes to everyone in your network.
Communicate payment terms in the contract.

Create separate brochures for each market segment you serve.

Describe past successes, *not* past clients. A client list is OK.

Develop seminars, brochures, newsletters, manuals, software.

Develop three or four speeches you can give to promote your practice.

Do smart networking.

Don't do a cold sales call; do an "interview for an article."

Don't know so much that clients will think you have a "package."

Don't nickel-and-dime clients with small expenses.

Don't rely solely on rational selling. People buy on feelings.

Don't oversell or overpromise.

Don't combine the proposal and the contract.

Don't give away too much "how to" in proposals or when selling.

Don't take on clients with whom you have or could have conflicts.

Don't market with a resume (use it later).

Don't be too accommodating.

Don't "sell" at lunch, "pick the client's brain" for info.

Don't hand out brochures at a lecture, get cards and follow up.

Fee cuts for more business? Get it in writing!

Find out what reservations the client has about working with you.

First interview—find the "crying baby/gold bricks," listen!

First interview—tell if you charge for the first interview.

First interview—interview them before they interview you.

Follow up subtly, giving new information, new ideas, not bugging.

Get advance fees if you want them.

Get out the client's responsibilities in the contract.

Get to the decision makers.

Get listed in trade, professional, and other directories.

Get published.

Get legal advice on your liability exposure.

Hand annotate copies of articles, etc., and send them to clients.

Have the client smooth your way with others in the organization.

If you don't have the time to market—hire someone.

If you are asked to cut fees, offer to cut services.

In direct marketing, use a response coupon.

Include a photo (professional quality) with your press releases.

Keep your business card relatively clean.

Keep up your relationship with the client—work hard at it.

Learn to write and use effective proposals.

Learn to make your proposals *sell*, not just inform.

Lecture, publish, etc., to build an image of your expertise.

Let others in the company get credit—the client will know.

Listen!

Market and sell to those who are responsible for results.

Market and subcontract with competitors.

Market regularly—50 percent at first, 25 percent when full.

Match the quality of your materials to those your clients use.

Match your mode of dress to that of your clients.

Prequalify prospects. When in doubt—charge.

Price products for maximum long-term income.

Provide services to small clients in a group format.

Provide a series of free seminars to your clients, four to six a year.

Provide a schedule to the client.

Put a handwritten P.S. on communications.

Quote fee on a fixed price, not an hourly basis.

Quote "unround" fees, not even thousands.

Save for retirement.

Sell yourself, don't bad mouth the competition.

Set fees on the value of what you do.

Survey past and present clients to learn what is needed.

Tape record your consultations as a tangible product for clients.

Tell the clients what action you want them to take.

Test your written material on four readers (no friends or family).

Try to charge for your "products," brochures, etc.

Twice a year, attack the reference room of a library.

Use the phone to network, but only to people who count.

Use the brochure to interest and sell, not as a reference work.

Use the Yellow Pages. A small ad is enough.

Use "act now kickers" in your promotional efforts.

Watch!

When in doubt, charge for your services to weed out nonprospects.

When selling to committees or boards, presell them individually.

When selling to committees, attend the meeting on your proposal.

When raising fees, add a benefit for present clients.

Work present clients weekly for more business and new clients.

Write at the reading level of the daily paper.

Write letters to the editors.

You *can* charge for doing a diagnosis.

You can waste time and money selling to the wrong people.

You must answer these questions for the prospective client:

- How will I profit from your advice and services?
- Why will I profit from working with you?
- How can you demonstrate that I will profit?
- How much will I benefit from your advice and service?
- When will I realize these benefits?

Worksheet 16

Skills and Knowledge Involved in Consulting

	Your Skills Rating (1 to 10)

Technical skills required:

_____

_____

_____

_____

Business skills required:

_____

_____

_____

_____

Interpersonal skills required:

_____

_____

_____

_____

Consulting skills required:

_____

_____

_____

_____

Worksheet 17

Defining Your Consulting Services

I. What are your marketable skills and knowledge? What do you *know* more about than most people? What can you *do* better than most people? What do you enjoy working on?

_____

_____

_____

_____

II. What broad market needs exist for your skills and knowledge? Is there a need for your special skills, something you can do? Are there functional needs in a variety of industries and other settings? Are there general needs in a particular industry or setting?

_____

_____

_____

_____

III. List some specific applications of your skills and knowledge to the needs in part II. List them in order of marketability, that is, what the client would want most and be most willing to pay for.

_____

_____

Worksheet 18
Evaluating Market Opportunities

Criterion	Market Opportunity 1	Market Opportunity 2	Market Opportunity 3	Market Opportunity 4
Market needs match my services	———	———	———	———
Market size	———	———	———	———
Growth rate	———	———	———	———
Ease of selling	———	———	———	———
Ease of serving	———	———	———	———
Competition	———	———	———	———
Ability to pay	———	———	———	———
Willingness to pay	———	———	———	———
Expansion potential	———	———	———	———
Long-term benefit	———	———	———	———
Profitability	———	———	———	———
Enjoyment	———	———	———	———

Rate each market opportunity 1 to 10 against each criterion. Weight the criteria according to your preferences. Simple inspection of the worksheet table should provide a reasonable evaluation.

Note: This evaluation should be repeated periodically as you gain more experience.

Worksheet 19
Developing Your Brochure

I. Preparation
   A. Who is the audience?

_____

_____

_____

_____

   B. What are their interests/needs?

_____

_____

_____

_____

   C. How will the brochure be used? What are its functions?

_____

_____

_____

_____

   D. What is the single most important thing you want the brochure to accomplish?

_____

_____

_____

II. Copy points
   A. *Who are you?* A succinct introduction to your practice.

_____

_____

_____

   B. *What do you do? How do you do it?* This is the "features" section of your brochure.

_____

_____

_____

   C. *What do I get? What's in this for me?* Describe the benefits the client gets. Show how you lower costs or add to revenue. ***This is the most important section and is often entirely missing in consulting brochures.***

_____

_____

_____

Worksheet 19 *(Continued)*

    D. *Why should I choose you?* Provide some success stories or references if you can. At the least cite some examples of applications. If appropriate, present your personal qualifications.

    _____

    _____

    E. *What do you want me to do?* Make your call for action. You may want the reader to telephone you, fill out a return card, or give you an appointment. This section is optional and depends on your sales strategy.

    _____

    _____

    F. *How much money and time will this take?* If appropriate, present your fee schedule and timetable. This section is also optional and will depend on your sales strategy.

    _____

    _____

III. Production considerations
Before completing this section, get several brochures from other consultants. If you can, let a graphic designer show you the many options available. Work with a printer on this section. Most are helpful.
A. Size and format

    _____

    _____

B. Mailability and postage cost

    _____

    _____

C. Color and paper

    _____

D. Quantity needed

    _____

    _____

    _____

(Continued)

Worksheet 19 *(Continued)*

E. Design costs

_____

_____

_____

F. Production costs

_____

_____

Worksheet 20
Starting a Network Group

I. *Who.* List five kinds of people who can buy or recommend your services. Think about others who call on your potential clients. Avoid competitors.

_____

_____

_____

_____

_____

Use simple detective work to get actual names and phone numbers. Set up a pre-liminary meeting.

II. *Where and when.* Decide where and when you and the group can best exchange your leads.

_____

_____

_____

_____

_____

III. *How.* Set up your procedures. Some groups are very formal, others have almost no rules about attendance, minimum degree of participation, and so on.

_____

_____

_____

_____

_____

Index